'…as a record of courage and endurance it deserves to stand in an honoured place on any shelf devoted to the self-punishing experiences of Anglo-Saxons up the Amazon.'

The Times Literary Supplement

About the Author

After seven canoeing expeditions to the Amazon, John Harrison is regarded as one of the world's experts on independent jungle exploration. He has also canoed the Niger and many rivers in North America and Europe, has been profiled by National Geographic TV, and chaired tropical forest workshops at the Royal Geographical Society. Find out more at www.johnharrisonexplorer.com

He lives in Bristol.

D0107042

An Amazon Adventure

by John Harrison

Bradt

First published in 1986

This revised edition published 2012 by
Bradt Travel Guides Ltd
IDC House, The Vale, Chalfont St Peter, Bucks SL9 9RZ, England
www.bradtguides.com

Published in the USA by The Globe Pequot Press Inc,
PO Box 480, Guilford, Connecticut 06437-0480

ISBN: 978 1 84162 384 9

British Library Cataloguing in Publication Data
A catalogue record for this book is available from the British Library

Production managed by Jellyfish Print Solutions; printed in India

Contents

Foreword

During recent years a sinister shadow has fallen across the world of travel and travel-writing. Its name is 'Sponsorship'.

The quest for sponsors was, I suppose, inspired by the example of mountaineering expeditions. And its rapid spread may not be entirely dissociated from those State-dependent attitudes so dismally prevalent among the post-war generations. Even in modern Britain the State is not expected to subsidize long trips abroad; but the notion of someone else paying for one's thrills is lamentably congenial to a certain type of young traveller. During the 1970s more and more firms advertised their goods by backing phoney 'adventures' and 'expeditions'. These much-publicized stunt journeys, televised at appropriate stages, have all too often been followed by lavishly illustrated books of remarkable tedium and questionable veracity. Such volumes are presented to the public as 'travel books', which does no good to the blood pressure of genuine travel-writers. Happily their numbers seem now to be dwindling: perhaps a beneficial result of the recession. Or it may be that publishers have discovered sales-resistance to the latest heavily hyped account of descending the Indus in a beer barrel with an outboard motor or crossing the Gobi Desert in a golf-buggy.

In the course of duty I have been compelled to read many descriptions of sponsored expeditions. These develop one's sensitivity to travel pseuds and heighten one's appreciation of authentic adventurers like John Harrison, whose unsponsored Amazonian journey is recounted here with humour, honesty and enthusiasm. This is a thoroughly satisfying description of a hazardous and gruelling canoe trip on one of the more obscure tributaries of the Amazon – an adventure undertaken just for the hell of it and completely convincing in all its details. John Harrison uses vigorous, unpretentious language and has blended his ingredients most skilfully. We have good old-fashioned suspense (if anything does seriously go wrong hundreds of miles from the nearest village no sponsored helicopter will fly to the rescue) – and marvellous descriptions of Amazonian wildlife (sometimes viewed from the inside, as when John observed that a certain species of monkey, a favourite for the pot, was always riddled with worms) – and witty analyses of how and why things went wrong between John and his companion (he had two companions over different stages: there may not be any other man who could have withstood all that hardship, disease and danger).

By the last page one's strongest feeling is of sheer admiration for this traveller's courage. It is the courage of a sort not often found nowadays, because not often needed. John Harrison was born a century too late. He should have been out there with Livingstone, Speke, Selous and all that lot. For people like him, our shrunken planet offers too few challenges. His readers, however, will hope that he soon finds another – and writes about it.

DERVLA MURPHY

1
Prophecies and Preparations

'I'm a father at last,' he beamed proudly, blocking my path, 'and in my country it is a custom to invite a total stranger to a meal so that the child might grow up strong and healthy.'

It seemed a charming and commendable custom, and with nothing but the welfare of his son in mind I accompanied him. As we walked he told me he'd come from Khartoum so that his wife might have the baby there in Cairo, and this was his first visit to Egypt.

'In Khartoum I live in an apartment where the balcony overhangs the Nile. In the evenings I can sit up there getting splashed by crocodiles slapping the water with their tails.'

We stopped at a street stall and he bought me a cup of coffee and a dirt-encrusted honey cake. And that was it. He didn't seem concerned that his son might grow up to be a sickly runt because of his stinginess.

Having nothing better to do I let him lead me round the alleys of Cairo where for a visitor he seemed to be extraordinarily well-known. He tried to lure me into all the shops to gain a commission, and offered me Egyptian artefacts 'dug up by tomb robbers just last week', hashish, girls, boys and semi-precious

stones, growing more and more sulky with every refusal. Finally, as we passed
an old man sitting on a doorstep, he suggested I have my fortune told. Never
a believer in divination in any form, I nevertheless thought I'd better agree to
something to get him off my back, so after establishing a price, I sat down.

The old man looked unblinkingly into my eyes before reaching for my
hand to read my palm. It was a relief when his piercing gaze left my face since
one stray, dead eye wandered in different directions from the other. He had
a wrinkled, authoritarian face, a white stubbled chin, and the hand that held
mine felt leathery and dry. I waited impatiently for his prophecy, my guide
chattering irritatingly all the while.

'This man is very wise. He can see into the future: your life next year,
twenty years, even fifty years ahead!'

The old man was silent, bent myopically over the mysteries of my palm.
I was not expecting much revelation and the pretence at thoroughness was
a tedious delay.

'This old man told me two weeks ago that I will have a boy. What did my
wife give me this morning? A boy! He is very, very wise!'

'You told me you only got to Cairo three days ago,' I reminded him
mischievously, and he looked embarrassed.

The old man finally sat up straight, looked into my face briefly, painfully
uncoiled himself from the doorstep and said something in Arabic.

'What did he say?' I asked.

'He says that the things he can see are best left untold,' said my companion,
looking genuinely perplexed as the old man began to shuffle away.

Probably a ploy to squeeze more money out of me, I thought, pursuing
him much as I'd chase an evasive doctor after a chest x-ray.

'Tell him I want to know, whatever it is.'

They talked gutturally while I studied their faces. If this was play-acting
they were very, very good. My guide turned to me.

'He says it is better not to know. You're very young. How old are you?'

'Twenty.'

'Twenty. That's very young. When you're young you need hope, and you think that you will live for ever and ever. It's not good to learn bad news. Best forget it.'

'Tell him I want to know. I prefer to know.'

'You'll regret it if you do.'

'That's my worry. Now go on and tell me.'

'You're going to die young and it will be death by water.'

'At what age?' I foolishly demanded, half-hoping this time he would refuse to tell me.

'When you're thirty-three,' translated my crooked friend, and the fortune-teller disappeared into the crowds, not even accepting payment. That was cause for concern in itself, and I stood in the alley feeling goose-pimply even in the Cairo heat.

There's a lesson there. Never mess with fortune-tellers. Once threatened with a prophecy like that how can you forget it? You ridicule the idea of seeing into the future as hogwash, superstition and baloney, but the memory stays and subtly comes to alter your life. In my case that prophecy justified much misspent youth. I could never make any long-term plans and a career seemed pointless. What was the point of spending six or seven of my prime and dwindling years securing a profession if it only led to the Big Gurgle at thirty-three? Or would it be my thirty-third year? This distinction did not seem particularly important when I was twenty, but assumed major significance on March 21st 1983 when I celebrated my thirty-third birthday. Was I already safe, or was the fateful year just beginning?

Certainly it was not the time to go canoeing in the Amazon, thought my friends. Why on earth was I going to one of the most watery places on earth when I shouldn't even be filling the bath more than 2 centimetres deep?

And what about water-borne disease? Everyone knows that a glass of water in South America is a potential cocktail of death.

'Stay at home,' I was told, 'no swimming, no deep baths, only drink Perrier and you'll be all right.'

I tried to convince them, and myself, that it was just coincidence that I felt the urge to return to the Amazon during this particular year. Really, of course, I knew that staying at home would afford me no protection if the fates were out to get me. I might spend a year living timidly in London, only to fall over on my way home from a party and drown in a puddle. Wouldn't dying in an Amazon rapid or from a virulent Brazilian typhoid seem a touch more stylish? Hopefully I'd get through the year unscathed, and as I made preparations for the canoeing trip I did my best to put the prophecy out of my mind.

This was to be my fifth Amazonian river journey, and I had a pretty good idea of the sort of river I wanted to explore. The previous trips had started as simple apprenticeships on easy rivers – the Branco and Guaporé – and gone on to harder stuff, the Verde and Teles Pires. This time I wanted a river with very few people living along its banks, where the wildlife would be abundant and the jungle undisturbed. That meant a river with rapids.

Before the road-building programme of the 1970s the pattern of population along Amazon rivers used to depend on the ease, or otherwise, of river travel. Rivers free of rapids on their lower or middle reaches – the Madeira, Purus, Tocantins, Juruá, Branco, Amazon and Solimões, for example – carry a scattered population of perhaps one house every kilometre on either bank, and have communication by riverboats with nearby towns. This is a tiny population density, but enough to banish two of the main attractions for me – isolation and the chance to see a lot of wildlife. Now, of course, new roads have opened up areas only reachable by unnavigable rivers in the past, where rapids previously made travel too difficult and deterred settlers.

Another important consideration to me was the size of the river. I find huge wide expanses of water boring to paddle, and in Amazonia many tributaries are more than a kilometre wide. Only one bank can be seen clearly at a time, the water conditions are often choppy and tiring, and there are few things more psychologically withering than to see the river in front of you merging with the sky kilometres away. It's far more interesting to have twists, turns, islands, shallows, sandbanks, narrows and a few rapids.

As the states of Mato Grosso, Rondônia, Amazonas and much of Pará are already too developed to meet these requirements, I concentrated my attentions on northern Brazil between the Amazon river and the borders of Venezuela and the Guianas. Here were several possible rivers – the Trombetas, Paru d'Oeste and Jari – all descending from the Guiana Shield, some of the oldest highlands in South America. All of them have a barrier of rapids to deter settlement. They flow from one of the last truly virgin areas of rainforest in Brazil and are relatively small rivers in comparison to those of south and eastern Amazonia. I say 'small' in strictly Amazon terms: the Trombetas is 750 kilometres long, and the Jari 600.

There were a few logistical problems to canoeing these rivers, however. It seemed we'd have to paddle up them for a start. What would it be like to paddle against the current for that distance? Like most canoeists I had no idea. It's not something we normally do. Where to end the trip posed a problem too. I did not relish paddling all the way up a river only to paddle all the way down again, but as there were no towns or roads in the north where we could leave the rivers I began to consider a more ambitious project. The headwaters are up in the Tumucumaque hills on the border between Brazil and her northern neighbours, and these hills mark a watershed with rivers running north and south. If it were possible to paddle to the top of the Jari, for example, it might be feasible to portage over the top and descend the river Litani into French Guiana, or cross from the Paru d'Oeste to the Tapanahoni in Surinam.

The idea was exciting. It would give a real goal to the trip, and be an enormous challenge. The distance between one river and another appeared to be about 15–20 kilometres, and from the comfort of an armchair in England, with a glass of wine in my hand, such distances seemed trifling. Twenty kilometres can be cycled in an hour, or walked in three. How hard could it be? A week spent hiking across the hills to find the other stream. Another couple of weeks cutting a trail through the jungle, and then a few days of humping the canoe and gear across. Easy.

I finally decided on the Jari. It seemed to provide all the necessary ingredients for an exciting trip and to have fewer rapids than the others. It 'connected' with rivers in French Guiana, which was a more politically stable country than Surinam or Guyana, and it had the added interest of Daniel Ludwig's Jari project on its lowest reaches. This pulp and timber project has aroused such controversy I was keen to have a look at it for myself.

Now I just needed a companion to go with. Friends know me too well to want to go anywhere with me, or they have organized their lives so badly that they can't take six months off work on a whim. Once or twice in the past I had flown out to Manaus on the Amazon river and hung around the cheaper bars and hotels until an interested traveller appeared. That way I had done canoe trips with a Chilean, an Australian and an Italian that had all worked out well. None of them had ever paddled a canoe before (but neither had I on my first river trip), but curiosity had lured them to Amazonia, they'd got there by themselves, and the brief look they'd had of the jungle when travelling to Manaus by riverboat or along the Transamazonian roads had given them some idea of what to expect.

In England I never know where to start when recruiting a companion. Canoe clubs seem a possible source, but I find that the average canoe enthusiast and I don't speak the same language. They are usually kayakers, whereas I have always used local dug-outs or 'Canadian' canoes, and they are passionate about technique and white water, using mysterious technical terms like 'sculling draw', 'high brace' and 'reverse ferry glide' that mean little to me. I've probably picked up some technical canoeing strokes after paddling for a few thousand kilometres, but I wouldn't know what they are called. Between trips to Amazonia I rarely canoe, so though I find white water exhilarating, it can also be downright frightening and a nuisance too. It is like talking to a rally driver before setting off on a motoring holiday around Europe. You are both using cars, but enthusiasms, language, type of vehicle and passions are different.

An alternative method of recruitment is to put adverts in several journals and newspapers, and sit back hoping to be swamped with applicants. But then how should I conduct the selection process? By taking them all on some endurance test to spot their strengths and weaknesses, or by meeting them one by one in a pub where a beery evening can easily give us both the wrong impression? Unless they have done a similar trip before, the uncertainty remains. However much I might emphasize the dangers and discomforts, the majority would still insist that they could handle it. Only a few would run away, grateful for a lucky escape.

For a long and ambitious trip like this one, the option of hanging around in Brazil until the right person appeared seemed too haphazard. There would be too much to do in England before departure, and it's more fun to plan and prepare with a companion. There would also be expenses I couldn't meet alone. Imagine if no one suitable appeared at my backpackers' hostel, leaving me with my canoe and huge pile of equipment, forlornly scouring the streets, with dwindling funds and growing desperation.

This Jari trip was going to be extremely tough and I needed to find someone to match. Paddling against the current, with long portages round the rapids, would demand a high level of fitness. There were obvious risks and dangers too, and the expedition would last a minimum of five months.

Where could I find the right sort of imbecile? I contacted one or two canoe clubs without any joy, and was reluctantly facing the necessity of inserting some newspaper adverts when I was introduced to Mark. He was a rangy Australian of well over 2 metres tall who had done the overland route from his country and was therefore familiar with travel in the developing world. That seemed to be the sum of his relevant qualifications, but he was enthusiastic, capable and keen to go. And as no one else was, I agreed to take him.

I had slight reservations about Mark from very early on, and a hunch that things might not work out smoothly. However, he seemed tough enough, and that was my prime concern. I made a point of warning him again and again of the physical hardship of the expedition, exaggerating the monotony, the heat, the insects, the bland diet, the slow progress and the long, back-breaking portages. He seemed to relish my descriptions, confident of his stamina and endurance.

Any reservations were over our slight incompatibility of character. Meeting once a week in a London pub in the months before our departure, I think we both found each other's company a bit of a strain. Conversation would flag, and it was hard to find topics of mutual interest. Put it this way: if we had been on a first date there wouldn't have been a second. It's foolish to embark on an expedition with such doubts, but time was running out. So I put it down to our difference in age (Mark was twenty-two) and got on with the preparations. As I expressed it to a friend, 'The chances of finding the ideal combination of wit, raconteur and beast of burden in one powerful body are remote. Better a humourless beast of burden than a wimpish wit.'

Incidentally, I never mentioned the dreaded prophecy to Mark. I didn't think it would improve his morale knowing he would have to share a canoe and drink out of the same water container as someone condemned to die a watery death.

One immediate problem was finding a canoe to fit him. On previous trips I had used either local dug-outs bought for a few dollars at the riverside, or plank canoes that I built myself at the nearest sawmill to the river. The latter were pretty basic constructions but very strong and stable. Their big defect, as with the dug-outs, was their great weight. Any portage over long distances or over rough terrain was out of the question with only two people, and on the Jari we would frequently have to portage past rapids – and of course there would be the 15–20 kilometres of trail over the Tumucumaque to reach the river Litani in French Guiana. Also the lighter the canoe, the easier it would be to make headway against the current when paddling upstream.

Preferring to take a canoe out with us from England this time, we had four options to choose from. In the kayak range, there were costly folding models that could take two people and a lot of gear. While they had the advantage of being light, strong, easy to repair and could be folded up and taken on the plane, they had their disadvantages. Although they could reputedly carry two people and 200 kilos of gear, they would be tedious to load and unload with everything crammed down the bow and stern. To get in and out of them you really need shallow water or 7 metres of clear bank that you can pull alongside, neither feature being typical of Amazon creeks. Generally you nose your canoe into the bank at right angles and walk along the canoe to get out. All my canoeing experience had been gained in 'Canadian' canoes with a single-bladed paddle, and they come in aluminium, plastic or fibreglass. The plastic ones were almost indestructible, the fibreglass ones easy to repair and the metal ones too expensive. What ruled them all out was the cost of shipping them to Brazil and the inevitable customs problems when they got there.

Finally we hit on the perfect solution – a 6-metre wooden 'Canadian' that came in kit form. Cheap enough not to break our hearts to leave it behind at the end of our journey, it was also within the size limitation for airline luggage. It was made by Granta of Cambridgeshire, where their designer, Ken Littledyke, advised on certain strengthening modifications.

As the canoe kit was to be assembled using fibreglass, we first had to check whether polyester resin would be available in Amazonia because airlines do not accept such volatile chemicals. An acquaintance in Brazil assured us that we would be able to get it in the cities of Manaus and Belém.

Mark and I drove up to Granta's factory one beautiful June day to try out a canoe and were relieved there was no one around to watch as we launched it onto a dyke near the factory. Mark had never paddled a canoe before, and for some reason I ended up in the bow when I'm accustomed to the stern. The sternsman controls the direction, while the one in front supplies the brawn and only helps with the steering in tight manoeuvres. We launched off, turned in a circle and ran into a nearby bridge. After changing over in midstream and performing a giggling dance as we passed in the violently wobbling craft, we got sorted out and paddled a few kilometres. We ended stiff and tired, but so pleased with the responsiveness of the canoe that we placed an order.

2

Departure

London life always improves enormously just before I leave on a trip. I make more effort to get together with friends, and use the last few weeks as a pretext for parties, rowdy restaurant meals and nights on the town. The grind of work and routine is ending and the anticipation of escape is at hand, along with feelings of regret at leaving, and certain fears of what lies in store.

Many expedition accounts talk about the months of hectic preparation before the trip: the leader tirelessly chasing up last-minute supplies, giving press conferences, raising sponsorship money and joining the other team members on a punishing training schedule. His house has crates of equipment spilling out of every room and rugged, super-fit expeditionaries sleeping in every nook and cranny. The leader's wife (who usually stays at home) must heave a sigh of relief when hubby, his boring cronies and all their bloody gear have gone, perhaps never to return.

I usually set off overweight and out of condition. I may have made a practice of cycling to work instead of driving, but nothing more. I figure that two weeks on the river will make me lean and fit, and the tropics will soon sweat off the paunch. As for all the other preparations, they don't seem hectic at all. Some letters, phone calls and a few days' shopping and it's all done. It's all so easy that I lie awake at night worrying about the dozens of things I must be forgetting. Nice though it would be to receive sponsorship and financial backing, life is a lot simpler without it. To stand a good chance of eliciting funds or materials, you need to mount a formidable public relations exercise. After all, you're trying to get someone to pay for your unusual holiday.

In a pamphlet that gives advice on how to approach firms for help I note the following tactics. First you give the expedition a glamorous name such as 'Tumucumaque Traverse' and have some notepaper printed with the title and a little logo. Your chances of getting funds are vastly improved if you say you are undertaking some sort of research, because this gives the enterprise the stamp of serious endeavour. Without it a trip is regarded as a stunt or an adventure.

I've always preferred to finance a trip myself with a period of frugality and by working a bit of overtime. They are modest, low-tech expeditions that don't cost a great deal. An unsponsored venture can be more fun – and it's much simpler to keep the trip cheap and small, unpublicized, unauthorized, flexible and unscientific. Escapism, pure and simple.

So at the end of June we were finally on our way. With us were Martin and Tanis Jordan, old friends who have travelled on many rivers in Venezuela, Peru and Surinam using inflatable craft. This was to be their first trip to Brazil, and they planned to ascend the Mapuera river, a tributary of the Trombetas. We assembled at Heathrow in high spirits.

The dominant item in our luggage was, of course, the canoe kit. Its box was 2.5 metres long, 75 centimetres wide and 15 centimetres deep and weighed 40 kilos. Mark and I weighed it in as joint luggage and managed to get on three extra bags with no charge.

Mark had planned to join the army in Australia when he returned home, and he had a passion for everything military. He now sported a haircut that would have delighted a marine sergeant, with 'white-walls' running 5 centimetres above the ear. He also wore an olive-green combat jacket, stuffed with syringes, ampoules, bottles of pills and lotions, in an attempt to reduce the weight of our checked-in bags. For the same reason we both wore several layers of clothing and had every pocket filled. Mark looked like a mercenary off to another hot spot and the security guards quickly pulled him to one side. Fortunately we had persuaded our doctor to write a letter to say that he had prescribed us the medicines, and they were all essential for our exploit.

After an apparently uneventful flight to Cayenne, French Guiana, we were informed that one of the engines had developed a fault and we were blessed with two nights in a luxury hotel with a swimming pool and good food, all at the airline's expense. The other passengers with more pressing engagements were impatient and irritated, but we felt our rivers would wait for us. We sunbathed, ate hugely and prayed that the engine would not be fixed for five or six days more.

In fact Air France were not able to repair it in those two days, so they chartered an old crate from one of the least illustrious Peruvian airlines to take us on to Manaus. It was one of the most unnerving flights of my life. On take-off all the ceiling panels groaned under the stress and large gaps appeared between them. Our oxygen masks kept popping down in front of our faces, and for much of the flight there seemed to be a crisis on the flight deck. Taut-faced stewardesses raced to and fro along the aisle (one of them once clutching a fire extinguisher), with no attempt to dispel our alarm by breezy smiles.

'Not much chance of finding us, or the black box, down in that lot,' said Martin encouragingly, staring out of the window at the unbroken jungle below. It was a very relieved group that arrived in Manaus, and we looked on in pity at the poor passengers who had to continue on that plane over the Andes to Lima.

Visitors who reach Manaus by plane are often disappointed in the city. Because of its location 1,200 kilometres up the Amazon they expect to find a small river settlement fighting a losing battle against termites and the encroaching jungle. The reality of course is quite different: a busy city of over half a million people at that time, with skyscrapers and the attendant traffic congestion and shanty towns. Because of its 'free port' status it also has shops full of cameras, computers and stereos.

For the new arrival to the Amazon, only the busy port area on the Rio Negro lives up to expectations. The sweating stevedores shouldering cargo into the riverboats, and the passengers assembling for the evening departures to Benjamin Constant on the Colombian border, Porto Velho up the Madeira near Bolivia, or Belém down at the mouth of the Amazon. A powerful stench of rotting fish, fruit and vegetables hangs over the scene, and the rooftops are lined with urubus – the black vultures that do more to keep the rubbish from overrunning the port than the municipal authorities.

Manaus certainly doesn't disappoint the visitor who approaches it after a period in the forest. It's a place of rest and recreation for combatants of the interior. After weeks or months of deprivation and craving here is satisfaction: pretty women, cold beer, a bed instead of a hammock, cinemas, crowded streets and a break from mosquitoes, rice, beans and farinha. If all you have seen for weeks has been jungle or dusty little frontier towns, Manaus seems like heaven. It's all there for a price, and it's easy to forget that you are in the middle of the world's largest rainforest.

Arriving in 1983 at the international airport we lacked that combatant mentality, but it felt wonderful to be back in Brazil with a new river to explore. The customs officers did not spoil that pleasure by asking us to open the canoe box or Tanis and Martin's large holdall, or questioning us about the pharmacy of medicines we were carrying. Nor did the taxi drivers moan, complain or charge us extra for the problem of getting our bulky gear to the city centre.

During the taxi ride I noticed how the city had grown since my previous visit, and that some of the new suburban sprawl consisted of motels catering for sexual liaisons. These places charge by the hour and generally have circular beds, orange lighting that is reckoned to be the most flattering to one's skin, luxurious bathrooms and ample TVs or radios so that unfaithful husbands who are supposed to be at the football match can return home at least knowing the score. Video cameras are also on offer to record one's performance. Or so I'm told.

We had preparations and shopping to do in Manaus and that meant a lot of walking; our activities were too hectic for gradual acclimatization to the oppressive humidity. We trooped around in sodden shirts and with sweat running down our faces, and found temporary relief by popping into air-conditioned banks and leaving damp stains on their furniture. Our appetites diminished, and over the next two weeks our flesh dripped away, leaving us leaner and more comfortable. Tanis, Martin and Mark hadn't been to Manaus before, so we did the sights. There aren't many of them, apart from the port, fish market and the Teatro Amazonas (the opera house). This has a lovely interior and is interesting for the period it represents. It was finished in 1896 in the extraordinary period when Amazonia held a world monopoly in rubber, an export that financed an era of ostentation, extravagance and bad taste.

Of course the rubber tree, *Hevea brasiliensis*, had always been in Amazonia, but apart from a certain curiosity value for its latex in the shape of erasers and rubber balls, demand was very small at the beginning of the nineteenth century. However, two scientific developments changed all that. In 1839 Charles Goodyear developed the vulcanization process that kept rubber consistently pliable (before that it became stiff in the cold and soft in the heat) and, equally importantly, John Dunlop invented the pneumatic tyre in 1888.

Suddenly rubber was in huge demand, for industrial machine belts, footwear, raincoats and bicycle tyres, as well as for the emergent motor industry. The collection of latex from trees scattered through the jungle required a huge network of tappers and traders, covering almost every tributary from the mouth of the Amazon to Bolivia. Some local Indians were used, but the drought-ridden northeast of Brazil provided most of the work force. These men were often tricked into a form of debt dependency that was little more than slavery by another name. To get to his new place of work and equip himself with a gun, machete, hammock and staple foods, the tapper or *seringueiro* needed an advance from his boss. After that, however much rubber he collected, he never quite managed to erase the debt because he periodically needed to make new purchases – from the company store, of course. Instead of making the fortune he had been promised, he never broke even.

The life of the *seringueiro* was, and still is, a hard and lonely one. Usually on his own up some pestilential tributary, perhaps with hostile Indians nearby, his days began before dawn. Following the hilly, swampy trail from tree to tree, he cut a 'V' in each trunk and placed a cup underneath. Several hours later, after a quick lunch, it would be time for him to go round and empty the cups. Finally, before he could rest, he had to sit over a fire solidifying the latex on a slowly rotating ball in the smoke. His life was usually short, and the chance of escape almost nil.

From all this forgotten, unacknowledged labour, Manaus and the rubber barons made a fortune. In 1897 $49 million worth of rubber was shipped from Manaus alone, and the city took 20 per cent in tax. It became one of the first cities in Brazil to have piped water and sewage or trams powered by electricity. Extravagances had to be imported from Europe – the latest fashions, food, wines and building materials – and the rich competed to build the flashiest private residence, a few of which survive today. The city authorities began work on the opera house, importing the necessary steel, marble, decorative tiles and chandeliers.

The steel tycoon Andrew Carnegie supposedly said with sadness, 'I ought to have chosen rubber'; yet as the traders in Manaus were outdoing each other in displays of excess, the seeds of their decline had been sown. Literally. Henry Wickham, an Englishman who had spent a year in Amazonia, left Belém in 1876 with 70,000 smuggled *Havea* seeds. After some initial setbacks at London's Botanical Gardens in Kew, the new seedlings were shipped to plantations in Ceylon and Singapore, and later throughout most of Southeast Asia. In 1906 Ceylon produced 500 tons (as opposed to Amazonia's 35,000 tons that year), but by 1914 Asia dominated the market. In 1918 the Amazon produced 30,700 tons and Asia 256,000 tons. An Asian tapper could cover five times as many trees as he went down the ordered plantation rows than the poor *seringueiro* stumbling along in the jungle gloom. So Asian rubber was 50 per cent cheaper, and Manaus' decline was abrupt and catastrophic. Attempts to cultivate rubber trees in Amazon plantations, particularly by Henry Ford on the lower Tapajós, were frustrated by leaf blight, and the plantation of Fordlândia was abandoned in 1946.

During our stay there seemed to be very few travellers passing through Manaus, and I was glad I'd brought Mark with me and wasn't sitting forlornly in the bars waiting for a travelling companion. We did meet an adventurous American, but he was returning home after ten years in Latin America. He'd owned a farm in Belize until it was destroyed by a hurricane that buried him under the ruins of the house (he had malaria at the time and hadn't heard the radio warnings). Then he had gone to Nicaragua to work with the Sandinistas as a nurse, before spending four years as an agronomist in Paraguay.

Dick had been with the Special Forces in Vietnam, and his platoon had frequently parachuted behind enemy lines to gather information. He had completed his year's draft and returned to the States, but like so many other veterans found he couldn't adapt to civilian life, so had re-enlisted for a further year. He'd also felt that he had a responsibility towards the new recruits.

'After all, it had been the older guys who'd kept me alive when I first got there,' he said. 'How could I leave those young kids to fend for themselves?'

On hearing that Mark was Australian he told us this story.

'One night my platoon boarded a plane for a night drop into the North, and before we took off a group of four Australian guys with an amphibious jeep got on too. After we'd been airborne for an hour or so the signal light came on, and the Australians climbed in the vehicle, fastened their seat belts and one yelled out, "Clunk Click every trip!" We didn't know what he was talking about, but an English newsman explained a few weeks later that the phrase came from a government advertisement for seat belts. Anyway, the big doors at the end of the plane opened, and with a whoop and a yell those Aussies started the engine and just drove off the edge!

'My platoon sat there open-mouthed staring at the darkness beyond the doors. What a way to arrive in enemy-held swamps, tumbling down with only the vehicle's parachute! Shit, we thought we were a mean bunch, but those Australians were something else!'

Mark could have talked to Dick for hours about the thrill of combat, the whiff of cordite and weaponry. I made many attempts to dissuade him from army life over the next few weeks, because it was a mystery to me how someone could enjoy the freedom and irresponsibility of three years' travelling, and then voluntarily submit to blind discipline and the abuse of drill sergeants. Mark was determined he could. Anyway at that stage I was pleased to find riddles in Mark's character. Subject for future campfire conversations.

We didn't have much time for chatting as we had shopping to do. We were leaving the bulk of the food supplies for later, but in Manaus we had to buy some of the other gear, including polyester resin, tools for making the canoe, rope, machetes, pots and pans, water containers, knives, hammocks, tarpaulins, mosquito nets, shotguns and ammunition. A few years earlier a foreigner in Brazil had been permitted to buy a firearm over the counter. Not any longer. Now it was a lengthy business that had us running from office to office, pleading and cajoling with bureaucrats until we obtained the necessary authorization. A shotgun was an essential item. Without it we'd be unable to supplement our diet with fresh meat when supplies grew low, or defend ourselves if attacked, so we would have found a way of getting one illegally if they had turned us down.

In the evenings we savoured the last opportunities for restaurant meals, ice-cold beers and, above all, each other's company. We found ourselves clutching at pretexts for delaying our departure, admitting to nervousness about what lay in store. Well-prepared and experienced we might be, to a degree at least, but these were risky ventures. Being so far from help could make a minor accident fatal. We might wreck the canoe in a rapid, losing most of our equipment, get seriously ill or break a limb. We might be attacked by Indians who had been abused by other trespassers on their territory. We joked about such fears, but our stay in Manaus lasted ten days instead of the five we had originally planned.

Finally we forced ourselves on to a riverboat going downstream. Mark and I were going to Santarém, but Martin and Tanis would get off at Obidos. We made thirteen trips between the hotel and boat with all our equipment, and this didn't escape the attention of the captain. He informed me that he would be charging freight, but didn't tell us the price until the following day. The figure was so extortionate that we had to protest, and it wasn't a ritual prelude to some good-natured haggling – his charges would have cleaned out our kitty.

'I have the right to charge 15 per cent of the value of any cargo on board, and I know the cost price of that Yamaha outboard motor (that Martin and Tanis had bought), and I've calculated the value of the remaining items.'

'What's in that cardboard box then?' I asked, pointing at the canoe kit. Of course he had no idea, so I pressed on. 'You don't know what's in it, or what it's worth, so how do you arrive at such a ridiculous sum?'

He was unwilling to negotiate.

'This is my boat. You will pay the freight charges or I'll call the police at the next stop.'

I consulted Martin, Tanis and Mark. It was unfortunate that I was the only one in our group who spoke Portuguese, being temperamentally unsuited to delicate negotiations. Dealings with authority, especially with policemen abroad, have got me into a lot of trouble. I find it very hard to be civil with uncivil characters, and I only have to see one of those swaggering, brutal cops with mirrored sunglasses and a sort of red mist descends. I want to go and knock his beret off. I spoke to the captain a second time and he dropped his charges to 10 per cent, but I needed to get him to accept a flat fee that we could afford.

Our argument was watched by three of his crew who grinned supportively at me when the negotiations grew heated, urging me on with shadow-boxing encouragement from behind the captain's back.

'Just because we're gringos, you think we're made of money and you're out to fleece us!' I said at one point.

The little man puffed out his chest.

'I've been travelling these waters for thirty years!' he shouted, quivering with rage. 'I've trained for this job, studied the changing course of this river longer than any man, transported hundreds of thousands of people safely up and down it, and never, never, has anyone called me a *bandido* before.'

We retreated to our respective corners and calmed down. Opting belatedly for the conciliatory approach, I then shook him by the hand, patted him on the shoulder and apologized for any offence, which of course had been unintentional. But surely he understood that we hadn't budgeted for these charges, and that we were very short of money?

At this moment Tanis managed to squeeze out a tear, no doubt of pity at seeing me grovelling so abjectly, and the mood immediately became warmer. He had not realized we were English, he said. ('And Australian,' added Mark.) He thought we were Americans. The English had always done a lot for Brazil (he hadn't heard of Henry Wickham, it seems), unlike those damn Yankees who only plundered her wealth. He dropped the charges to a fee that we could just afford.

At 2 a.m. on the second night we arrived at Obidos and said goodbye to Martin and Tanis. It was a sad moment. We hugged farewell, surrounded by their piles of gear on the quayside, and the realization of what we planned to do suddenly sank home. We were all thinking it would be a long time before we met again, and that, at the worst, it might be never.

Mark and I arrived in Santarém at dawn the next day. After checking into a hotel we began the quest for a place to assemble the canoe. One of the nice things about being a foreigner in South America is that people seem to expect you to behave eccentrically. Spying some houses with large gardens we knocked on their doors and explained our needs. We were entertainingly odd, but they didn't want us setting up a boatyard on their lawn, thank you. They edged the door shut while dredging up numerous factors that made their particular garden unsuitable for our purposes. Undaunted we approached a large college on a hillside and spoke to a man sitting in the gardens.

He let me explain our requirements in Portuguese before revealing that he was an American priest. The college was run by the Order of the Holy Cross with ten or fifteen American teachers, and they very kindly offered us the use of a thatched, open-sided shelter with a flat earth floor. They also provided a store room for us to lock away all our materials at night.

We could not have asked for a better place, and as the college was closed for the holidays we wouldn't even be surrounded by hundreds of kids as we worked.

In England we had wondered how we would transport the assembled canoe from Santarém to the mouth of the Jari, 250 kilometres downstream. Perhaps we would take the Belém boat and be dropped off on the south bank, and then have to paddle right across the Amazon at nearly its widest point? That wasn't a prospect we relished. However, when we walked along the waterfront enquiring about boats, we found there was one direct to Monte Dourado (paper magnate Daniel Ludwig's town 100 kilometres up the Jari). Things seemed to be clicking into place.

We set to work at once. Neither of us had used fibreglass before and we were apprehensive that we would waste a lot of resin before we got the hang of it. The ratio of resin to catalyst was crucial: too much catalyst and the mixture would solidify in the pot before we had time to apply it. The setting time also varied according to the air temperature, so we bought a calibrated baby's bottle and soon found the ideal ratio that wasted very little.

Assembling the canoe gave us a feeling of personal involvement in the project that we would have missed in buying a ready-made model. Moreover, we could include modifications, like waterproof hatches and extra strengthening, and position the seats just where we wanted them. We were also well aware that the strength of the finished craft was going to depend on our workmanship, so we took our time over it.

Those kits are ingenious, yet simple. The pieces of the hull are supplied cut to shape, and have to be joined together by a combination of stitching, wire twists and fibreglass tape. As the plywood hull is only 6 millimetres thick, we lined the inside with fibreglass matting to give it extra strength. It was fun and interesting to do, and pretty straightforward; although it was six days of hot, sweaty work and we were irked by inadequate tools, we produced quite a fine craft.

Only one problem. We had underestimated the quantity of resin we would need for the job. Even though we had bought two extra litres to allow for repairs while on the river, the internal matting soaked up so much that we had to use it all, and there was nowhere to buy any more unless we made a special trip back to Manaus or Belém.

We did buy some pitch to take with us, but that seemed a poor substitute. It would cover small holes and scrapes, but if something drastic happened, like the canoe cracking open, it would be worthless.

I had a narrow escape when we were tidying up at the end of the job. Having some liquid catalyst left over, I found an oil-drum which was used for rubbish and started to empty the bottle into it. Fortunately a little puff of steam gave me a second's warning and I leapt back just as a mushroom fireball whooshed 3 metres above the top of the drum, singeing my hair and eyebrows. The bottom of the drum had contained hot ashes from a fire that morning, and if it hadn't steamed and warned my turgid brain, I'd have ended up in the burns unit of Santarém hospital – if they had such a thing.

We carried the finished craft down to the river Amazon for trials, and it looked very handsome with its many gleaming coats of varnish. Would it float? In front of the crowd of onlookers that had gathered we would look bloody silly if it didn't. We launched the canoe-with-no-name, and to our relief and pride it floated without listing or leaks. Unfortunately the watertight compartments weren't quite, and as we had no more fibreglass to rectify that, we decided to use them for storing tins of food rather than the more precious items. While making the canoe we'd had help from five or six charming kids, so we rewarded them with canoe rides along the waterfront. They also provided the perfect way to find out the canoe's carrying capacity without risking our belongings. By seeing how many children could be fitted in before it sank, we could then march them to a chemist to be weighed on the scales. Apparently the canoe could take

400 kilos comfortably. Just as well, because our hotel room was becoming congested with supplies.

When planning how much food you'll need for six months you have to think big, even if you intend to live off the land to a degree, as we did. We gathered together kilos and kilos of rice, beans, spaghetti, oats, wheat flour, sugar, salt, coffee, tea, spices, cooking oil, garlic, onions, powdered milk, drinking chocolate and rum. Then there were pots and pans, torch batteries, water containers, machetes, rope, string, tools, clothing, spare paddles, knives, sharpening stones, books, mosquito repellent, fishing rod, reel and tackle, shotgun, 200 cartridges, presents for Indians, tarpaulins, hammocks, mosquito nets and blankets, medical supplies, photographic equipment and other bits and pieces. It all added up to an alarming pile. Would it weigh more or less than seven kids? We wouldn't know until we reached Monte Dourado and loaded up.

We would have loved to take dozens of books with us on a trip into the jungle, but the limitations of weight prevented such a luxury. It is difficult to choose the ideal book for a trip. Even fat, meaty novels would last only a few days each, so we searched for more substantial books that could be read in fits and starts. I opted for *A History of the World* by M Roberts, a formidable piece of scholarship well over a thousand pages long. It was going to fill in a lot of gaps in my knowledge, and I'd be unlikely to read more than twenty pages at any one sitting.

Mark's choice was more unusual, and the source of a great deal of teasing on my part. In pride of place was Debrett's *Etiquette and Modern Manners*. A weird choice of book for a trip where one generally goes naked, eats with the fingers and becomes uninhibited about releasing wind and picking one's nose. I'd skimmed through it – what to wear at Ascot and Wimbledon, the duties of a best man, how to handle funeral arrangements and the correct way to tackle an artichoke and a plate of spaghetti without getting sauce down your tuxedo. I wasn't sure I'd ever get sufficiently bored in the jungle to face Debrett, but Mark clearly felt that spare time should be spent on self-improvement. Second on his list was an English grammar. Finally there was a depressing little manual on emergency war surgery. This was full of colourful descriptions of the devastation caused by tumbling high-velocity bullets, and contained detailed instructions on how to carry out an amputation in the field.

Before we left England Mark had assembled an excellent medical kit that included suturing for wounds, plaster for broken limbs, antibiotics for infection, ampoules of local anaesthetic and painkillers, adrenaline to combat shock, anti-histamines for allergies, eye-drops and creams, multi-vitamins, pills for tapeworm and other parasitical infections, quinine and chloroquine for malaria, temporary fillings for teeth, and a large assortment of dressings. He also spent some time with doctors learning how to administer an injection or set a broken limb. He discovered that in cases of coma after a head injury a build-up of blood can occur in the skull. After a few days this should be drained by getting out your Swiss Army knife and searching for the blade used for drilling little holes in skulls. I drew the line there. I'd rather he let my coma run its course, thank you very much.

We had four days' wait before the riverboat arrived. Travelling often involves a lot of waiting and hanging around, but we were now impatient to get going, and Santarém was a boring little place to spend our last moments in civilization. We could eat well, go swimming in the blue Tapajós from beautiful sandy beaches, and get a little drunk each night, but time dragged.

Compared to some Amazon riverboats the one that took us to Monte Dourado was relatively empty, the food was edible and the journey of two nights and one day short enough to be enjoyable. Having spent a total of more than two months of my life on such boats, I find that the thrill, if there ever was a thrill, has gone. The engine thumps, the jungle flows monotonously past, and waiting for your next bland meal is the highlight of the day. The

BEIRADAO

ceilings are so low that after a few days you disembark with a lumpy skull and curvature of the spine. Then there are competing radios and music players to contend with and the stinking toilets. Amazonia must be a disappointment to the many tourists who confine themselves to a trip up the Amazon by riverboat and a stop at Manaus.

On both sides of the lower Jari lies the land of Jari Florestal e Agropecuaria – the concern headed, until 1982, by American billionaire Daniel Ludwig. He purchased 13.5 million hectares of rainforest for $3 million in 1967, a time when the new military government of Brazil was fully committed to a policy of attracting foreign capital. Ludwig anticipated a world paper shortage in the future and the major part of his operation was the production of pulp for export. He cleared 250,000 hectares and planted them with three fast-growing species of tree – Caribbean pine, eucalyptus and melina – the latter apparently growing to 6 metres high and 8 centimetres in diameter in a mere twelve months. To reach all corners of this vast plantation, he built 4,200 kilometres of road, 36 kilometres of railway and three airfields.

The pulp mill and power plant were assembled on barge-like hulls in Japan and towed 23,300 kilometres across the Indian and Atlantic oceans by tug – a journey that took three months. That was typical of Ludwig's style. Thought to be America's richest man, he pumped an estimated billion dollars into the project over thirteen years. In addition to the pulp operations he also planted a large area of floodplain with rice, and discovered the third-largest Kaolin deposit in the world on his land – a bonus he said he knew nothing about when he bought it.

The project attracted controversy from the beginning. Brazilian citizens resented the acquisition of such a huge area by a foreign concern and, as Ludwig refused to allow visitors during the first years of development, rumours abounded as to what was really going on there. Environmentalists expressed concern about the long-term viability of the project. Would Jari become a failure like so many other grandiose projects in the region, ending only in the bequest of useless, worked-out scrub to future generations of Brazilians? When the delicate tropical rainforest was replaced with three species of foreign tree, would disease and blight run riot down the ordered rows, as had happened in Fordlandia? Surely the fragile soils would not be able to support single-species cultivation for long? Why had he chosen a tract of virgin forest for such a scheme, when it might have worked on previously cleared land?

Many of the people who were initially hostile to the project seemed to change their views when they were finally allowed to visit. Certainly Ludwig had the capital, resources and expert staff to research each stage of development and to overcome most of the problems. The danger was that he would attract less than expert imitators in other parts of Amazonia. He employed over 13,000 people for clearing the forest and establishing the infrastructure, but this number dropped to 4,000 as he was forced to make economies.

Most of Ludwig's grandiose plans failed to come to fruition. Power was generated by burning timber and the bark from the trees he was about to pulp, but he was applying for permission to build a dam on the Jari to provide hydro-electric power. He intended to extend the 4,000 hectares of rice to 13,500, thus producing 140,000 tonnes a year, and introduce enough livestock to make the project self-sufficient in food.

Yet despite all this massive investment Jari was losing an estimated $100 million a year by 1980. The melina, the key tree species, had not grown as fast as anticipated on the sandy soils. Hundreds of millions of dollars more would have to be invested before the project became viable, and even then profitability wasn't guaranteed. Ludwig appealed to the Brazilian government to be guarantor for the import of a second pulp mill. It refused. It also delayed in giving him the definitive legal title to about half the land and turned down his request for $6 million a year to pay for the running of the hospitals, schools and other social amenities he was providing.

In 1982 Ludwig passed control over to a consortium of twenty-three of Brazil's largest companies, and the government put in $180 million. This saved Brazilian face and pride, but the pulp output would have to double or treble before it became a viable concern. All Ludwig could expect to recoup was a small percentage of any profits from 1987 to 2021, and it seems unlikely that there will be any.

3
Early Days

Mark and I would have liked to stay a few days at Monte Dourado. However we had no letters of introduction to help us gain a visit to the project, and we were nervous that some official might demand to see our authorization to travel up the Jari. The longer we hung around, and the longer our canoe was left moored at the jetty, the more risk we ran of arousing unwelcome curiosity. We had not applied for authorization because we were certain it would be refused. We were planning to canoe into a 'security area' (all Brazil's border areas are classified as such), then to cross a frontier that had no controls – or so we hoped – and possibly to cross through an Indian area too. Even a large and prestigious group of accredited scientists would have been lucky to gain permission for such a journey. Best, we felt, to go pleading innocence and ignorance, and hoping to meet no officialdom.

As we loaded the canoe at the waterfront in Monte Dourado that morning, we could see a police post only 100 metres away with a policeman lounging in the doorway. A crowd of onlookers was gathering.

'Where are you going?' one asked.

'Oh, 50 kilometres or so up there,' we gestured vaguely, 'to make a camp and fish for a few weeks.' It must have seemed an awful lot of stuff we were loading into the canoe for a mere fishing trip, but we continued with indecent haste. The present financial state of the Jari project and the success or otherwise of the operation since it changed hands, issues we had been keen to look into before, held no further interest. We wanted to be off, round that bend, out of sight, out of mind.

We launched the canoe in trepidation, not sure whether it would be able to take all the gear, and us as well. We dreaded climbing in and sinking to the bottom in front of all these spectators. However the water level rose to about 2 centimetres below the gunwales and stayed there, and our load could only get lighter as we munched our way through it. We grabbed paddles, waved goodbye and pushed off into the current. Past the police post we went, expecting to hear a shouted command and see a uniformed figure marching down the bank. Nothing. Within five minutes we had rounded the bend and could breathe more easily. At least we had not been stopped before we started.

Fortunately for our debut the Jari was calm and sluggish, and with this canoe we seemed to go as fast upstream as I had gone down in the heavy plank canoes I used on previous trips. The river was about 100 metres wide, the water greeny-black, and apart from one or two glimpses of Ludwig's plantations on the hillsides the jungle along the banks was intact.

Paddling a canoe is hard work for the first few days. There can be few muscles in the upper body that are not called into play – but the back, shoulders and arms ache most. With the sun beating down it is not much fun until the right muscles get into shape. It never becomes fun, exactly, but you develop a rhythm that can be kept up easily for five or six hours a day. So that first day we felt exhausted by the time we stopped to make camp. We still had to sort out our gear properly. The food (all triple-wrapped in plastic bags) we put into a large zipped nylon sack. That stayed in the canoe every night along with our two backpacks and a polystyrene box that held our medical supplies and film. A large kitbag held everything we would need in the way of clothing and bedding each night. Another bag had small quantities of all the staples (rice, beans, sugar, salt, oil, coffee etc) that we would need for cooking at each stop. In a third bag were our camera equipment, a small first-aid kit, books, notebooks and shotgun cartridges. One final sack held all the cooking utensils.

As we brewed up a well-deserved pot of coffee I felt an itching on my ankle, looked down and cursed.

'What's the matter?' asked Mark.

'That,' I said, pointing at my ankle.

'I don't see anything,' he replied, peering closer. 'You mean that little fly there?'

I explained about the pium fly: not much to look at admittedly, but the winged scourge of daytime Amazonia. It can make tough men break down and weep or leap fully clothed into the river, and draw forth a string of obscenities from the lips of the most saintly men. If they had them in Africa, Katharine Hepburn would have gone through *The African Queen* fouler-mouthed than Bogart.

Mark's eyebrows rose in scepticism as he regarded the little speck that was now struggling to get airborne with its load of blood.

'Doesn't look much,' he muttered, but soon he was scratching his arms and legs where little spots of blood and welts marked each bite.

Pium flies had taken a lot of pleasure out of my trips to the Mato Grosso, especially on sections of the river Teles Pires, where they had forced us to travel fully clothed with sleeves rolled down, trousers tucked into socks, and often towels wrapped over our heads. It was ominous to see them so soon on the Jari , although they only attacked when we were ashore. Thankfully, after the first week we never saw them again, but their place was taken by mosquitoes. More about those little bastards later.

We slung our hammocks and mosquito nets, finding a 'triangle' of trees that allowed us to tie both hammocks to the same tree at one end and to different ones at the other. This is a sociable arrangement, and facilitates the use of the tarpaulin to protect you from the rain. The colourful local hammocks are very comfortable once you are accustomed to sleeping on your back and, though mosquito nets make it stuffy on a warm night, they are absolutely essential. Specially made to fit the hammocks they taper around the ropes at each end to stop ants and other creepy-crawlies from joining you in the night. The chore is keeping them in good repair as they get snagged and torn repeatedly by the vegetation.

Having no energy for a fishing excursion we cooked spaghetti for supper, then stretched out in the hammocks listening to the jungle noises. All the aching muscles, the sting of sunburn and itch of bites couldn't overcome the feeling of excitement at being on our way at last. It was good to be back.

The next day we paddled steadily, passing a few houses, until in the afternoon we could hear the roar of rapids up ahead. Although we were over 400 kilometres from the Atlantic, we were helped by a tidal rise of nearly a metre in the morning, which for a while kindly reversed the current. A man fishing from a canoe told us that the sound of rushing water we could hear was the falls of Santo Antônio.

'Will we have to portage round them?' we asked.

He chuckled. 'Well, they'd be hard to paddle up.'

The roar increased, gradually growing in volume, but the river twisted and turned and always hid the falls from sight. On one of these bends was a small cemetery, and towering over the humble crosses was one that looked ornately carved. Curious, we went ashore, and found that it bore a swastika and marked the last resting place of Joseph Greiner. There had been a German Jari Expedition in 1932, and this individual had died of fever. He had either not got very far or had died on the way back and relatively close to civilization. I remarked idly that the cross must have been erected later: it wasn't the sort of memorial that expedition members could knock up in a day or two.

'Perhaps they left Germany with one prepared for each member just in case,' suggested Mark, and our sacrilegious laughter echoed across the graveyard.

When we saw the falls we understood why the fisherman had laughed. The river dropped vertically for over 25 metres, and a haze of spray hung over the gorge. We passed the few dilapidated buildings of the village of Santo Antônio, and fought the crosscurrents below the falls looking for a place to begin our portage. An inlet on the right bank looked as though it had been used for that purpose, so we made camp and went for a reccy. From the water's edge there was a steep, vertical scramble up to the top of the falls, then 300 metres through jungle, followed by an expanse of shallow water littered with slippery rocks, to emerge on an old clearing and finally a large track. We went no further that evening, assuming that the track would join the river upstream after a few hundred metres. Next morning we discovered how wrong we were. It continued for over 4 kilometres, passing another set of rapids before finally reaching calm water. It was going to be a hard day.

We made four trips each with our gear, and came to appreciate what a lot of it there was. Filling our packs to capacity with 30 to 35 kilos, we struggled up the side of the gorge, clinging on to rocks and saplings, hearts threatening to burst, then hopped from rock to rock across the shallows before finally reaching the trail. At least we were on level ground now, but these were early days and we had been lazy about our physical preparation. Rubber-legged we tottered along, with sweat plopping steadily into the dust and pium and ticks feasting on our bare legs and torsos. Forty-five minutes later we reached calm water at last, shrugged off our loads and plunged into the river where we soaked until we could face the walk back. We walked over 30 kilometres that day, half the time laden like mules, but by late afternoon we had everything portaged except the canoe. We struggled up the gorge with it; in our weary state it was three steps up and two back down, with the cheering possibility of toppling to the bottom and the canoe smashing on top of us. We got it over the other obstacles and a few hundred metres further up the trail before our muscles gave out and we abandoned the task till next morning.

Mark had come through the first test with flying colours. He had carried huge loads, and from his comments I gathered he was trying out the sort of burdens under which the troops had 'yomped' in the Falklands war. He was proving an excellent beast of burden, and cheerful company too.

It was nearly dark and we still had to make camp and cook something, but all our sacks of food were dumped on a section of open grassy bank with no trees for the hammocks. So we had to lay them on the ground, fix up mosquito nets with sticks, and put plastic sheeting above that. We were just in time: before we started the cooking, down came the rain. Oh what a jolly end to a fun day! Uncomfortable, hungry and exhausted, we sweated under our airless shelter and broke open the booze supplies. Two mugs of rum got us giggly and helped us forget our troubles. Four local fishermen passed – they had been out in a canoe to position nets – and we all laughed at our unorthodox shelter which was, moreover, proving to be ineffective, with water seeping upwards from our feet.

Next day it took over an hour to coax a fire into life using every trick in the book. On a past trip some gold prospectors had showed me that an old inner tyre tube scrounged from a garage or bike shop makes an effective and economical firelighter. Cut into small pieces, it will burn long enough to first dry and then ignite twigs in most circumstances. With dry kindling a piece less than a centimetre square is plenty, but that morning we scraped the wet bark off twigs searching for the dry interior, shaved chippings from a log and eventually coaxed a reluctant fire into life. Ninety minutes work to cook up some oats and make tea. Nostalgia was growing for high-speed electric kettles and packets of muesli. It needed several brews of tea and coffee to get us moving, and we lounged around in the early morning sun, delaying the hike to fetch the canoe. Meanwhile the fishermen returned, bearing three huge armoured catfish which they tied to a pole and carried home on their shoulders with the tails of the fish dragging along the ground. For some reason I was too weary to hunt for the camera and take their picture. A lapse that I still regret.

The next part of the river was full of rocks just below the surface, without enough current to set up warning ripples. We paddled gently but rammed several and hit others with our paddles. These we had brought out from England and they were a joy to use compared with the heavy local hardwood ones I had used previously. Worried that they wouldn't be strong enough to cope with conditions like this we strapped the blades with insulating tape to prevent any chance of them splitting.

Officially this was supposed to be the dry season, which in northern Amazonia begins in May and ends in November or December. It was now the beginning of July, so it really shouldn't have been raining at all. Yet rain it did almost every day for the first five weeks of our trip, and they were often torrential downpours lasting several hours. If a shower caught us out on the river, it was no big deal so long as it stopped before we got too chilled. The sun came out again and everything dried in a cloud of steam. The jungle, however, continued dripping for many hours, becoming a sodden and cheerless place.

The dry season usually means day after day of cloudless skies. The jungle floor becomes tinder dry, and a tarpaulin is not necessary over the hammocks. However the Jari was never predictable, as we were to learn over the next few months. Perhaps the extra rain was due to its proximity to the Atlantic? Certainly the bad weather rolled in from the east.

We were without fish for the first few days. On previous trips I had relied on hand-lines with pieces of fish for bait, but you have to catch one fish in order to snare others. We tried water-snails, crickets, bugs and grubs with no luck, so we finally shot a medium-sized bird and used that to catch a pintado, a grey-and-black-striped catfish. However it was a long time before we started to catch fish regularly. We had decided that a rod, reel and spinning lures would be a more efficient way of getting fish, and avoid always having some rank piece of bait turning green and stinking in the bottom of the canoe. However during those first days the spinner did not seem to deceive the Jari fish, so we ate large quantities of our rice, beans and spaghetti.

By the fifth day we'd developed a bit of teamwork, with Mark getting the hang of paddling. There was a strong tailwind for much of the day, creating quite a swell and white horses, but we felt secure enough in the canoe. The river was wider here – over 200 metres – and seeing a large house ahead we stayed on the opposite bank, still being paranoid about officialdom. We could see people waving at us, perhaps signalling that we should call in, and someone fired a shot in the air, but we just waved back and kept on going. Perhaps it was an invitation to lunch, but that did not seem worth the risk of too many questions.

To our alarm a few minutes later a motorboat headed our way with a man in the bow training binoculars on us. Three men and a woman drew alongside, and it was the latter who did most of the talking – or rather most of the questioning. We had no map of the lower Jari (ours began at a point where a tributary called the Ipitinga entered from the west) so we told them we were going to that area to camp and fish. They seemed impressed.

'That's a long way. Loads of difficult *cachoeiras* (rapids),' said the boatman, but I was warily watching the man with the binoculars who sat there in silence, regarding us unsmilingly. It was only through the woman that we learnt he was one of the two remaining American technicians working on Ludwig's project, and a surly, morose character he was too. When he did finally speak it was like an interrogation, punctuated by barks of scornful laughter at our plans. It was a sweltering midday, and he had the front to reach into a cooler and pull out a beer in front of us. Just the one. Plop, fizz, went the ring pull, and the can covered with pearly droplets as it came into contact with the hot air. We watched as he drank deeply, sighed contentedly and wiped the froth off his lips with the back of his hand. Deciding that we had no reason to put up with his boorish interrogation any longer, we continued on our way. A few weeks later we discovered that he had reported us to the authorities in Monte Dourado for acting suspiciously.

We had, however, gathered a bit of information about the river from his Indian boatman. It seemed that the Ipitinga was a gold-prospecting area, and that the section up to the confluence was very tricky. As these goldfields were serviced by motorized canoes, we could expect to see a lot of people in the week or so that he thought it might take to get there. After that, on the Jari, there were no more gold camps and we were unlikely to meet anyone.

I went for a long walk that afternoon – clambering up a steep hillside behind our camp. Mark and I were getting on fine, but everyone needs some space. I carried the shotgun in the unlikely event that I needed defending, and I made such a din that all the animals had plenty of warning of my approach. I am full of admiration for hunters who manage to shoot anything in the jungle. Visibility is reduced to about 30 or 40 metres, often less, and if an animal stays still it is almost impossible to spot. Movement is the great betrayer, and as the hunter has to cover a large section of forest he has to betray himself all the time. Also he has to try to walk silently over a carpet of crunchy leaves and debris, pushing past bushes and creepers that clutch at his clothing and rarely allow an unhindered step. It still seems an impossible task to me.

Good Amazon hunters tell me that they usually go barefoot, walk at a snail's pace and pause frequently to look or listen for movement. I have tried all that in more desperate times, but generally the only creatures I've managed to kill are birds and monkeys, either too curious, or over-confident of their safety in the trees. As for deer, well I often see them bounding away in the distance. How on earth do hunters manage to get within shotgun range of a nervous animal that has all its senses in tip-top working order? Beats me.

I have never hunted anywhere else in the world, and feel no urge to do so: the idea of shooting anything that you can't eat seems ridiculous. Occasionally hunting for the pot has become a pressing necessity due to dwindling food stocks, but I wouldn't last long if my life depended on it. Very rarely I find myself moving well in the jungle. I seem to be flitting along for a change instead of fighting it, and briefly I feel silent and deadly. I scan the forest with eagle eyes, my hearing acute, floating almost soundlessly over the ground. At any moment I am going to stumble upon a snoring deer and return to camp with abundant meat. John the city boy transformed into mountain man. The feeling of proficiency usually ends abruptly when I trip over a creeper, fall through a rotten log or get tangled in a thorny thicket. But when I see some potential victim and attempt to sneak up and get in position, the adrenaline and excitement make me quiver like a jelly. At that moment I understand why people hunt for sport. However, when I retrieve the bloody heap of feathers or fur the emotion is at once replaced by sadness and guilt.

That day I followed a ridge for a while before the ground dropped to a marshy hollow. So far all I had seen was a bush turkey that flew up and away, and I was beginning to wonder why I hadn't stayed in my hammock with a good book. Resting the gun against a large tree I squatted down to dry off the sweat and roll a cigarette, but a movement made me glance up, and there was a wild pig trotting my way, 40 metres off and briskly narrowing the gap. Later I cursed my slowness in responding. The animal could not have scented me and movements on my part would not have alarmed it too much. However I reached with ridiculous slowness for the gun, pulling it to my side and cocking the hammer. The click made the pig stop 10 metres away, nose up and twitching, and looking straight at me. A smooth raise to the shoulder, bang, and it would have been pork chops for the boys. However the gun was still only halfway to my shoulder when the pig turned without panic and trotted away. A tree hid it from sight for a while and by the time it reappeared it was just out of range.

Oh well. My strongest emotion was relief that I hadn't ruined the day with bloodshed. The way the little fellow had wrinkled his piggy little snout had been most endearing, and its eyes had met mine in trust.

Mark was passionate about firearms and made little attempt to conceal his scorn for our single-barrelled 20-gauge shotgun. Robust and uncomplicated, it was a good weapon for jungle conditions, but the hammer had to be cocked before each shot, and that was its one defect. That 'click' sounded deafening when stalking any nervous creature.

Mark gave me lengthy dissertations on the ideal choice of firearm for our situation. They all seemed to be Magnum something or others powerful enough to blow doors off barns, and if you hit some small creature you would be picking fur and feathers out of the trees in a 100-metre radius.

When I returned to camp and told him about the pig Mark felt motivated to go on a hunt himself, his first in the jungle. I watched in amusement as he put on his heavy jacket, strapped on the compass, stuffed his pockets with cartridges and set off full of optimism and assurances that I should prepare a hot fire for tonight's roast.

Three-quarters of an hour later he was back, sweaty, scratched, empty-handed and disillusioned.

'How the hell can you hunt in that stuff?' he muttered, and for the rest of the trip he never tried hunting again.

'Of course it's not like shooting kangaroos with a spotlight from the back of a Landrover,' I jibed cruelly. In all fairness, though, Mark at over 2 metres tall was not built for the jungle. I'm also too tall. The Indian's short, stocky stature is ideal.

Our progress up the river became more and more difficult. We asked some passing boatmen about the river up ahead and they all mentioned a large rapid called Tracajá, which would need a portage, and three or four others. That would have been all right, but there were also many stretches of fast water that gave us problems and that the boatmen hadn't considered worth a mention. A tweak of the throttle would get them safely through, but we often had to wade up them or, if the water was too deep to get a secure footing, one of us had to go ahead with the rope while the other swam and guided the boat. One boatman told us we would reach Tracajá the next day – but four days later we still hadn't got there.

After negotiating a maze of fast-flowing channels we emerged into a narrow sluggish river that looked nothing like the Jari that we knew. Lacking a detailed map we were concerned that we might have strayed from the main river and entered a tributary, and after passing two small rapids we brewed some tea and debated what to do. We didn't want to go several days upstream only to have to return, and why had no boats passed us all morning? Deciding to retrace our steps, we'd just run one of the rapids when we heard a motor and hailed the boatmen.

'Is this the Jari or one of its tributaries?" I asked. It must have seemed a dumb question, and the ruffians regarded us stonily.

'Of course it's the Jari,' answered the *motorista*, cursing us under his breath, because in stopping to speak to us his ancient outboard had died. We thanked him and turned around, but until we rounded the next bend we could see the guy repeatedly tugging at his starter cord, and no doubt insulting our parentage.

We began to catch more fish, because rapids are where fish congregate in greatest numbers. My favourite is the tucunaré – a yellow-green predator with an eye-like marking on its flank. Game fishermen know it as the peacock bass and it reminds me of the European perch in shape and by its dorsal fin that becomes erect when it is angry or frightened. When filleted, coated in flour and fried it is delicious. We also caught a brown, scaly fish with pink eyes that I had never seen before. I later learnt it was a traira, but for a few weeks we scientifically named it 'the bony bastard', and we were to catch many of them.

The Amazon is an angler's paradise, containing over 3,000 species of fish, making it by far the richest freshwater habitat in the world. The Congo, by comparison, has a paltry 500 species, and all the rivers of Europe together only 150. The pirarucú is the largest freshwater fish in the world, growing to more than 3 metres and 150 kilos. It's unusual in other respects, too, caring for its young for the first four months of life by secreting a milky fluid from pores in its head. While it has gills it also has a lung, and comes up for air every three minutes. Its scales are bony and abrasive and make excellent nail files should you be worried about the effect of paddling on your manicure.

There are over 500 members of the catfish family in the Amazon – twenty-five times more than in the Mississippi. The largest is the piraiba, which attains over 2 metres and 170 kilos, and there have been cases of piraiba devouring swimming children. The surubim, pintado, pirarara and cuiu-cuiu are other catfish, some covered with armoured plates and with bony pectoral fins behind their gills that can be used to 'walk' across the jungle floor from one pool to another.

The matrinchá is one of the best eating fish, because when it is boiled it gives off a rich, red sauce. The Brazilians say 'it has ketchup included'. Some fish have a firm, red flesh that is indistinguishable from veal when cooked. Others seem to lack bone structure. They sag in your hands in a repulsive manner, and when opened up seem to have a disproportionate amount of intestines. Yet if the process of cleaning them does not upset your appetite, they are good to eat.

Some species of fish – the tambaqui and pacu, for example – are vegetarian, and can be seen splashing under trees when a breeze is shaking off the ripe fruit. Bait a hook and flick it under the tree and the take is immediate, or not at all. A 6-kilo tambaqui gives a hell of a fight with its high-sided shape catching the current and adding to the strain. Some fish will leap to snatch insects off bushes, or raise half of their bodies out of the water (without jumping) to pluck berries off overhanging branches.

Naturally there are a lot of predators and it was these that we caught on the spinners – tucunaré, trairão, pirapopo, piranha, and others we never learnt the names of.

That night, after filling up with fish and rice, I went down to the water's edge to rinse my plate and heard a scuttling in front of me in the dark. Stopping in mid-stride I called to Mark to bring a torch. There a metre away was a large tarantula 12 centimetres across, rocking slightly on its hairy legs. It was debating whether to run away, and that made three of us. There is a temptation, a primeval urge almost, to kill any poisonous creature on sight, especially if it is threatening your territory. This we overcame, as we were feeling benevolent and in harmony with all God's creatures. We shooed it into the undergrowth with much banging of saucepans and encouragements. Mark in fact used to keep a pet bird-eating spider in his bedroom in England and had an affinity for these creatures. He said it had been entertaining to try the spider-in-the-bath routine when he had a girl call round.

Later that night I regretted not killing the tarantula because I kept imagining it was creeping up inside my mosquito net, or at the very least would be in my shoe in the morning. Tarantulas are not particularly venomous, actually, but to have one trot across your face in the night might banish peaceful slumber for a lifetime.

After two portages and a lot of struggle we finally came to the Tracajá rapid. The river fell at 45 degrees over a drop of about 15 metres, but it was not a very long portage and there was a well-trodden path around it. We made some coffee before we started, and got talking to a young prospector who was waiting for a canoe down river. After chatting for a while about our trip and plans he asked me a question that made me doubt my Portuguese.

'Has a loved one been ill recently?'

'No,' I answered, wondering what that had to do with a conversation about the Jari and her difficulties.

'Here in Brazil,' he explained, 'when someone is ill and looks as though he might die, people make vows in church to undertake some sort of painful venture as thanks should there be a recovery.'

I laughed, and reassured him that was not the reason we were there.

'Oh, gold then?'

On every trip I've made to the Amazon I have found that the locals, although invariably friendly and hospitable, assume that I am some agent for a multinational mining company prospecting the big find. However many times I deny this, or even invent other plausible motives such as being a wildlife photographer, I still hear them telling friends that I am a geologist.

This young man kindly helped us get all the gear round the rapid, but it became a race against time because he was drinking steadily all the while. I remember he had his fly buttons undone and no underpants on, but he was totally indifferent to his indecent exposure. At first we trusted him with some sacks that contained fragile objects, but he was swigging with such abandon that by the third trip he could barely get over the rocks unladen. That *cachaça* is so potent it can transform you from a sedate, upright human being to a weaving, slurring liability in five good gulps. By the time we carried the canoe he was leaning on it for support rather than actually lifting it. When sober he had assured us that he was helping out of the kindness of his heart and because he had nothing else to do. Later he tried to demand $100 for his services.

Even once we were past Tracajá we could only paddle a few metres before having to unload the canoe again to negotiate a fast stretch of turbulent water. Then before nightfall we had to carry the gear for over 500 metres and haul the empty canoe through the shallows. It was a pretty tough day, but we ended it with a smile and joke on the lips. A sign that we were getting fitter.

That evening we met the Indian who had been boatman for the American. As he seemed knowledgeable about the river we told him of our plans to portage over the Tumucumaque hills. From the maps there seemed to be three possible tributaries which entered the Jari and which would take us to the border of French Guiana or Surinam: the Cuc, the Ximim-Ximim and the Mapaoni. The Indian had worked in 1967 with a team demarcating the boundary region, and knew the Mapaoni and the Cuc. He reckoned the Ximim-Ximim would be too small and difficult, and thought we would have trouble on the Cuc finding a portage point. There used to be an Indian village and trail up there, he told us, but they would have disappeared long ago.

He recommended the Mapaoni and told us a trail had been cut in 1967 by the Surinamese government to the river Litani. It was in fact marked on two of our maps, and he thought there would be enough Indians using it regularly to keep it open. That was encouraging news, but we had planned to avoid Surinam owing to the political situation there. Just before we left England it was announced that Brazil was sending a task force to the border, complaining of Cuban presence in Surinam. We did not want to blunder unauthorized into a tense military area. With one rusty 20-gauge shotgun we would hardly look like crack soldiers of fortune, but to some bored, bush-crazy frontier guard, we might be of interest.

So we favoured the Cuc, which 'connects' with rivers in more stable French Guiana, and asked the man no further questions about the Mapaoni. We were to regret that later. However, we did learn that the Cuc only had two major rapids – the rest was calm – and also that after the confluence with the Ipitinga the Jari was easier. The present stretch was the worst on the whole river. It had apparently taken the Indian's party twenty-eight days to get to the headwaters of the Mapaoni by motorized canoe. He was envious of our trip.

'You'll have a great time,' he said, and listened to our plans without surprise or amusement. I asked him the names of rapids between Monte Dourado and Ipitinga, and it was a long list: Santo Antônio, Itapeara, Escalão, Tracajá, Acaipé, Cumarú, Itace, Veriverina, Sete Pancadas, Cajú, Inajá, Aurora, Marcaranduba and Ipitinga, in addition, no doubt, to a lot of small stuff in between not worth a mention. (A dismissive term for the smaller rapids among the Jari boatmen was 'bubbles'. These 'bubbles' would frequently take us an hour or two of danger, strain and discomfort to ascend.) At least that list did not have the evocative names of some Brazilian rapids that I had met in the past: 'Hell', 'Purgatory', 'Disaster', ' Disillusion'.

The boatman's assurances that the stretch of the Jari up to the Ipitinga was the worst on the whole river gave us much-needed encouragement over the next couple of weeks. There was never more than ten minutes' quiet paddling at any one time. Either the current became so fast we had to churn the water to a froth just to make headway, or small rapids would make us get out and wade. Luckily it was still a novel experience, so we hopped in and out of the water with good humour and stoicism. We had expected rapids and we were gaining experience in the teamwork and technique needed to get past them.

We evidently had a lot to learn, for on the tenth day we came near to disaster. We had just stopped at one of the rare houses to inquire about the river up ahead, and the owner told us that we were just below the rapid of Itacé which flowed round dozens of islands in channels of varying ferocity. Like all the people hereabouts he had his favourite disaster story. Two rainy seasons previously a canoe with ten people on board had mistaken a channel and overturned. Pieces of canoe and one or two personal effects were found, but not a single body was recovered.

Cheered by this information we followed his advice and set off up the right-hand channel. Half an hour later as we were struggling to get past a small fall we were overtaken by two men in a dug-out and we watched their technique with admiration. The one in the bow stood up and used a punting pole; the other sat in the stern with a paddle. Reaching the metre-high fall, the poler ran back down the canoe to make the bow rear up, gave a fast jab with the pole and banged the bow down on the rocky lip of the drop. A few more pushes and they were above it and on their way. Waist deep in water, unloading sacks, we were impressed and envious. Of course our canoe would not have withstood such treatment, and we were fully laden with provisions. You can't have great strength *and* lightness. 'Flash buggers,' we muttered, and got on with it our way.

Soon we came across a section of river where the water poured down a small chute, and we decided that if we used the rope it would give us few problems. I took up position on a rock 10 metres in front, while Mark stayed at the bow and began to walk the canoe up. We had done this type of operation numerous times that day already, and perhaps we were too off-hand. Mark lost his footing in the deep, fast water and the bow swung sideways and tipped.

'Look out!' I yelled. 'Let go of the canoe, let it go!' But as Mark couldn't get a footing he naturally held on to the bow for dear life, and by doing so he pushed it across the current and added his weight to the rope.

As Mark said later, 'It was fine for you up there on that dry rock to shout, "Let go!" I just thought, "Up yours!" and held on like a bloody limpet.'

Understandable – there was a lot of fast water below this rapid, but the canoe had started to fill and the strain on the rope grew impossible.

'I'm letting go of the rope! Try to straighten it up!'

There was still a chance that if the canoe was put bow-on to the current it would zip straight down the rapid to the calm water below. No such luck. It filled and turned on its side; our stuff spilled out and started to float away.

Leaping into the water I helped Mark throw gear onto the rocks. The canoe meanwhile had ended up broadside to the current, wedged between two rocks with the full force of the water pouring into and over it. It was imperative we did something, but to get the canoe off we had to lift it full of water, causing even greater strain, before it floated clear. We hung on and were swept downstream, with Mark being sucked under before we could get into a quiet eddy. The canoe was still intact, so full marks to Granta Boats (and our craftsmanship, of course).

A lot of gear had disappeared, including the shotgun and machete. Some bags of provisions were wedged in the overhanging bushes by the bank, heavier ones were on the bottom where the canoe had tipped over. We spent the next two hours wading in the fast water, feeling in every crevice with our toes (not now, electric eel, I'm busy). That way we found the gun, machete and nearly everything else.

It had been a narrow escape, and we had got off very lightly. Everything was soaked, water had penetrated all our triple-wrapped food supplies, and our two cameras were full of water. As mine was a sophisticated model with an electronic shutter, absolutely nothing was working. Mark's was a mechanical one that he could dismantle and spread out to dry in the sun, and we were hopeful that it might be all right. Fortunately it was a sunny day for a change, so we laid the tarpaulins on rocks and spread the wet food supplies over them to dry.

A sobering lesson. Having previously always travelled downstream I still had to learn the different techniques for negotiating rapids against the current. When roping downstream you can often get hastily through tricky bits by slackening the rope and letting the canoe buck over. Going upstream you are crawling up through these sections for much longer and it only needs the shipping of a couple of dozen litres of water before the canoe becomes too heavy to hold.

We had also learnt that in deep, fast water the 'swimmer' is no help at all. He can't get a firm footing, so flounders and leans on the canoe for support, thus pushing the bow sideways. Most important, and tedious though it is, it is essential to unload a few bags of gear first. It makes the canoe much easier to handle, and by selecting the bags you unload you can make sure that the important stuff is safely on the rocks should things go wrong.

That night it poured with rain for five hours. The Jari likes to put the boot in when you're down. Already a love-hate relationship was developing between us and the river. It was beautiful but mean, unpredictable and intolerant of mistakes. 'Not for boys,' we would joke as we struggled up yet another fierce section. 'A man's river.' But we weren't sure in which category we belonged.

Wild food remained scarce. As we were only doing 4 or 5 kilometres a day, we felt compelled to work longer and camp later. Longer days meant less time for fishing, so we just delved into our food rations with enormous appetite but no fish supplement. We had a self-imposed hunting ban in force. It seemed too early to be killing anything.

An hour or two a day was spent checking out the river ahead, finding the easiest channel and seeing if it would be impassable upstream. We saw a lot of monkeys and one day I encountered the largest, blackest tapir I have ever seen. I was within 3 metres before I saw it half-hidden in some bushes; we stood and contemplated each other for a while before it caught my scent and crashed away with a thunder of hooves.

The tapir is the largest land animal in Amazonia (the manatee being the largest creature) and it is solitary, shy, short-sighted and hard of hearing. Its sense of smell, however, is acute. With its short proboscis and great bulk it is reminiscent of a small elephant, and we frequently saw its deeply punched tracks in the muddy margins of the river – three toes on the forefoot, and four on the hind. The river is the tapir's second home, where it feeds on the water plants and wallows during the heat of the day. When alarmed it can submerge and stay under water for several minutes. Carrying 150 kilos of tasty meat, it is considered a very desirable prey by hunters.

On we pushed. Being rocky, the banks were often difficult to negotiate when portaging. It was a matter of hopping over huge boulders with the gear and canoe, risking a fall and an injury. Several times we had to return downstream to find alternative channels and our spirits started to flag for the first time. It was an unmitigated slog with no respite and without even the encouragement of good progress. We had no idea where we were. Although we'd been given the names of rapids, they were more or less continuous, so we didn't know where one ended and the next began. For example Sete Pancadas is, as you'd expect from the name, seven separate drops over a kilometre or more. But there were similar little cascades all through this section. Our legs and feet were suffering most. While walking in the deep, rocky water we often banged our knees or shins, so we were covered in bruises and cuts that re-opened several times a day. These were not the only perils of spending so much time in the water. Twice we saw snakes swimming nearby – a metre-long venomous coral, and another dark brown one of nearly 2 metres.

At least I had been in Amazonia long enough not to be worried about piranha. They were everywhere, and we grew pretty blasé about them. I've never heard of anyone being attacked by piranha, only bitten when taking them off the hook, and the locals show little concern. Like sharks, they probably have mad moments when they attack – when cut off in stagnant pools in the dry season with a shortage of food, for example. But we certainly gave them every chance on this trip – wading, swimming, often oozing a bit of blood – and they were a disappointment. Poor piranha, stars of Hollywood movies, lurid travellers' tales and all: a tough reputation to live up to. The only fish that did bite us were the little minnows that made us jump by nibbling at the pus of infected cuts. If you could stand it they did a great job of debriding wounds, leaving them clear of dead tissue.

I had always associated piranha with slow, sluggish water, but we caught plenty in rapids on a spinner. While they never provided us with first-hand experience of their flesh-stripping ability, they are ghoulish little horrors. We were mystified as to why so many of the tucunaré and trairão we caught had bloody, semi-circular chunks taken out of fins and flanks. Then we realized that, while they were fighting the hook, groups of piranha had taken advantage to nip in for a nibble.

Piranha grunt, and these grunts can be heard before you've pulled the fish to the surface, so that you know what is on the end of the line should you not have recognized the feeble tugging fight. I have seen piranha bite through a hook, and if you put a knife blade in their jaws they will snap and snap at it until rendered toothless. They also grew very large on the Jari – 2 kilos was common – and they are reasonably tasty although hard to scale. It's easiest to remove their guts, pop them on hot coals, let them blacken on both sides and then peel the skin off before eating.

I do have one piranha story. In 1980 I canoed a section of the upper Teles Pires, and my companion on this trip was an Italian, Andrea Bettella, whom I'd picked up in a Manaus bar. (Actually I'd arrived in Brazil with two guys from England, and we'd been grateful to recruit Andrea because three is an awkward number to fit in one canoe. A couple of weeks later while we were making two canoes at a sawmill in the town of Sinop in the Mato Grosso, the two Englishmen did a flit from the hotel, just leaving me a note: *'Had enough. Gone to Rio.'*)

I'd turned to Andrea in stunned disbelief. 'They've buggered off,' I said.

'Oh good,' he'd replied. 'I always thought they were a couple of wankers, but what could I say when you'd recruited them? We'll have a much better trip now.'

And so we did. Anyway, one day on the Teles Pires, we came across a camp of São Paulo businessmen. They had come to spend a week's holiday hunting and fishing in the jungle, and they were a friendly crowd, if a conservationist's nightmare. They shot everything in sight, and by placing gill nets everywhere caught hundreds of kilos of fish which they dried and salted to take home. We stayed with them for three days without much persuasion; after all they had coolers filled with cold beer, bottles of whisky and all sorts of tasty food.

They had a huge piraiba catfish tethered to a tree to keep it alive and fresh until just before they departed, and it was the biggest specimen I've ever seen. Over 100 kilos they reckoned, 2.5 metres long, and with a whiskery mouth wide enough to hold a beach ball. It was truly awesome.

Time passed in an inebriated haze, but I clearly remember that one of the Brazilians became argumentative and aggressive, and loved to blast away with his arsenal of weapons. He once gave me a shock by shooting a can of beer away just as I was reaching to pick it up. One regular chore was to bring in the catch from the gill nets, and I estimate we had over 80 kilos of fish to clean on the riverbank each time. All the entrails, heads and muck were tossed into the slow current in front of us. On one occasion when we had finished, the tiresome Brazilian announced he was going for a swim. Everyone tried to stop him – after all, we had just dumped 20 kilos of blood and guts right there and the water should have been swarming with piranha. He paid us no heed, so I furtively got out my camera. I wasn't going to miss this scoop of the century, and the first authentic case of a piranha attack. Already I could picture the water boiling and the stripped skeleton of a hand appearing and waving a couple of times before it disappeared. One photo could pay for the whole trip. In he went, and I followed him through the viewfinder as we all held our breath. Well, the guy swam for ten minutes and nothing happened. Nothing. Not even when in my disappointment I suggested he went out further and tried swimming downstream.

4

Slow Progress

During the days we spent struggling with Sete Pancadas (or was it Cajú or Veriverina?) we were aware of the beauty of the river, but without much time to appreciate it. We paddled past dozens of jungle-clad islands, and large black boulders jutting out from the swirling waters. Steep hillsides rose 40 metres or more on either bank, and we negotiated little channels full of exotic scents, butterflies and flowers, while raucous macaws flew overhead. We enjoyed some beautiful campsites on rocky islets with mica-strewn sandy beaches, so occasionally we would forget the difficulties, try not to look at all those rapids upstream, and just open our eyes to the good things around us. We came to regard getting past the Ipitinga as the true beginning of the trip, and what we were going through now was a hard and unfortunate initiation. Up there we should live better and hopefully make better progress.

After not seeing anybody for five days we happened to be chest-deep in another rapid when a canoe pulled alongside. It was not the most dignified position from which to conduct a conversation, and the occupants of the canoe, gold-prospectors and whores from upstream, must have thought we were crazy. We had begun to share those sentiments. Our fame was apparently spreading, because they had heard about us. But we were going very slowly, weren't we? We smiled through clenched teeth and muttered that naturally we could not go as fast as they could with their motor.

'*Muito corajem* (very brave),' said the boatman. What he really meant was, 'You gringos are a bit soft in the head; and with all the money those multinational mining corporations have, you'd think they could buy you a motor.'

We learned that we had passed Sete Pancadas and were now just below Cajú rapid. This is one of the fiercest rapids on the river – it only drops once, but down a chute and across submerged rocks that create huge waves. We camped below it in one of the loveliest campsites we'd found to date. There was a huge bay over 500 metres across before the river separated again to depart down seven major channels. Round the bay were numerous sandy beaches that I walked along, occasionally casting the spinner, hoping to catch some supper. It looked a superb fishing spot, with deep pools and swirling eddies, but to my surprise there was not a bite.

That evening black clouds started to roll in from the east yet again. We quickly rigged up our tarpaulins and collected enough dry wood to cook both supper and next day's breakfast. All we had was rice again, and a packet of dried soup – insufficient reward after a hard day. The trees near our fire proved too flimsy to take our weight, so we hung the hammocks 50 metres away and, since the clear and star-filled sky now seemed to promise no rain, decided to leave the tarpaulin off. For a while, anointed with insect repellent, we lounged on the beach, and Mark gave me an hour's tuition on complex star constellations.

The heavens were ablaze. It would have been pleasant to lie there companionably watching the shooting stars for several hours, but we were suffering from insect bites through our clothing. For repellent to be 100 per cent effective on the Jari, you have to put it all over the body before getting dressed. Our thick shirts and trousers alone were no protection against the mosquitoes' lances.

After a mug of rum we settled into the hammocks and went to sleep in a good mood. At midnight it began to pour with rain. It is always the same story – put up the tarp and you are guaranteed a dry night, leave it off and it will rain for sure. As we were blundering around in the dark I felt a searing pain in my ankle that made me cry out. Mark shone the torch and it was a relief not to see a snake slithering away. We never found out what had stung me. A scorpion probably, or one of those solitary black ants, but although my ankle swelled a bit and I felt feverish that night, I suffered no long-term effects.

The next morning brought some good news to start the day. I had taken to sleeping with the camera batteries inside my trouser pockets to warm them up and dry them out, and when I tried one in the camera at breakfast time everything seemed to be working again. I reloaded with film and looked forward to being able to record our progress once more.

We were lucky with the rapid, too. On the left bank of the river there was a shallow section that we could wade up, although only 3 metres to our right the water boiled up into back-curling waves higher than our heads. Gingerly we crept along, knowing that with one false move we'd be sucked that way and our bodies might not surface for weeks. Best not to look there, best not to even think about it. The roar of the water was so loud that we had to shout to hear each other even though barely a metre apart.

Somehow we kept in pretty good spirits. Occasionally we had little tantrums and cyclical depressions, but were generally amazingly cheerful. We sang and joked, or swore and cursed. We took each new difficulty that the Jari threw up as one more challenge to be overcome. We were not going to let that river break us, even if it came near to it several times. After Cajú we had five days when we never paddled more than 100 metres at a stretch without having to get out to wade, rope up or portage.

It seemed like it was never going to end. A couple of boats passed us, and it made us feel better to see that even with their motors they were having a hard time. With the engine at full throttle the crew still leapt out and heaved on ropes.

The six days we were told we would need to get to Ipitinga had stretched to three weeks. We gave up asking people how many days they thought it would take us. No one had paddled up here for years, and all they did was double the time it took by motor, which wasn't realistic at all. Finally, on the twenty-first day, we had a much-deserved stroke of luck. It had been a bad morning of the usual kind and we had nearly had another disaster when the canoe turned broadside and hit a rock. We shipped a lot of water but luckily were able to leap out and bring it under control. We then had a very tiresome kilometre during which we paddled like crazy and saw the jungle crawl by. If we stopped paddling to wipe the sweat out of our eyes or scratch an insect bite we would be swept back to where we had been five minutes before. We had become adept at 'hedge-hopping', keeping right into the bank using the protection afforded by the bushes. We were lashed by branches as we zigzagged along, but saved a little bit of effort by escaping the worst of the current.

Soon the water was so fast we were making no headway by paddling. Yet it was too deep for us to wade. It was up to my chest, and there are few more frustrating experiences than wading in deep fast water. Lift one foot off the bottom, try to move it forward, and it seems paralysed, so we often hung on to bushes and pulled ourselves up hand over hand with our legs swept out horizontally behind us, the canoe being towed by a rope around our chests.

It was while we were in this dispiriting situation that a canoe came up behind us. We waved it over.

'Are we near the Ipitinga?' we asked.

'Oh no,' came the reply. 'It's still a long way.'

Seeing our crestfallen faces they offered us a tow to a place called Carecaru. We transferred Mark and all our gear into their large dug-out and I stayed in ours so I could steer and follow their line.

It was exciting to roar along while the boatmen zigzagged across the river choosing the easiest sections and dodging rocks. By ruddering with the paddle I tried to keep exactly on his line or risk holing the canoe. Once the motor stalled in a fast section and all the men jumped out to hold on, but the canoes began to slip backwards with me dangling on the rope in the fiercest turbulence, unable to do a damn thing as the canoe reared and weaved. On other occasions the motor was not powerful enough, and one of the crew would need to get up ahead to haul on the rope. As the current stopped him getting there direct, he would jump overboard, swim to the bank, make his way upstream on land and then swim out to a rock where the rope would be thrown to him. Not a job I would have relished. But in three or four hours we covered what would have taken us two or three days to paddle and we got to Carecaru at dusk.

The last part of the towing exercise had been misery for me. I felt frozen stiff, and in the breeze of our progress my teeth were chattering and I was covered in goose-pimples. Unfortunately my clothing was in the other canoe, so I had to sit there in only my shorts for an hour trying desperately to concentrate on steering. Had we entered a new climate zone or was it me? I looked at the others. Everyone seemed warm and comfortable. Why then were my fingertips blue?

There is really only one plausible reason for people to shiver in a tropical afternoon with the air temperature over 80 degrees F. Malaria. It was a truth I did not want to accept, and once we reached our destination I put on a couple of sweatshirts and tried to put it out of my mind.

There were three houses opposite the mouth of the Rio Carecaru, and a goldfield two days' journey upstream. People hang around there waiting for a boat up to Ipitinga, or down to Monte Dourado. Mark and I stayed two days and the people were good to us, letting us use their butane stove (which seemed unbelievably luxurious after our open-fire cooking), and giving us food, a shelter to hang our hammocks, coffee and booze.

We gathered as much information as we could about the river up ahead. By now we had dropped the pretence of going no further than the Ipitinga, and told the inhabitants of our project to try to cross to French Guiana. No one we spoke to had actually travelled beyond the Ipitinga, so information was scarce and based only on hearsay. Two people did tell us that there was a FUNAI post (the Brazilian Indian Protection Agency) at a place called Molocopote, positioned to stop anyone from going any further upstream. Where exactly this Molocopote was no one could agree. At the mouth of the Cuc, said one. Forty kilometres beyond the Cuc, said another. However the information did reinforce our choice of the Cuc for that section of our route. It seemed we would not get up to the Mapaoni without passing this control.

On our first night at Carecaru two men went hunting and shot a puma and a paca (a large nocturnal rodent prized for its meat). Seeing only the eyes of the cat in the torch beam they had shot it, but discovering it was a puma, whose coat is considered worthless, and not a jaguar, they cut off one of its paws as a memento and left the rest to rot. Fortunately the number of professional cat hunters (*gateiros*) has declined in recent years. In the early 1960s they were taking an estimated 15,000 jaguars and 80,000 ocelots a year, but that has now dropped to about a quarter of those figures. In 1967 the Brazilian government banned the commercial exploitation of all wildlife. The powerful skin exporters complained bitterly that they were left with large quantities of stock-piled furs, so the government gave them until 1971 to liquidate these. Naturally the firms had inflated the size of their stocks, so the hunting actually intensified between 1967 and 1971. In 1968, 6,389 jaguar and 81,226 ocelot skins were exported from Brazil to the United States. Even in 1975 the UK imported nearly 50,000 ocelot skins from Brazil.

The hunting obviously still goes on – Amazonia is far too large to be effectively policed. You cannot condemn a Brazilian homesteader for shooting these cats – he can earn two or three months' pay for each one – and as long as the demand exists he will continue to do so. Yet the consensus of opinion on the rivers I have travelled was that there are now too many obstacles placed in the way of the *gateiro* to make it worth his while. Most importantly some of the countries which were the main markets for these furs have imposed a ban on their import through CITES, and fashions have changed.

An ex-*gateiro* told me how he went about his business. A *patrão* (boss) equipped a team of three or four men with food and ammunition on the understanding that any furs would be sold to him on their return. They would set off up the remoter tributaries at the beginning of the dry season and hunt for four or five months. Ocelots were generally caught in baited traps with a sliding or weighted door, and the men would construct a hundred or more of these along the riverbank. A far crueller method was to tie three large fish hooks together and cover them with a lump of meat. This was suspended about 2 metres off the ground so that the ocelot would leap for it, impale itself in the mouth and be left dangling there until the hunter returned and strangled it. This method was often favoured as it entailed less work than trap-making.

Jaguars were generally attracted by dragging a monkey carcass along the jungle floor to leave a scent trail, and then shot by a hunter at night from a hammock suspended a safe distance above the ground. Or they could be called by imitating the panting groan of a cat. The instrument used to do this is a hollow tube of wood covered at one end with a stretched hide. A horsehair cord was passed through a hole in the hide and through the tube, and wetting the finger and rubbing it down the cord reproduce the call.

A team of men working intensively like this could account for a large number of kills. If the take fell below two cats a night they would consider the area to be poor and would move on. Five or six cats a night was common, and naturally any other animal with a commercially valuable skin – giant otter, brocket deer, peccary or caiman – was also taken.

These days it is habitat destruction that presents the greatest threat to Amazonian wildlife, and while men continue to take animals for the pot and do not pass up the opportunity to shoot commercially valuable animals, not many are engaged in the activity full time. Others, like the guys at Carecaru, will shoot because it is supposedly manly to confront a jaguar or puma with a 20-gauge shotgun. Probably the fur would be damaged anyhow or improperly cured, but the hunter would have risen in his own esteem and in the eyes of his fellows. Machismo probably accounts for a good proportion of jaguar deaths in Amazonia.

We used the time at Carecaru to go through our stuff and count our dwindling food stocks. We had eaten much more than expected, owing to our lack of success at fishing. One of the men was taking sacks of provisions up to the goldfields, so from him we bought 15 kilos of *farinha* (manioc flour), some oil, torch batteries, rice and sugar at prices four times those in Monte Dourado. A bottle of rum was 20 times more expensive, but we still had loads of that.

Farinha is a gritty flour that hasn't much flavour, but that adds a welcome crunch to a plate of rice. It's prepared by soaking the manioc tubers for a day or two and then crushing them to remove the poisonous prussic acid before they are grated and toasted. Surveys have revealed that most *caboclos* (Brazilians of mixed Indian and European descent) have dangerously high levels of this poison in their bodies owing to years of eating inadequately prepared farinha.

My suspicions of having malaria proved well-founded during our stay. Having had it before, I was able to recognize the symptoms – headache, muscular pains, shivers, tender midriff and weakness. Several people at Carecaru were suffering from the disease and we handed out a few Fansidar tablets to control it for a while. Rural Brazilians have a blind faith in anything pharmaceutical. Rarely able to afford a visit to a doctor (or indeed find one in remoter areas) they are prey to the pharmacies which are big business in all South America. There seems to be one on every corner, and on their shelves one sees medications that are banned in the developed world but have been dumped there by unscrupulous drug companies. There are 14,000 types of drug available in Brazil as opposed to 7,000 in Britain.

Brazilians stress the need for vitamins after a malaria attack – and I think there is some justification in that, because malaria does make you anaemic. Yet strength can easily be regained by a good diet and taking vitamins orally. Not good enough. A pill is always better than a syrup, and an injection better than a pill. We saw the boss of Carecaru giving his daughter a huge intravenous injection of vitamins taken from an unsterilized bottle – liquid that was probably designed to be taken orally anyway. We did try to mention tactfully that it was not such a great idea, but as he had done it several times and so far got away without killing anybody, he was not to be dissuaded.

We set off wearily at dawn, as there had been a bit of a party next door until 3 a.m. Had I felt better I would have joined them, but I was buried under about five blankets feeling sorry for myself.

A couple of kilometres upstream we passed the airstrip belonging to CPRM, the government agency that explores mineral resources. I was beginning to feel very unwell but tried to ignore it as we dipped our paddles against a strong current for the next two hours. Finally I suggested a rest to brew up some coffee, and out of curiosity took my temperature. One hundred and three degrees. This was malaria, no doubt about it.

5
Malaria

Back in 1980 I had been naïve and trusting about the effectiveness of my anti-malaria medication.

'No, it can't be,' I told Brazilians who had just told me that my symptoms could be nothing else, and who should recognize malaria when they see it, 'I take Maloprim once a week.' Anyway I was twelve days from the nearest hospital where I could be diagnosed or get any treatment, so I just had to let it run its course.

It started when I was riding on the top of a truck from the Mato Grosso up to Santarém on the Amazon. Sun-whipped and covered in red dust during the day, and frozen at night, conditions weren't perfect for an invalid, and the journey took five days instead of two because we were delayed by a collapsing bridge. Several trucks had drawn up on both sides of the creek, no one daring to cross. The bridge was tilting alarmingly, and the drivers decided they would shore it up themselves rather than wait two weeks for the authorities to send a team. They cut medium-sized trees into 3-metre lengths with a chain saw, and we carried them 200 metres to the bridge. I tried my best to help but as I'd had attacks of fever for the previous three days,

I felt very weak and retired to the shade after two hours. The two drivers of my truck were fairly sympathetic, having seen that I was ill, but the others weren't at all. I've noticed this in developing countries – ill people do not receive the pampering and fuss we have come to expect, and a sick tourist is often a source of entertainment. One of the drivers commented that no wonder the British economy was in such a state if everyone lay down instead of working! Another, when I said I'd had fever for three days, spat and said he had once had it for ten days but still drove his truck. Conveniently the malarial chills started shortly afterwards, and even the most insensitive can't fail to be impressed by the sight of a guy lying groaning in the full sun, wrapped in a cocoon of blankets, body shaking and teeth chattering.

At Santarém the delays weren't over as there was no boat to Manaus for three days, so I lay in a hotel room wracked with rigours and fever. My problems were compounded by a shortage of money. I'd just come off the Teles Pires river, and after putting aside enough for my boat ticket to Manaus (where money was waiting), I had to choose between a hotel and eating. Good job I wasn't hungry. Even when treated to a meal by another traveller I found I couldn't eat more than a mouthful anyway. Everything tasted unpleasant, and just the sight or smell of it made me retch.

So I had not eaten for several days by the time the boat set sail. The most alarming development was that I had started to see blood in my urine, which was a sign of something bad, but I didn't know what. Kidneys? Liver? I slung my hammock and crawled into it, knowing that at least food was provided with the fare if I felt like it, and that within three days I would have money to see a doctor in Manaus.

However, life always chooses such moments for delays. Twelve hours out from Santarém the propeller broke and another two days passed before we got underway again. By now I'd had fever for nine days and each afternoon the attacks seemed more severe. Trying to fight the violent shivers left me totally exhausted, and then I poured with sweat until my shirt and trousers didn't have a dry patch on them. After a few hours, feeling marginally better, I needed to get up for a pee and to drink some water. By this time it was usually midnight and everyone was asleep.

The deck was completely obstructed by hammocks and the easiest way for someone of my size to get to the toilets at the far end was to crawl along the floor, over the luggage and under the low-slung hammocks. After risking other diseases by gulping a litre or two of untreated river water I returned the same way. Before retiring to my sodden hammock I dug out some aspirin from my backpack – although they did little to relieve the appalling headaches.

Perhaps it was paranoia, but the passengers on the boat seemed hostile and unfriendly – two very rare characteristics in Brazil. This may have been partly explained by my lack of sociability. I wasn't in the mood, and made no effort to pick up the conversational openers thrown in my direction. I wanted to lie there and suffer in peace and privacy.

On the second night of the renewed boat journey I crawled to the far end for the usual reasons, and found several men still up and playing cards. Finding the water container empty, I asked one of them if he would mind filling it for me. That meant hanging over the side of the lower deck and scooping it from the river, and I didn't trust my strength and feared I would fall overboard.

'Fill it yourself, gringo,' he replied, not looking up from his cards. I must have looked ill – hair plastered to my head with sweat, clothes sodden, swaying on rubbery legs – but I explained I was sick.

One of them got up reluctantly to fill the jug, but another commented that a fall into the river was the best thing that could happen to me. I then surprised us all by bursting into tears. I felt so bloody ill, miserable, weak and far from home.

That night the paranoid nightmares started: gold was hidden on me and everyone was out to kill me. No one could be trusted. My illness was their chance to get the gold and toss me overboard. By morning I could barely distinguish between dream and reality, and with a temperature of 104 degrees those delusions continued all day. Everyone passing my hammock was a potential assailant, and anyone regarding me with mild curiosity was a jackal waiting for my end. That end did not seem far away: my clothing, after repeated soakings in sweat, seemed to have the sickly sweet odour of death. My body was beginning to rot already.

In the late afternoon when I started to shake, rattle and roll in another attack, I became aware of a commotion around my hammock. Summoning reserves of strength I listened to the shouting voices.

'Every night I see him crawling around under the hammocks opening suitcases,' said one.

'Let's search his pack to see if he's hidden it in there,' suggested another. People then grabbed my pack and began to pull out the contents. When they found my camera they let out a cry of delight.

'If we don't find the money, this must be worth something.' I sat up, shivering violently, and asked what the hell was going on. Someone had had a large sum of money stolen from his suitcase, I was told, and I was the prime suspect. An excited crowd had gathered, so I asked who it was that was accusing me. Two men came sheepishly forward and I tried to conduct my defence through chattering teeth. I said they were welcome to look through my pack, and if it were really necessary I would even get up and let them search my clothing and body too.

'Why do you open people's suitcases at night?' one asked me. So I explained that the only baggage I opened was my own to get aspirin. Without even finishing the search of my luggage, the men departed and the passengers collected in little groups discussing the case out of earshot. I realized I was crying again, and I'd probably been sobbing when replying to my accusers. Later the captain came over and said that I was cleared of suspicion; they'd decided the thief must have got off at the previous stop.

'You've got malaria,' he told me.

'Oh no, it can't be. I take a pill called Maloprim,' I replied and even refused some chloroquine that he offered me.

We got to Manaus the next day. Just getting my hammock untied and stowed away in my pack took over an hour, then I fainted twice in the street on the way to the bank. But with money in my pocket at last I got a taxi to the hospital where they diagnosed falciparum malaria.

Now, when I think back on that boat trip, one thing bothers me. Did the incident of the stolen money ever happen? Or was it all mixed up with the nightmare about the stash of gold? There is no doubt that I believed it at the time – and probably even sat up sobbing a defence – but did I imagine the rest? Three days after arriving in Manaus, when I was starting to feel stronger after some treatment, I spent half an hour searching my possessions for that gold. The nightmare had taken hold. Had it been stolen, or had it never existed?

Well, here on the Jari three years later, malaria was back. This time I was more sceptical and had been expecting it despite taking the preventive pills. That naivety and blind faith in their effectiveness had gone. Fortunately we had plenty of drugs to cure or control the disease: enough quinine for six treatments if the malaria was falciparum (the fatal, cerebral strain), and plenty of chloroquine for vivax. Vivax is the most common of the four human malarias (*Plasmodium falciparum*, *malariae*, *ovale* and *vivax*), but is rarely fatal except through cases of enlarged or rupturing spleens. It can cause more relapses and recurrences, however, because the parasite can become dormant in your liver for months or even years. In my experience, though, there's no difference in the symptoms and misery of either strain.

Obviously without a blood test we couldn't be sure which type it was at the time, but attacked the possibility of falciparum first. Two days previously I'd been able to paddle, portage and toil all day without feeling particularly tired. Now a walk to the river to fetch water would have me leaning on trees for support, my heart thumping wildly. This is the most dangerous aspect of malaria for jungle travellers. They become too weak to fish, hunt or feed themselves, nor can they get in the canoe and paddle to the nearest help.

Quinine is still the most effective treatment for falciparum malaria and it's been in widespread use for over 300 years. Malaria has killed many millions of people throughout the world since ancient times, and was rife in Europe until quite recently. Alexander the Great and Oliver Cromwell are thought to have been among its victims. Mussolini eradicated the disease in Italy by draining certain swamps. In 1633, Father Calancha, a Jesuit priest, learned of the healing powers of the bark of the cinchona tree while living in Peru, and the Jesuits brought the first samples to Europe. As a result it became known as 'Jesuits' powder', and for many years was shunned by the medical profession, which is often slow to accept herbal or folk remedies. In any case it threatened to impinge on their existing lucrative malaria 'treatments'. In parts of Europe, it was apparently regarded as a Papist plot to exterminate Protestants.

The cinchona tree grows in the wettest parts of the Andean rainforest in Ecuador, Bolivia, Colombia and Peru, and it was 200 years before a proper study was made of it. The most tragic attempt was that of the Frenchman Jussieu, who spent thirty years living among the Indians, identifying and collecting bark from different species of tree, only to have all his papers and specimens stolen by a servant the day before he was due to sail triumphantly back to Europe in 1761. Poor Jussieu never recovered from the shock and ended his life in an asylum.

Alexander von Humboldt and the French botanist Aimé Bonpland were the first to publish a serious study of different species of cinchona in the early 19th century. Soon afterwards two French doctors, Joseph Pelletier and Joseph Caventou, discovered the alkaloid that made the bark effective against malaria, and called it quinine after the Indian name *quinaquina*, meaning bark of barks.

Meanwhile in South America the Spanish and Portuguese had imposed a ban on the export of seeds or seedlings in an attempt to maintain a monopoly of this increasingly important commodity, and collectors were beginning to ruin the trees by over-collecting and carelessness. But the British and Dutch, both with malaria-ridden colonies, sent expeditions to the Andes and managed to get seeds out. The Dutch planted two million trees in Java but none contained useful amounts of quinine. Richard Spruce collected hundreds of thousands of seeds of different species, but when they were planted in India and Ceylon these too proved worthless.

It was a Bolivian Indian, Manuel Incra Mamari, who eventually passed on seeds from the best trees to Charles Ledger in the 1870s, and he was executed for treason in consequence. Ledger offered them to the British Government, which refused them, and in desperation, knowing that the seeds would soon die, he turned to the Dutch, who reluctantly bought one pound (about 450 grams). Ledger sold the rest to a planter from India who was home on leave in London. These seeds were to prove the most potent type of cinchona ever found, yielding up to 13 per cent quinine, but the Indian plantation manager failed to grow any of Ledger's one million seeds to maturity. Fortunately the Dutch were more successful with their pound of seeds: these grew to 12,000 trees in Java and gave the Dutch a European monopoly for more than a century.

In 1942 this monopoly was interrupted when the Japanese invaded Java. Moreover, in 1940 the Germans had taken Amsterdam and all the quinine reserves in Europe, precipitating a crisis for the Allied troops. The war effort in the Far East was threatened by the number of servicemen who were incapacitated through malaria. Fortunately the US Government sent a team of botanists to Colombia, where they collected 5.5 million kilos of dried bark, which kept the Allies supplied during the war. In 1944 William Doering and Robert Woodward synthesized quinine but, although it seemed for a while that malaria was on the wane, the disease began to increase in the 1970s and is now estimated to kill more than 2 million people a year worldwide. In India in 1952 there were 100 million cases. This figure dropped radically to 60,000 in 1962, but rose again to 6 million in 1976.

Natural quinine is now back in demand throughout the world, as it has superior properties to its synthesized counterpart, and in the 1970s abandoned plantations were reopened in Zaire, Guatemala and Java. The story of quinine should teach us some valuable lessons about the natural remedies of the rainforest, and the Indians' knowledge of them. Yet it seems probable that we shall destroy both.

On the second day of this enforced rest, while I struggled to overcome the malaria, Mark almost trod on a bushmaster – one of the most poisonous snakes in Amazonia. He went down to the river for water and spotted the snake on the path, its brown skin almost invisible on the carpet of leaves and sticks. We usually had a live-and-let-live policy towards snakes, but this one was too dangerous to have around the camp. We shot it and added it to a stew we were cooking at the time. We had no snakebite serum with us. Doctors had advised against it, saying the serum was frequently more dangerous than the bite itself and should be administered only in a hospital environment. It also needs to be kept in a fridge. Other arguments were that over 60 per cent of people bitten by snakes recover anyway, because the snake fails to inject a lethal quantity of venom, or because its toxicity is affected by factors like how recently it has eaten. They also told us not to suck or cut the wound, or apply tourniquets. What should we do then? Oh, relax, they said: relax and rest. Relax? Pick up a novel, and sit down with a cup of tea? That would be a hard test indeed. Running around the jungle yelling, 'I'm going to die! Why me?' would be a more likely response. I have also received interesting advice from *caboclos* on their remedies for snakebite. Drink a litre of kerosene, say some. Cut across the bite marks, empty the gunpowder of two cartridges into the wound and set fire to it, say others. Run away from *caboclos*, I say, before you put the kettle on and settle down to a good read.

Late one afternoon on the Teles Pires Andrea and I had seen a house in the distance, and quickened the pace of our paddling. It is customary in Amazonia to ask to spend the night at any house rather than sleep in the jungle, and you are unlikely to be refused.

There was a man taking his evening wash on the rough wooden jetty where two other canoes were moored, and with the self-control showed by all the Brazilian *caboclos* he kept his face impassive and refrained from staring as we approached out of nowhere, so obviously alien. He returned our greeting and consented to our staying the night, asking us a few friendly questions about our trip and where we were from. He was missing his right hand, the forearm ending in an ugly stump.

We took what we needed from the canoe, followed him up the bank where some neat steps had been cut, and emerged into a big clearing with a large thatched hut at the far end. The tinkling of a cow bell made us look round to see it attached to the neck of a playful, well-fed dog that leapt and frolicked around its master.

'It stops the jaguars eating him,' he explained, pretending to be stern with the creature. 'Dogs are their favourite food.'

On the way across the clearing we passed a strange sight. A large tarpaulin had been rigged up into a peculiar igloo-like construction that you would have to enter on hands and knees. Outside it, cooking his supper, was a rather scruffy man who barely looked up as we passed and returned our greetings with a grunt.

We entered the large hut and were very impressed with the cleanliness and order of the interior. A swept earth floor, sacks of provisions placed on trestles, possessions hanging from the rafters, and a gleaming collection of pots, pans and utensils around an earthenware oven. The place reinforced our impression of being the guests of a very capable individual, well-versed in jungle life and able to make himself comfortable in it. Little things like the jetty, the steps in the bank, the well-fed dog (most Amazonian dogs are mangy, scrap-fed curs) and his clean clothes and neat appearance were all unusual in remote dwellings where men lived alone. We felt ashamed of our wild beards, tattered shorts and grimy fingernails.

Jorge insisted that there was plenty of food already cooking for all, and soon we were tucking into a delicious curassow stew with rice and beans. I went to get our plastic container of rum from the canoe, and on the way back asked the other man if he'd like to join us for a drink.

'No,' he replied, 'thank you' coming as an afterthought, so I shrugged and left him staring glumly into his fire.

We spent a pleasant, inebriated evening with our host, chatting about our respective lives. He was employed by a São Paulo businessman to clear a *fazenda* or cattle ranch. There was an airstrip nearby, and every month the owner would fly in, bring pay and provisions, spend a day fishing and depart.

All the time we were talking I couldn't help but stare curiously at the stump and wonder at the missing right hand. It had obviously occurred a few years before because he had become so adept at life without it. For example he rolled cigarettes one-handed with ease. I decided to ask him about it after another drink or two. Meanwhile I broached the subject of his strange companion. His face clouded for a moment and I was concerned that I had offended him. However he shrugged, grinned ruefully and began to talk.

'Yes, it must seem strange to you, I suppose. Here are two men living a long way from any company, and yet I live here, and he lives over there in that…construction,' he said ironically, gesturing towards the glow with his stump.

'A few months ago I was feeling a bit lonely so I asked the boss if he could find me another man to help.' He gave a pleasant laugh. 'In fact I asked him to get me a woman, but he couldn't find one who wanted to leave the city and live out here!

'It's difficult to believe now, but I was very, very pleased to see him. I'd been here by myself for over a year, and to have company was like a dream. He moved in here, I cooked and cleaned for him, and we talked and talked; or rather I talked and talked.'

He sighed.

'And yet slowly, my eyes cleared, and I saw him for what he is. A dirty, slovenly and lazy man. Not at work, mind you, I've no complaints on that score, but in personal habits and hygiene. He never washes, his clothes and hammock stink, he spits fish bones on the floor so every insect around began to invade the place. So after a time things began to get cold between us, and in the end I gave him a tarp and told him to build himself another hut in the clearing. I was going to cut timber and help him build it, but he refused, and he rigged up that strange place that he has to enter like an animal. Now it's the dry season but when the rains come he'll be floundering in the mud.'

'Do you talk at all now?' I asked.

'Only about matters of work,' he replied, 'and then only the necessary.'

'In a way it must make you feel more lonely,' I ventured, the booze making me less concerned about asking too personal a question.

'Yes it does,' he answered willingly enough. 'Sometimes at night I look across from here at him sitting over there, and feel like calling him over. But I don't.'

A bit later, after a discussion of the animals of the region, we finally got around to the subject of his hand. It emerged quite naturally in fact. He looked up as I was watching the dexterity with which he rolled a cigarette, and he grinned. 'Now it's easy to do, but at first it would all end up on the floor!

'It happened seven years ago when I was working in Mato Grosso do Sul, doing the same sort of work, but for another boss. I was out hunting one day a kilometre or two from my hut when I came to a place where a big tree had fallen across my path. It seemed easier to climb over it than to go round, so I reached up over the trunk to pull myself over, and got bitten at the base of the thumb by a surucucú.'

We winced. Of all the snakes in the jungle, this is the one we feared most. The bushmaster. I could remember some facts I'd read about it. Growing to 4 metres long, it is a fairly slender snake with a rough skin of pale, reddish-brown which has dark brown or black diamond-shaped patches. It can vibrate its tail like a rattler, but having no rattle it only produces a warning buzz in dry vegetation. It has fangs over 3 centimetres long, capable of penetrating clothing that would protect you against most other species, and injects a considerable amount of venom. The bitten limb starts to swell, and blisters to appear. Sometimes the skin will become tight and shiny from the internal tension and even split open. You become faint and experience profuse cold sweat, the pulse becomes rapid, feeble or frail. Bleeding occurs in lungs, heart, kidneys and brain, and you soon enter a coma or convulsions and die.

'I knew I didn't stand much chance,' Jorge went on, 'it had bitten me too deeply and I could tell from the burning pain that the venom was in there.'

He drew on his cigarette. 'So I decided to cut my hand off, thinking that so long as I did it in the first thirty seconds after the bite, most of the poison would come off with it.'

We gasped, and he grinned. 'Yes, it was a tough thing to do. I thought that if I spent too long thinking about it I'd never do it, and anyway delay wasn't an option, so I rested it against the tree trunk, put the machete in my left hand and chopped. Unfortunately, you know, I was right-handed and couldn't do much with my left, and also the machete wasn't as sharp as I would have liked. The first cut only half severed it, I had to chop again, screaming with pain and thinking I was going to pass out before the job was done.' He paused, staring down at the floor.

'But my troubles weren't over. I was still 2 kilometres from home, and at home there was no one to help. I tied my shirt around my arm up here until the blood stopped pumping and started to walk home. But I'd only gone a few paces when I looked back and saw my hand lying there on the jungle floor, and it didn't seem right to leave it there. So I picked it up and walked home – hand in hand, so to speak.' He laughed, and we joined in, relieved at a touch of black comedy.

'The pain was awful, but I made it home. I knew I couldn't leave the shirt tied around my arm much longer or the whole arm would die. So I had to do something that now I remember was worse than cutting it off. I heated a sheet of metal over the fire until it was red hot, and then plunged the stump down on it and sizzled it closed.' He sighed. 'And that hurt, my God, how that hurt. And all the time the metal was heating I sat there staring at it, gulping rum, and knowing how much it was going to hurt.'

'I then got into the canoe, which fortunately had an outboard motor, and travelled for three hours to the road, where a truck took me to the hospital. I still had the severed hand wrapped in a shirt. I think they took it off me and buried it.'

Well, we'd got the story of the missing hand. You couldn't really switch the conversation back to trivia after a tale like that, so we soon retired to our hammocks, and Andrea and I lay there for a long time in the darkness thinking about it. One thing was for sure – our admiration for Jorge was verging on awe.

The next morning we had breakfast with him, thanked him profusely, shook hands (left-handed) and departed.

As we paddled along Andrea and I had our first chance to discuss the tale, and he summed up our feelings neatly.

'That man has some courage, doesn't he?' he said. 'As we say back home, he's got a big pair of bollocks!'

We'd gone about a kilometre when we came across the scruffy man out fishing in his canoe. As we hadn't been impressed with his cordiality the night before we planned to say goodbye and paddle on past, but he smiled pleasantly and called us over. He seemed a different person now, asking us a lot of questions about our trip and showing us the three big catfish he'd caught. We exchanged tobacco and chatted for half an hour, and just before we left I made some comment about the terrible thing that had happened to Jorge's hand.

'Yes,' the man replied, shaking his head sadly, 'that place was a death trap.'

We looked at him, slightly confused.

'So many men had accidents in that sawmill. Jorge certainly wasn't the only one.'

We stared in amazement into his eyes expecting to see malice or deceit. They shone back clear and innocent, tinged with a bit of sadness at the cruelty of modern machinery.

6
Burnt Foot Camp

When I felt strong enough to move on Mark and I finally reached the mouth of the Ipitinga, its muddy waters spreading a stain into the clear Jari. As we paused to fish at the confluence a canoe came down the Ipitinga paddled by two villainous-looking characters. They had a sick companion lying under the shade of some banana leaves, and told us they were going down to Carecaru so that their friend could be flown to hospital. He had been stabbed in the back. As we talked their eyes were flitting interestedly over the contents of our canoe, and we began to feel uneasy.

When I first visited gold camps in Amazonia I was expecting to find them populated by the scum of the shanty towns and a bunch of psychopaths and homicidal maniacs. But they usually turned out to be a perfectly reasonable bunch of men. Codes of honour exist, with the fortunate helping out the less fortunate. After a lucky strike the whole camp would be treated to a feast, or prostitutes flown in from a nearby town. Incidents of murder were very rare, especially in the remoter camps where there were no women to fight over and not much alcohol to fuel tempers. Maybe I'd just been lucky in the choice of the five *garimpos*

I'd visited. There are larger goldfields of several thousand men, with bars and brothels that are more dangerous, I'm sure.

We didn't know what the *garimpo* of Flechão further up the Ipitinga was like, but judging from these two characters it might have been a rough one. One had a scar running from the corner of the eye to the edge of his jaw, and the other had a dead eye that had turned as white as that of a fish after cooking.

Mark and I said a hurried goodbye and set off upstream, having to stop and wade through a rapid.

'Shit, they were a mean-looking couple of cut-throats, weren't they?' he said, and glancing back, we saw the men still hadn't moved. They just sat in their canoe and continued to watch us.

'I don't like this at all,' I said. 'Did you see the way they were checking out our gear? I think we'd better push on until late and put some distance between us.'

Mark agreed. 'They couldn't follow us up these rapids with their heavy canoe, but it would be easy for them to walk up and see our fire.'

'Let's face it, we're the easiest couple of guys in the world to bump off and get away with it,' I contributed cheerfully.

We travelled hard for two hours until we felt we'd covered enough ground to be safe. For once we were grateful that the river had so many channels. It would make it much more difficult for them to find us.

Martin and Tanis, when we separated at Obidos, had given us five of their dried dinners – beef and chicken curries – and we had decided to eat one at each significant milestone of our journey. Number one was opened to celebrate the passing of the Ipitinga at last. We poured a stiff shot of rum and toasted our venture.

'From what they tell us, we're over the worst,' I said. 'Here's to more wildlife, less rapids…'

'No more malaria, easier going and easier living,' contributed Mark, 'fat juicy pigs, giant fish…'

'…and not so many fucking mosquitoes.'

While Mark prepared the feast I took the canoe out and fished the channels of the rapids. I caught a sleek, torpedo-shaped predator of about 4 kilos that gave an incredible fight, like a small freshwater marlin. It performed huge head-wagging leaps, stripping line off the reel with long dashes, and then doubling back to nip under the canoe. The confrontation was made even more exciting by the fact that the canoe was drifting steadily towards some small falls, and it was touch and go whether I'd get the fish on board before I went over the edge. Mark said all he could hear was SPLASH. 'Jesus!!' Zing from the reel. 'Bloody hell!' SPLASH. Just in time I managed to scoop the fish out by the gills, throw it aboard and grab a paddle.

We had a marvellous two-course meal. Meanwhile it had poured with rain yet again, so during a lull I decided to go and bail out the canoe. The batteries in my torch were getting low, and I directed the feeble glow a metre ahead of my feet – Indians say a snake is more likely to bite after rain, and I figure they should know. I reached the steep bank and shone the torch down on the water.

'Strange,' I thought, 'wasn't this were we left the canoe? Must be further along here.' I walked to the left, and then to the right. There was no canoe to be seen.

'Mark!' I yelled. 'Come here!'

'What is it?' he called.

'I think the canoe's gone!'

That got him running, and while I waited for him to arrive, I considered the possibilities. The weight of the rainwater might have sunk the canoe, in which case the bulk of our possessions would have been swept away.

Or perhaps we had not tied it up securely and it had drifted away to be wrecked in the rapids? Or possibly those *garimpeiros* had followed us and stolen our canoe.

Mark appeared at my side.

'I reckon the *garimpeiros* have stolen it,' I told him, trying to control my panic.

'No way,' said Mark calmly, flashing his bright torch about.

'What makes you so sure? Where the hell is it then?'

'Well, it's not here.'

He was getting exasperating.

'I know it's not bloody well here! Have you got any idea where it might be perhaps?'

'It's not here because we didn't leave it here.'

'What?'

'We're on an island, and the canoe is on the other side.'

He was right.

The incident reminded me of my first-ever canoe trip in Amazonia, when Patricio, a Chilean, and I paddled most of the way from Boa Vista to Manaus down the Rio Branco. It was a very incompetent, ill-equipped and uncomfortable initiation – made worse by the rainy season that was at its peak. It rained every day and every night, and once it rained torrentially for thirty-six hours without a pause, without the tiniest break in the greyness.

One morning we packed up our camp and carried out gear down to the riverbank to load the canoe. We reached the spot, and stopped dead. The place was empty. The canoe had gone. We dropped the stuff and ran to and fro along the bank in a panic. No canoe.

'You tied it up last night,' said Patricio accusingly. 'Did you do it properly?'

'Yes. Yes, I did,' I answered, but the evidence wasn't looking good.

'You can't have, can you?'

We slumped to the ground and watched the muddy river flow by.

'What shall we do now?' I asked.

'We'll have to walk downstream until we find a house. There must be one within a couple of days' walk.'

What a mess. What a pair of incompetents.

I stared gloomily down at the water, and suddenly let out a cry of excitement. I'd seen the canoe's rope – it was still tied to a tree to the left, and it was pointed straight down to the depths. We pulled on it, and the great weight confirmed that the canoe was still attached to the end.

We sat down and laughed. The dug-out canoe had always leaked profusely, and the rainwater had obviously helped push it under.

Despite reaching a landmark in getting past the Ipitinga, our spell of optimism was doomed to be short-lived. For one thing, the rain was relentless. What sort of dry season was this supposed to be? A nice sunny spell might help to reduce the numbers of mosquitoes which plagued us from dusk till dawn.

We found that insect bites have a cumulative action. Our skin did not react visibly at the time of the bite, but every three or four nights all the hundreds of old bites would suddenly start to itch in unison, and we would be reduced to a scratching, cursing frenzy.

The river did seem to be easier, though, and for two days we had long stretches of calm water, a rare treat indeed. The rapids were traversed quickly with a short wade or portage.

One evening we camped below a small falls and put out night lines baited with large pieces of piranha. We used nylon cord and large hooks for this lazy fishing method, but we often found them broken or the hook straightened by morning. However as we were eating supper that night a splashing and commotion announced a catch. It was a pirarara of about 10 kilos, a red-tailed catfish with an armoured plate over the neck. We got him beached with difficulty, giving Mark a bit of amusement as I got my hand trapped between the line and the torch I was holding as the fish tugged with all its considerable strength.

The question was how to kill a fish like this? We could leave it out of the water – but several hours later it would still be alive and gasping, and probably with a column of ants entering its mouth and attacking its intestines. Any blow with the machete to the head would bounce off its bony armour. The only way seemed to be to roll the fish over and chop the head off from underneath.

We baited up the line again before turning in, and were woken before midnight by the rattling of the pebble-filled can that we tied to the bush as a bite alarm. Heading towards the river with the torch I told Mark to stay put, but he misunderstood, and got up in the dark to give me a hand.

We had left a pot of beans to simmer overnight on the remains of the fire, and disaster struck. Mark tripped over it and upset the contents over his foot. He was wearing thick socks at the time as protection against mosquitoes, and the wool soaked up the boiling water. He ran down to the river to plunge it into cold water, but when he removed the sock a lot of skin came off with it. It was a very nasty scald indeed and he was in a great deal of pain. Sitting on the edge of the canoe in the dark with the mosquitoes making the most of our vulnerability we bathed the foot and gave him an injection of the strongest painkiller we carried.

Obviously we were going to have to stay put to give the foot time to heal, and Mark started a course of penicillin to combat possible infection.

But any healing is a slow process in the jungle, and what should have been an overnight stop became Burnt Foot Camp, the scene of eight days of inactivity, frustration, hostility and crises.

It may sound selfish, but there are bound to be mixed feelings in a situation like this. Of course I felt sympathy for Mark, but it was so frustrating to be held up just when we'd started to feel that the tide had turned in our favour. I felt exasperated, impatient – and guilty, too, because of all my uncharitable reactions. When travelling, only one thing is worse than being ill; and that is someone else being ill. One good reason for travelling with only one companion is that such delays are less frequent. In a large group someone always seems to be laid up.

The fish that caused all the trouble was a small surubim of 2 kilos which we had for breakfast. I gutted and sliced the pirarara from the previous evening into fillets which I then salted and took across to some rocks in mid-river to dry in the sun. Half an hour later I glanced across to see the rock black with contentedly belching vultures that had eaten the lot. I should have known better. However it seemed a good place for fishing: we felt sure we would catch a lot more and be able to continue on our way with a large supply of dried fish. In fact over the next eight days we caught lots of piranha, but only one more large pirarara.

This period was hard on both of us. I could pass some of the time trekking in the forest and fishing, but Mark had to stay and rest up in his hammock all day. Once the mosquitoes discovered us they began to work day shifts too, and we were only able to relax under the nets. The terrain was very tough – steep hillsides covered with fallen trees and thick tangles of bamboo, and my jungle sorties were sweaty and unrewarding. I'd motivate myself by treating them as hunting safaris, but one monkey and one curassow was the sum total of those days.

The curassow or *mutum* is the largest of the jungle fowl. A handsome bird, larger than a chicken and black except for its yellow face and a few white feathers on its rump, it is the ideal size for feeding two hungry people. On other trips I had eaten plenty of curassow, because it is a good quarry for inept hunters. It feeds on the ground and when scared flies up to the lower branches where it feels safe, making a sort of clucking tweet alarm call. That strategy may work when it is pursued by jungle cats, but doesn't put it out of shotgun range. Curassows also betray their presence with their alarm call; many times we wouldn't have seen them if they'd just kept quiet. They often go around in groups of four or six, so it is sometimes possible to shoot more than one at a time.

The species of monkey we were to see most of over the next months was the tufted capuchin – one of the commonest in Amazonia, and one of the most intelligent. It has a golden-brown coat with darker back and head. The larger, gangly spider monkey is even more endearing, being marvellously agile, curious and having a wide range of facial expressions. We also heard howler monkeys nearly every night, but hardly ever saw those, the largest of the New World primates. We were less likely to see the attractive woolly monkey, as we were on the fringes of its habitat, or the rare sakis or uakaris. The latter has a very unusual appearance, with long fur and a bald red face that grows redder with excitement. The Brazilians call it the *macaco inglés* – the English monkey – and it does remind you of an apoplectic squire after a heavy luncheon.

We had finally lifted our moratorium on hunting as we needed to eke out our food supplies in any way we could, and sentiment could no longer be allowed to interfere. As I write this, stomach full, with a vast array of food in the supermarket round the corner (much of it killed by others, and packaged in a way that almost makes you forget that it was once a living creature), I feel mortified at my actions.

But our food sacks were already half empty and we had four or five months travelling ahead of us. Regretfully monkeys are easier to kill than most other creatures because they are numerous, their commotion in the tree-tops betrays their presence from far away, and they are just too curious and trusting for their own good. It's unpleasant and shameful to kill such endearing creatures, and we hoped to find alternative victims. Hunting monkeys was always upsetting because they had such human responses to danger. They shook the branches in outrage, screeched defiance, pelted us with fruit and sticks (and urine sometimes) and often stayed loyally by a wounded companion. You could always see the conflict in them between the instinct to flee and the overwhelming desire for just one more peep. Yet when they ended up in our stews, their meat was much appreciated. It is rather gamey and lean, somewhat akin to wild rabbit in flavour.

The one I shot was a squirrel monkey – one of the smallest monkeys in these forests. By the time it was skinned and gutted there was a pitiful amount of meat left and we ruled this species out for further consumption. Even in populated areas they are numerous because their small size has proved their salvation. Brazilian hunters need a large creature to justify the expense of their shotgun cartridges. Squirrel monkeys have golden-green coloured fur and a black muzzle, and are the only species of primate where the male becomes spermatogenic, being unable to breed for most of the year. Just prior to the breeding season, they take on 20 per cent in body weight, all of which is lost in their campaign to gain control of receptive females. The mortality rate among males is high, and the sex ratio among adults is four females to one male.

Hanging around for so long was bound to bring despondency, and we had plenty of time to assess our situation. Obviously we were short of food. Did we want to reach the Tumucumaque hills totally dependent on living off the land? The canoe, although scraped and battered along the external joints, seemed to be holding up okay, but was it wise to continue with no polyester resin for emergency repairs? In addition to all these doubts, Mark's foot was healing very slowly and we were running out of sterilized dressings for any future injuries. There were also quite a few other important items that had run short, or we had realized too late that we needed – spinning lures, wire for fishing traces, a larger tarpaulin if it was going to continue raining so much, and new shoes as we had worn through two pairs each already.

We discussed the situation, and Mark viewed it with more realism (I'd say pessimism) than I did.

'We're in trouble,' he said. 'We're short of food, medical supplies and materials for mending the canoe. All fairly important items, I'm sure you'll agree. Adventure is one thing, and bloody recklessness is another. I love adventure, but I like to keep the odds on my side.' He paused, and stared glumly at the grimy bandage that covered his foot. 'Nothing has gone right on this bloody trip since we started. Hundreds of rapids, no hunting, lousy fishing, malaria, a burnt foot, too much rain and slow progress. I expected it to be hard, but not like this. I expected the going to be hard, but the living to be easy, know what I mean? That's what you said it would be like,' he added accusingly.

'That's how I thought it would be,' I replied. 'But with so many rapids there's been no time for leisure or collecting food. It'll be easier from now on, you wait and see.'

Mark wasn't convinced. 'The Jari easy! I don't believe this bloody river would ever be easy! It's crazy to go on without more supplies.'

I knew he was right, but I wanted to carry on and risk it. Reckless perhaps, but preferable to retracing our steps to Belém, which was the nearest place that would have everything we needed. Personally I've always had unjustified confidence in my ability to muddle through difficult situations. This isn't something that you can infect others with, and Mark did not share my optimism. It seemed to me that he was clutching at pretexts to have an excuse for pulling out. He wasn't really assessing the problems and thinking of ways to overcome them, but using each as a prop for his defeatism. I, on the other hand, was shrugging off the risks and ignoring common sense.

'The trip has been disappointing,' he continued, 'and it all seems pretty meaningless. We might get through, and succeed in crossing the Tumucumaque hills. But what's the point?'

That did it. Such heresy and mutiny in the ranks! Once you fail to treat your goal as a sort of holy grail and start ridiculing it, you're doomed. How could we quit now after only five weeks with so little achievement? So much planning, expense and hard work had gone into this venture that quitting was out of the question. Of course I didn't have a burnt foot, so my mood was more buoyant, but Mark's defeatism aggravated my normal stubbornness.

'You'll feel better about continuing after we've had a rest and your foot has healed,' I tried to reassure him, but I knew all too well that once the enthusiasm has gone on a jungle expedition, it's gone for good.

Our relationship began to sour at this point, which was a shame because we had got on well up to then. He had proved to be a cheerful and resourceful companion. Yet in England I'd warned him repeatedly that I was looking for someone who had the determination to stick things out when the going was hard. That did not mean I would carry on in the face of disaster, I'd explained reassuringly, but there would have to be a good reason for quitting. Now he could see that we had different ideas of what the good reasons would be.

'A burnt foot, malaria, no canoe repairs, a shortage of food and medical dressings: all that's not a sufficient warning for you, is it?' he muttered, avoiding my eyes. 'What would stop you then? Death?'

We spent long hours in tense silence after that, and Burnt Foot Camp became a miserable place. I went on long, exhausting hunts to purge my frustration and worry, and Mark swung in his hammock, his face closed to scrutiny behind the mosquito net. After we completed this trip he planned to go to the USA before he returned to Australia. Now he spent hours poring ostentatiously over maps of that country and consulting guide books. It was psychological warfare.

'What's Montana like?' he would ask, out of the blue.

'Why are you asking me that?'

'You've been there, haven't you?'

'Yeah, but why ask me that now?'

'It gives me something to think about.'

'Are you giving up this trip then?'

'I don't know yet.'

This used to infuriate me so much that I'd have to go on an extra-long trek to calm down and God help any creature crossing my path.

We spent three days without exchanging a word, which appeared to get on his nerves less than on mine. He held the trumps. He knew I couldn't carry on without him, and there was no danger of me deserting him. There were far too many portages involved for me to contemplate continuing alone. So I was at his mercy and I hated him for it.

We each kept a diary, and I became obsessed with the idea that if I could get a peek at his recent entries I'd find out what was going on in his mind. I assumed he might have the same curiosity and more opportunity to read my scribblings, because he only left the camp to take a crap, but I was gone for hours at a time. So I began to write devious entries expressly for his eyes, indicating disappointment and criticism, or challenges to his pride and masculinity. From what I had learnt of his character, he was into machismo and tough guy pursuits, so I wrote things like *'Mark's tough, and he's keen to join a tough elite – the Australian army. I don't take him for a quitter; I reckon it would take a really rough run of luck to make him give up. If it proves otherwise, I've judged him wrong. I doubt whether the Australian army selection panel will be so easily fooled.'*

I penned a couple of pages of such childish nonsense every day, then I'd slam the diary closed to attract his attention, crawl out of my hammock, pick up the shotgun and depart. Hell, he might not usually sink as low as I did, but even a saint couldn't have resisted the temptation for a peek in those circumstances. I often chose somewhere very conspicuous to write the diary too, so every time he looked my way I'd be chewing thoughtfully on my pen as I regarded him. Laughable, but it passed the time.

Yet when I finally got a look at his diary, I found it contained no real surprises. He was concerned at my recklessness, and he was demoralized. It offered no glimpses of hope. *'John's only keen for me to go on because he needs me,'* said one entry. *'Without me he'd be stuck.'* He understood the situation, sure enough.

It made me question my apparent obsession for carrying on. Objectively we had stacks of reasons for calling it a day, and Mark had a point when he said the whole thing was a bit meaningless. So why was it so important to me to continue? Could I really pretend I had enjoyed the past five weeks? Was my obsession rational? It didn't seem so. And yet I didn't feel at all apprehensive about carrying on with the limited supplies, and was actually looking forward to it. I think (of course I don't know), but I think I would have kept that determination even if it had been my foot that had got cooked.

I suppose on a trip like this it is obsession that reinforces the willpower to keep going. We had the concrete goal of crossing the mountains into French Guiana, and objectively it was a meaningless and faintly ridiculous plan. Yet it provided a focus and target for the trip and I clutched hold of it obsessively. Mark viewed it differently and more objectively. We might get over the hills, but so what? So what indeed, but you can't have motivation without a goal.

After days of sulks, silence, bad temper, gloom and despondency, we finally sat down and thrashed it out. I admitted grudgingly that it would be more sensible to re-equip the expedition, and that we should return downstream to get more supplies. Yet at Carecaru we would not find a lot of the items we needed. Crucial things like fishing lures and polyester resin would be out of the question. Perhaps it would be better to leave the canoe there and journey down to Belém – do the thing properly, and get everything we needed at a reasonable price.

'I really can't afford all that expense,' countered Mark, and I reassured him that I would mail home for some more money and pay for it all. After all that would work out cheaper than returning to the Jari the following year. Having found a compromise solution, we shook hands and the camp became a more cheerful place.

Two days later we set off downstream, after sorting out some equipment to leave behind for our return. We hung this in a string hammock safely off the ground and positioned out of sight just in case anyone passed by. That left the canoe really light for our journey down to Carecaru, and after weeks of toiling against the current we seemed to fly along. Since Mark couldn't get his foot wet, we paddled through all the rapids. I would go for a reccy and return with complicated instructions about the stretch below us.

'There's a large eddy when we get past that big rock over there, and we have to head quickly over to the left to avoid a big wave in the middle. Then we should bear right and take a channel near the far bank. Be careful, as there are two rocks we should pass downstream of, etc.' Of course such a description is meaningless unless you can see it for yourself – and anyway it always looks different once you're paddling, so I couldn't even follow my own instructions. We took many risks and bounced off a few rocks, but reached Carecaru by four that afternoon.

At the airstrip we met a couple from the trading post who told us that there was a plane due and the pilot might take us for free because of Mark's foot and my malaria. We spoke to the pilot, and sure enough he agreed.

Having expected to wait several days for a canoe going downstream, we hadn't given any thought to sorting out our stuff. Suddenly faced with the good news, but also an impatient pilot in a hurry, we had just five minutes to grab some items from the canoe and to arrange hastily for the couple to look after everything until we returned in two or three weeks.

We climbed on board, bounced down the airstrip and twenty-five minutes later landed culture-shocked at Monte Dourado. Still wild and hairy, sunburnt, clothing in tatters and stinking of sweat and wood smoke, we shouldn't have been surprised that when we hailed a taxi to the town centre the driver asked to see the colour of our money first.

We were a couple of hobbling wrecks. Mark had his foot swathed in grimy bandages and I'd developed very painful sores on the soles of my feet that made walking agony. On the way to town the driver told us that there were no cheap hotels in Monte Dourado, and if we wanted something more basic we would have to cross the river to Beiradão. This boardwalk settlement developed during Ludwig's time, and there was an enormous contrast between Monte Dourado with its streets of identical American suburban bungalows, its tennis and social club, and Beiradão with its bars, clubs, slums, sleeze and smells. Beiradão looked more fun; we found an acceptable hotel and had a huge supper of steak, fried eggs, rice and beans. We tried to turn in early, but our room was right next to the bar with its blaring TV, and through the open window came the music and drunken yells from six or seven clubs that went on till three in the morning. Ah, civilization at last! Like it or not, the peace and quiet of the jungle permeates your soul, and the first contact with town life is always an affront with its squalor, crowds and lack of privacy. However the way those icy cold beers constricted my sinuses, made my brow ache and sent effervescent little shivers down my throat did something to smooth re-entry into the world. And one or two pretty girls returned my smiles.

While having supper we talked to a cargo-boat captain who said he would take us down to Belém for nothing in the next day or two. Even if he failed us, there promised to be a passenger boat very soon. The following day we went over to the hospital established by Ludwig in Monte Dourado, where we got prompt treatment and they cleaned and dressed Mark's foot. It hadn't become infected, but it wasn't showing much sign of healing either. Then I phoned home to reassure my anxious parents that the jungle hadn't killed me yet, and to ask them to get my bank to cable money to Belém.

That afternoon Mark's temperature soared to 104 degrees, so after sponging him down for a while in the hotel, I took him over to the hospital again. They diagnosed falciparum malaria, and started him on a course of quinine. Poor Mark – he wasn't having much of a holiday. He also discovered that sometime on the river (probably when the canoe overturned), his passport had been soaked and would have to be replaced before he could cross any borders.

By the next day we still hadn't heard from our cargo-boat captain and had discovered there were no passenger boats to Belém for five days. As we were swinging listlessly in our hammocks in the hotel room, a street vendor knocked on the door and told me that Senhor Araujo would like to see us. I said that if Araujo wanted to see us, whoever he was, why didn't he come in person? A pained look came over his face.

'Senhor Araujo would not come to a place like this,' he replied, glancing around at the grimy walls of our cell-like room.

Having nothing better to do and being curious to meet this character I followed the vendor to a supermarket and was shown into the manager's office. Senhor Araujo was about my age, but a lot richer and a lot less pleasant. The contrast couldn't have been greater between us. I was still in flip-flops and tattered shorts with hair and beard in need of a trim; my T shirt had faded and held stains from past meals and exertions. He wore polished shoes, a black silk shirt, his hair was slicked back from a low forehead, and he had evidently overdosed on after-shave. His front teeth had also been edged in gold, which reinforced the impression that I was dealing with a spiv with bad taste. A revolver sat on the desk in front of him. He made no move to shake hands, to get up or to hide his contempt, and his lovely secretary seemed to share his low opinion of me. But he wanted my dollars and gave me a reasonable exchange rate for them. I learnt later that Senhor Araujo is known as the 'Sheikh of Beiradão', with his finger in gold, skins, supermarkets, money-changing and no doubt much besides.

On the way back I bumped into the cargo-boat captain who said he had left several messages at our hotel and that he was leaving for Belém in fifteen minutes. So I ran back, dragged Mark out of his sick bed and we got on board. Jorge had travelled a great deal and spoke good English which made it easier for Mark. He had an enormous appetite for marijuana and was never seen without a spliff on the go – but seemed totally unaffected by it. The cargo that he carried between Belém and Beiradão was a more orthodox stimulant – beer – and he told us that 30,000 bottles are drunk in Beiradão a week. Knowing the place I'm not at all surprised.

The other crew members were Jucelino the mechanic and Oscar the pilot. It was a friendly ship, but not a very efficient one. Oscar's memory of the deep channels seemed to have become a bit hazy: we ran aground half an hour after leaving Beiradão and had to wait six hours for the tide to float us off. Mark and I didn't care. We tucked into a supper of steak, eggs and potatoes and turned in. At midnight we floated off, but at dawn Oscar made another miscalculation and we ran aground again; this time we had to wait all day for the tide. There was some concern as to whether we'd get off, because we had grounded at almost full tide, and as there was a full moon it was one of the highest of the month. It seemed ironic to be stranded there all day in that little boat while several ocean-going ships passed us on their way to Ludwig's pulp mill. We drove a stick into the mud, attached a rope to it, and by heaving on it and running the engines full astern we eventually managed to free the boat.

Jorge asked me to sit with Oscar from midnight to 5 a.m. to chat and help him stay awake. It was a real graveyard shift, but we managed to keep a conversation going and Oscar had a large supply of cloves that we sucked to let nausea keep sleep at bay. He dozed off quite frequently (he only slept an hour or two each day of the trip) and when he did so he would slump over the wheel and push it down so that the boat would have circled round and round across the busy shipping lanes if I hadn't been there. Tactfully and discreetly I would tap him with my foot so that he started guiltily awake and glanced shamefacedly in my direction. Being a gent, I'd always be gazing out of the porthole or lighting a cigarette at the time.

On the second night we had exhausted the conversational topics of football, family, travelling, sex, food, Amazonia and Ludwig, and it was barely two o'clock. I searched for a new theme.

'These boats seem really top-heavy. Don't they become unstable in bad weather?' I asked Oscar, whose head was beginning that gentle descent to the wheel.

'What?' he muttered, rubbing his face.

'Aren't there a lot of disasters on these rivers?'

I seem to have hit one of his specialist subjects. His sleepiness fell away and he became animated.

'Oh, yes. Every year we get two or three big ones, and there must be many more small ones we never hear about. There were two catastrophes in 1981 – one near Obidos and one near the mouth of the Jari. Many people from Beiradão died in that last one.'

'Tell me about it,' I urged.

'It was on the night of January 6th 1981,' he started, sitting on the bunk next to me and putting the boat on automatic pilot. That meant keeping one of his bare big toes on the spokes of the wheel. 'As you know January 6th is a public holiday here in Brazil and a lot of people from Beiradão were down in Macapá for the big *festa*. At midnight they piled on a boat for the journey home, and although the boat had a maximum load of four hundred passengers, eight hundred got on.'

'Don't they have any controls?' I interrupted.

'Oh, sure, but captains are greedy and the authorities are even greedier. The controls are broken and ninety-nine times out of a hundred they get away with it. This was one of the exceptions.' He sighed. 'It was a stormy night, but in the channels between the islands the river was calm. However when the boat emerged into a large bay it met a fierce side wind and swell, and it turned turtle. People were trapped behind the tarpaulins that had been lowered to keep out the wind, others who got free became disorientated in the dark and choppy water and swam away from a nearby island. Many were probably too drunk to swim anyway. Five hundred people drowned. Almost everyone in Beiradão lost relatives. One woman lost eight children, and many children were orphaned.'

'Did the captain survive?'

'Oh, yes. The guilty usually do, don't they? It's the innocent who die. He's still free and has another boat now, but he stays away from the Jari as there are too many people who want his blood. I was in Macapá when news of the disaster came through on the radio, and every boat went out to look for survivors and to collect the corpses. There were bodies everywhere – floating, caught up in the bushes, lying on sandbanks, covered with urubus pecking out their eyes. It was horrible. I collected fifty-six in my small boat and I hope I never have a cargo like that again. Within twenty-four hours they were all swollen like balloons and the gas started to escape, and in that small deck space we were forced to walk over them.' He shuddered. 'For several weeks afterwards other bodies would turn up, caught in fishermen's nets, and let me tell you, there's no corpse worse than a drowned one that's been nibbled by crabs and piranha.'

It was a cheery conversation for those dead hours before dawn, but it did have undeniable qualities for keeping us awake.

Small cargo boats weren't supposed to take passengers; if caught, Jorge faced a fine of twice the minimum wage for each illegal passenger. Twice we had to hide in a locked cupboard when a patrol boat approached, but no inspections were made. I found the journey enjoyable. Jorge was good company, said we could help ourselves to beers from the ice box, and he was a good cook – creating great meals with the fresh fish that he bought from the homesteaders. Mark, however, was increasingly morose and each time I sat down beside him or joined him on the roof for a sunbathe he would get up and move elsewhere. I knew he must still be feeling rotten from the malaria, but he'd started getting those damn maps of the States out again and I was in agonies of uncertainty. Meanwhile I paid for him and watched his moods in angry anxiety.

Although I'd agreed to pay for transport to Belém and back for re-equipping the expedition, I had assumed he would change a bit of money to pay for his own hotels and food. So far he had made no move to do so, and reading his diary (yes, I was still at it!) I found him complaining in Beiradão that he could only eat or drink beers when I felt like it because I controlled the purse strings. My dependence on him was making me take a lot of stick. Normally outspoken, I was pussy-footing around, anxious not to upset him, but my confidence in him had already gone, so I wondered why I bothered.

On the third night we ran aground again, and I commented to Mark that Oscar was not producing an academy award performance, which I found funny at least. This time the stranding seemed more serious because the boat was stuck on the edge of a shelf, with very shallow water on one side and deep water on the other. Jorge was worried that the boat could roll down the slope at low tide. To avoid being trapped inside if that happened, we slept on the roof clutching our possessions. The boat gave one lurch in the middle of the night that had us awake, hearts hammering, but then settled again at a rather alarming tilt until it refloated on the ebb.

Once we crossed a huge bay with no protection and a very strong swell, and Oscar somehow got the boat sideways onto the waves, which caused empty beer crates to hurtle all over the boat. I got the impression that he was going to be down at the employment office by the end of this trip, perhaps joined by Jucelino because, as we struggled into Belém against a fierce riptide, he was preening himself in the toilet for the girls of the big city and had forgotten to top up the fuel tank. The motor died, the generator with it, and we drifted unlit and sideways back up the busy waterways for ten minutes while the fuel lines had to be bled and the motor restarted.

We moored up a small creek near a brickworks and the next day I accompanied Mark to the hospital to have his foot checked. His malaria seemed to be well under control, his foot was scabbing over nicely and he was more cheerful. I wanted to take Jorge out for a meal to thank him and, as Mark still hadn't got round to changing any money, I paid for him as well. A few hours earlier he had phoned his parents in Australia, but it wasn't until the next day that he broke the news that they were sending money to Miami.

'I'm not going back to the Jari,' he said, as soon as I woke up. 'I'm sorry, but I've got no enthusiasm for that trip any longer.'

'When did you decide this?' I asked, as the news slowly sank into my sleep-sodden brain.

'I've been thinking about it for the last week, but I finally decided yesterday.'

'Why didn't you tell me then?'

'I didn't want to spoil our evening out with Jorge.'

'You didn't want to lose out on the meal, more like. Wanted to get one last good spread out of me, didn't you? How could you just sit there stuffing your face, knowing that you were going to tell me this morning?'

It felt good to shout at him. I had nearly forgotten how to be sarcastic and unpleasant. My disappointment in his decision was tempered by the relief that I could be myself at last.

'You made this decision before we even left Burnt Foot Camp, didn't you? We plan a trip of six months and after five bloody weeks you've had enough. All that macho talk, all that tough guy stuff – it's all bullshit. You've wasted my time and money, and talking of money I reckon you owe me about $100, which I want this morning.'

I got up out of the hammock and stood up. My anger turned to depression as I paused to consider my situation.

'Shit, you've really loused things up. What the hell am I supposed to do now? Go home with my tail between my legs? I warned you and warned you that this trip was going to be tough and you assured me that you were up to it. Well, we've both seen you for what you are now, haven't we? A bloody windbag.'

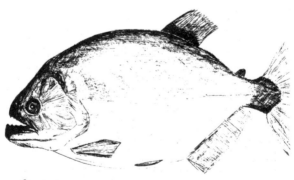

Piranha

7

Back to the Beginning

'Don't you realize that it probably needed more courage for Mark to tell you he was quitting, than to have carried on upstream?' said a friend to me several months later. 'The poor bloke! If I'd just spent weeks up some pestilential creek with you, you miserable, cantankerous old sod, I'd have packed it in too!'

Now that time has passed, I can sympathize with Mark and forgive him. Five weeks of hardship, a burnt foot and a dose of falciparum malaria were quite enough excitement for a first jungle trip. That morning in Belém, however, I felt differently. 'Gutless wimp,' I thought. 'All that macho military talk, and what happens? A little temperature comes along and kicks the stuffing out of the wuss.'

The whole trip had been a washout, a feeble anticlimax after so much dreaming and preparing. Now I had to return to England with this feeling of disappointment and frustration. I wandered the streets of Belém in a foul temper, answering smiles with scowls, and snapping at slow waiters. I could return the following dry season, but it would mean starting again from scratch. Although I had gear scattered all over the jungle – the canoe at

Carecaru, the hammock-full at Burnt Foot Camp – I couldn't rely on any of it still being there next year.

The money had arrived from home in record time. I didn't appear to need it now but had it transferred to the bank in Manaus in case I had problems there. I then went down to the port and bought a ticket for a boat leaving for Manaus that night. Later I met Mark in the street, and discovered he'd done the same. Oh, terrific.

The passenger boat was a giant steel catamaran mounted on two floats, and it was one of the biggest on the Amazon. I thought I'd be travelling in style until I got on board and found conditions were more basic than on the little wooden vessels. Over 700 passengers fought for places to hang their hammocks. The lower deck was divided into mesh cages according to marital status and sex: 'Single men', 'Single women', 'Couples with children', 'Couples without children', 'Unaccompanied women with children'. Single men predominated and in our cages the hammocks were slung under, over and across one another. Some touched the floor, others were so high that their occupants had to shin up pipes to get into them. It was so claustrophobic down there, that we spent most of the journey up on the only bit of deck open to the lowly masses.

The food was appalling: tiny portions served up on little airline trays with hollows for a piece of tough meat, a bit of farinha, a dollop of rice or beans. I commented to a Brazilian in front of me in the queue that in a country where people eat such enormous meals the food on this trip was downright stingy. He smiled.

'You've been in Brazil long enough to know how things work. If you want more food, or better food, all you have to do is visit the kitchen on the first day and give the staff a couple of dollars. Then you eat different food, more of it, and no queuing.' He was right, I should have learnt that lesson by now. I put the matter right straight away and treated him too.

There were more than twenty backpackers on board and a party of wealthy Americans tourists, and we got to know each other over the next five days. When I heard Mark impressing the ladies with his Amazon adventures I managed to control my tongue by keeping away from him as much as possible.

On the second day I became ill again, and spent the rest of the trip lying in my hammock with a fever. In my more lucid moments I discovered that two of the travellers were interested in taking Mark's place. It could have been regarded as a stroke of luck; but I was viewing life with a very jaded eye right then. I grunted a non-committal reply to their applications and watched them closely. After all, wouldn't they let me down too? 'Boys and wimps, the lot of them,' I muttered petulantly into my sweat-soaked blanket. In fact I was slightly awed by their vigour and youth. I felt I had neither.

Lutz was on the run from some trouble in Germany, although I never found out what. Frankly I wouldn't have cared if he'd chopped up his granny, as long as he showed the qualities necessary for a river trip. However, as he had been out of Germany for several months he was running short of cash and needed to combine pleasure with a bit of profit on the Jari. I couldn't see how this could be done without changing the trip in a way that I would find unacceptable.

Peter, from Switzerland, seemed the better bet. His motives were pure and he lacked Lutz's aggressiveness (Lutz and I would have been duelling with machetes within weeks). Peter had round gold-rimmed glasses, brown shoulder-length hair, and was quiet and introspective. He gave an impression of relaxed strength and competence. I had ignored my instincts when recruiting companions in the past; this time they told me that Peter would be all right. If I went back up the Jari myself that is.

When we got to Manaus I had a blood test and my malaria was diagnosed as falciparum. For several days I felt very low and weak, and I longed to go home. Occasionally I felt stronger and became enthusiastic about going back to the jungle. Peter had to live with this uncertainty for over a week.

One evening as I lay feverish in the squalor of Manaus' cheapest hotel, Mark ran up the stairs two at a time, brimming with health and enthusiasm. His burnt foot had healed, his malaria was cured and he was soon to leave for the USA. He was infuriatingly cheerful. He barged in through the door, and snapped on the single bare electric light-bulb.

'Hey,' he said, 'I've just met two fantastic English chicks. They're really gorgeous, and they're downstairs in the bar.'

I grunted unenthusiastically from under the cover of three blankets. I was shivery and miserable, and I wanted him to go.

'Man, they couldn't keep their hands off me. Practically ripped my trousers off. They're dying for it!'

'They must be blind and stupid then,' I muttered sarcastically. Mark didn't hear.

'Why don't I bring 'em up here and you can see what I mean? A good romp will do you the world of good!'

His memory of the effect of malaria on the libido had obviously grown hazy.

'No,' I answered. 'I feel lousy.'

'Ah, go on!' He insisted. 'Meet them at least. When you see the little darlings, you'll forget all your troubles.'

Isn't male pride a ridiculous thing? With a temperature of 103 degrees, the idea of flirtation and sex was absurd. Yet I had been in the jungle for six weeks and I was being mildly challenged.

'Are they nurses?' I asked.

'Nurses? I don't know.' Mark frowned, and then beamed. 'Ah, you like nurses! Yeah, so do I. They could be. I'll go and get 'em.'

'No, I just fancy the cool hand on my fevered brow,' I answered, but he'd gone, clattering down the stairs in his flip-flops.

I lay back, closed my eyes and waited. There were two thoughts in my mind: that if they fancied Mark, I would not fancy them, and how typical of

Mark that he only got excited about English, American or Australian girls. The fabulous Brazilian girls left him cold.

There was a knock on the door, I groaned inwardly and in walked a blonde. As my contact lenses were out at the time that was all that registered. Slight disappointment too because I do prefer brunettes. Then I gave a gasp of astonishment. It was Tanis Jordan! Behind her came Martin and a grinning Mark, and we had a noisy and emotional reunion. They looked thinner, but in pretty good shape and we babbled and laughed through the recounting of our adventures. They'd had a rough time on the Mapuera, with rapids all the way, and they had decided early on that their proposed route was out of the question. In many respects their journey seemed similar to ours on the Jari, but with two important differences. They had almost no rain and no mosquitoes. To Mark and me that sounded like paradise indeed. They had escaped malaria too.

We went downstairs to the restaurant and carried on our chat. They had a fund of good stories. One day when camped near a rapid, Martin saw a canoe full of Indians coming downstream, and called out a warning to Tanis, who was naked and scrubbing some pots at the time.

'Oh, pull the other one,' replied Tanis, carrying on with her chores while the Indians' canoe went sideways down the rapid as the occupants ogled her, then pulled into shore a few metres away.

It emerged they were from a tribe that crossed frequently into Guyana, and consequently one of them spoke a little English. Martin asked them about FUNAI, as this was the body empowered to stop people entering Indian territory without authorization.

'How many people live in your village?' asked Martin.

'Sixty-three,' replied the Indian confidently.

'Are there any FUNAI men living with you?'

'Oh yes.'

'How many?'

'One thousand, two hundred and twelve.'

All our tales of rivers and exciting adventure persuaded me to go back to the Jari. Why was I even thinking of returning to England with winter approaching and only a stint on building sites to look forward to? Once I regained my strength Peter and I could begin to make our preparations. We bought some polyester resin, fibreglass tape, spinners, fishing line and a large tarpaulin. Martin and Tanis kindly donated a lot of their medical kit, their shotgun, mosquito nets and even snakebite serum. In the evenings we sought out decent restaurants and gorged ourselves on meals that tasted extraordinarily good after the bland jungle menus.

Manaus oozes a sleezy sensuality. It is one of Brazil's sexiest cities, the Brazilian men assure you – probably meaning it has an abundance of red-light districts and prostitutes. Any walk at night is punctuated by whispered promises from doorways and enticing calls. The more daring girls block your path and try to encourage you with fumbling and squeezes. Faced with the prospect of several months' enforced abstinence in the jungle we felt that we should be storing up some memories for lonely nights in the hammocks. So after supper a small group of us would sometimes head off in search of sexual fulfilment, generally ending up at a club called, inappropriately, 'The Cathedral'. By Manaus standards this club was sophisticated, with dim lighting, modern decor and elegantly dressed cocktail waitresses. Ravishing girls did poorly choreographed striptease on a small stage, barely bothering to take their chewing gum out, and then put on the bare minimum of clothing before coming to sprawl on our laps. Gringos were courted with zeal, because we were supposedly wealthy, and we were different. I gathered that many Brazilian prostitutes hope that a gringo will one day fall in love, marry her and rescue her from the trade, and I have met one or two foreigners in Brazil whose wives had the unmistakable aura of, how shall I put it, fallen angels? No Brazilian is likely to marry them, so gringos are their only hope.

Ah, how convincing these girls seemed! How affectionate, how passionate, how sincere. 'I love you,' they whispered after five minutes' acquaintance, nibbling our ear lobes, and we, lonely, bush-crazy, far from home and inebriated, almost believed it. Yet we were fickle and inconstant. No sooner had we promised to go home with one than we saw another who seemed even more beautiful, and we changed allegiance. This caused different personalities to be exposed – the girls swore obscenely, spat, slapped our faces and fought each other. The aura of eroticism and excitement evaporated, and the atmosphere became recognizably squalid, tawdry and sad.

Anyway, I was still weak and sweaty from malaria and not really in the mood for it all. Undeniably the fear of nasty sexually transmitted souvenirs weighed on the mind: penicillin-resistant strains of syphilis and gonorrhoea, herpes and one or two new horrors rumoured to be present in Manaus. There reached a stage in every drunken carousal when I looked searchingly at the peachy-skinned girl on my lap and wondered whether she was really worth the gamble. If I had been feeling better I would perhaps have decided in her favour. Maybe malaria has its advantages after all.

On my last night in Manaus I was sitting on a park bench when a girl approached and we got talking. She had none of the mannerisms or dress of a prostitute. She was attractive, educated, warm and witty, just the company I needed before I set off back to the Jari. We had a lovely evening, a few beers, a meal, caught a bus to a funfair outside town and kissed as we went round on the big wheel. At 3 a.m. we found a cheap pension where they were unconcerned about couples arriving with no luggage, and made love.

Afterwards, I lay back contentedly on the pillows, smoking a cigarette, with her snuggled up beside me. During our earlier conversation she had mentioned that she knew some English, so I prompted her to speak a few of the sentences she had learnt. I expected language-school stuff – 'Hello, my name is Helena, I'm Brazilian' etc. I was in for a surprise.

'Hello, meester, what shipya from?'

'What?' I squawked, sitting up in bed.

'Hey, I like you, you like me. Wanna jigajig?'

'Holy shit!' I cried, getting out of bed. Where was the shower? The carbolic soap?

Peter and I flew to Santarém the next morning; we wanted to get to the river as soon as possible, and I was concerned at how quickly the water level might be dropping on the Jari. Despite all the rain that had fallen I had seen it drop nearly 25 centimetres in the nine days we were at Burnt Foot Camp. I wasn't sure whether less water would affect us on the lower reaches, but there was no doubt that too little water would make progress extremely difficult near the headwaters.

In Santarém we purchased all the new food supplies, and this time we bought considerably more: 20 litres of oil, 15 kilos of oats, 30 kilos of rice, 15 of beans, 10 of sugar, 10 of salt, 20 of wheat flour, 4 of powdered milk, 15 of spaghetti, 3 of coffee and 15 litres of cachaça. Added to the food we had left at Burnt Foot Camp, that should be plenty.

We also needed to replenish our fishing equipment. My original choice of spinners to bring out from England had been too flimsy and small. After being chomped by piranha several times they were bent and hookless. We bought two dozen robust ones designed for toothy Amazon species.

We also tried to buy more quinine, but in the chemist it was much too expensive for our budget, considering you needed at least fifty tablets for each treatment. We tried to get some from the hospital, but they refused to sell it. So, with the extra tablets that Martin and Tanis had given us, we returned to the Jari with only enough for four more bouts of malaria. As an alternative we bought a lot of Fansidar, which we had been told would control the disease, if not cure it. Had we known then what would happen three months later we would have spent every last penny on quinine.

We travelled on the boat to Monte Dourado, where we inquired about canoes up to Carecaru. We discovered they left from a point 50 kilometres upstream at the end of a road that bypassed Santo Antônio falls and several other rapids. I had to laugh when I learnt this. Mark and I had been in such a hurry to get out of town and avoid officialdom that we'd missed this vital information. That 5-kilometre portage round Santo Antônio had been unnecessary, and we could have saved six or seven days of toil if we'd stayed long enough to make inquiries.

We stayed one night at the same hotel in Beiradão that Mark and I had used three weeks previously. The girls who worked there were thrilled to see gringos again, and Peter and I could, no doubt, have spent the night accompanied. However, we were so concerned with our last blow-out meal and drinking our last beers that when thoughts finally turned amorous our indifference had offended them all. So we spent the last night in civilization alone. (In any case I was worried enough about what I might have caught on my last night in Manaus. Was our medical kit adequate for treating virulent clap?)

It was Sunday and everyone in Beiradão seemed to be drunk. Some lay sprawled across the broadwalk, while others bounced off the walls or stood swaying and trying to focus on us two – none too steady ourselves, but kept sober by the threat of violence. We went from bar to bar where a handful of people were aggressive and provocative, but most were just woozily friendly. Deafening music issued from every doorway. Naked kids crawled between the houses, and Beiradão was in urgent need of a rainy season to wash away the garbage piled deep under the stilts of the town.

As often happens in Brazil I found myself having long conversations about football and Liverpool FC, although I know absolutely nothing about either. Another bar was full of vociferous Argentina-haters telling us how they had enjoyed the Falklands war. In a third we met two prostitutes who could not have been more than thirteen and who brought out our paternal instincts by the fragile vulnerability, so badly concealed by their tough talk and posturing.

Early next morning after a last breakfast of fried eggs we took a taxi to the boat departure point. Delays looked certain – a dozen prospectors were already there, and some had been waiting a week. Peter and I were impatient to get moving, the biting pium flies were bad and it was hot and boring, so when a boat finally came we ran over eagerly. I had met the *motorista* before at Carecaru, and although he was only going as far as the Tracajá rapid, we asked to go with him.

There was the risk that any canoes going all the way to Carecaru would arrive at Tracajá already full, but we were keen to leave and were not even put off by the prospector who told us the *motorista* was an incompetent. The week before he had overturned and the prospector had lost his revolver, shotgun and spare clothing in a rapid.

'He's got no idea at all. I'd rather stay here two weeks than go with that idiot again!' he shouted.

The *motorista* certainly gave us some alarming moments. He took dubious routes in fast waters that had us all leaping out to haul the canoe forward, and his motor was badly in need of a service, tending to stall in the most awkward spots. Nevertheless we reached Tracajá in a few hours and camped two nights there. As there was a goldfield three hours' walk away, it was the arrival point for men and supplies, with a sprawling encampment waiting for canoes to Monte Dourado. We watched our mountain of provisions carefully as one by one the *garimpeiros* came over to check us out. We talked to one emaciated prostitute who told us she had suffered malaria thirty-one times. She also had a fresh bullet wound in her thigh from a bar brawl.

'It interferes with my trade,' she confided laughingly, with her hand on Peter's leg. 'I'll have to take a vacation, but I guess I can afford to. I've got one and a half kilos of gold stashed away.'

'Why don't you go home to Rio and leave this jungle before it kills you?' I asked.

'Well, it's not enough money to retire on, and in Rio I'd earn nothing. How could I hope to compete with those beautiful mulattas? I only got rich up here because I'm all there is. There are no other girls and the *garimpeiros* either go with me, or go without. I have a monopoly.' She laughed, revealing a solitary tooth sticking up discoloured in an expanse of gum.

One man strutted around with two revolvers stuck in the waistband of his shorts. He obviously considered himself to be one mean, macho bad-ass, so Peter and I called him over for a bit of gentle mockery. He was a gold buyer and carried a pair of jeweller's scales in a box. Out of curiosity I asked to see some gold dust. After cocking one revolver and placing it on the ground close to his hand, he unwrapped a sheet of newspaper and showed us a few grams – about $200 worth, I suppose. Peter and I sucked in our breath.

'What a lot of gold! Are you going to retire with that?'

'Good job you've got two revolvers: one wouldn't be enough if word got round that you were carrying so much gold!'

It was a dangerous game and he grew nasty and left. His place was taken by another guy who began to help himself liberally to our stock of rum. Out of hospitality we let him get away with it until he passed the half-litre mark and then the bar closed. I lost my temper with his pleadings, told him he was abusing our hospitality and suggested he got lost.

So it went on – a continual stream of visitors, some interesting, most not. Peter repaired Mark's old mosquito net that had so many tears and rips it had been more symbolic than effective. He also got into a hammock for the first time or, as frequently happens to novices, he got in on one side and was catapulted out the other. The prospectors loved that. You could see them describing it to every new arrival. Peter did however find a method of tucking the bottom of the net in such a way that it was completely closed to mosquitoes. I'd never thought of it, and it looked as though he was going to bring some Swiss resourcefulness into the venture.

Two prospectors told us that we were wanted for questioning by the police in Monte Dourado. They had left town a few hours after us, and it appeared we had got away just in time. Taxi drivers had been instructed to run us back into town to see the police.

'Why do they want to see us, do you know?' I asked.

'Well, they say that they've seen you leaving Monte Dourado twice now with a lot of provisions. Weren't you here a few months ago?'

'Yes I was. But we're not doing anything wrong.'

'Maybe not, but do you have authorization?'

'No.'

'Well, I guess that's what the police would want.'

I wouldn't normally have been too worried – we were already 70 kilometres from Monte Dourado – but we learnt that every Wednesday a policeman travelled up to the goldfields at Tracajá if there had been any trouble. It was now Tuesday morning, and in a gold camp one could imagine that there might be trouble every week. If he made us go back with him to Monte Dourado and apply to Macapá for travel authorization we would never get our trip off the ground. How we wished we had our own canoe with us so that we could disappear.

Luckily for us the next canoe contained not a cop but a pleasant *motorista* who was willing to take us to Carecaru. But he was infuriatingly relaxed and unhurried about everything he did. We portaged his 8-metre canoe using log rollers over the rocks, carried sacks of provisions around, had lunch and a little sleep, caulked the canoe, and it was by then so late that departure had to be postponed until the next morning. Our impatience seemed ill-mannered, but we were afraid another canoe would bring the policeman before we could get away. It turned out that this one canoe was to transport seventeen people, three dozen 50-kilo sacks and everyone's luggage to Carecaru. The only way to do it was in relays – three or four trips a day backwards and forwards. That meant agonizingly slow progress, travelling for one or two hours, and then having to camp and hang around the rest of the day while the canoe retrieved the rest of the passengers and cargo.

The *garimpeiros* apparently paid nothing for a passage upstream to the goldfields; they have little or no money then, and anyway all hands are needed to portage the sacks of provisions and to drag the canoe up the rapids. On the way downstream however they pay two grams of gold because the canoe has no cargo, and presumably the men are richer when they travel back. It seemed a fair system. We had to pay a modest sum because we had a lot of our own sacks.

It took us nine days to get back to Carecaru. It was interesting to retrace the route Mark and I had covered so burdensomely a few weeks before, but there were many places I could not recognize. We must have followed different channels. Peter was impressed.

'Mark said the Jari was difficult,' he said, 'but I never expected it to be like this. You did well to get as far as you did.'

I glanced anxiously at him. Was he overawed by his first glimpse of a tough Amazonian river? Would he let me down too? Once again I was embarking on a trip with a novice who'd never paddled a canoe before or set foot in a rainforest, and I knew next to nothing about him. All I had to go on was a gut feeling that he would prove to be all right. For the present I could merely observe his reactions and pray he would justify my untested confidence.

Our companions in the canoe were a friendly bunch. Seven were full-time crew, and it was a pleasure to watch their skill. They hopped barefoot from rock to rock with the rope and leant on punting poles to aid the struggling engine through the faster water. The outboard was obviously on its last legs and it was soon a standing joke that the engine would stall whenever its services were needed most, making us leap out into the turbulent water to stop us from drifting backwards.

One day I got the camera out to record these scenes, and the men were so chuffed at appearing on film that they returned downstream a little so that I could photograph them in the most dramatic setting possible. In Manaus the camera had recovered from its soaking when the canoe capsized. All it had needed was a fresh battery, and I had successfully tested it with a roll of film.

The men leaned on the rope, tensed their muscles and grinned at the camera. Even though the only full set of teeth belonged in Peter's smile, they looked a handsome team and it was going to make a fine shot. I pressed the shutter. Nothing happened.

'Oh bloody hell!' I yelled.

'What's the matter?' called Peter, relaxing his posture at the rope.

'This sophisticated piece of Japanese shit, that's what!' I yelled, for a moment debating whether to hurl it into the rapid. The battery had drained in two weeks, and everything had gone dead. Peter had no camera. Martin and Tanis had offered me the loan of theirs, but I had foolishly turned it down.

'I will have to start drawing,' said Peter. From that point he passed the quiet moments with his sketchbook, but we missed many opportunities to take wonderful photos over the coming months.

We ate well during this journey. The men placed a gill net every night and frequently caught loads of fish. Once they made us *açai*, a drink made from the fruit of a palm that I'd had before. Mixed with farinha and sugar it is delicious. The Brazilians stress its high vitamin and iron content, and obviously consider it a powerful aphrodisiac, because there was much winking, pumping actions with the fist and laughter. Its effects were wasted out here.

Arriving at Carecaru at last, we went straight round to the house where I had left our canoe and equipment.

'Who did you leave the canoe with?' Peter had asked the day before.

'Oh, a married couple who live up there.'

'You know them well?'

'No, not at all, really. They just happened to be at the airstrip when Mark and I were leaving.'

He had frowned.

'Can you trust them? I mean, will the canoe still be there?'

That was a worry. I had said I'd be back in a fortnight and nearly a month had passed. Had they assumed I wouldn't be coming and sold it? Or maybe someone had stolen it? Perhaps it had got smashed on the rocks of a rapid?

We walked briskly and apprehensively down the trail to their home. After such a long, tedious trip to get back, and with so many new provisions, it would be disastrous if the canoe were gone. The heavy local dug-outs would be impractical for the 15-kilometre portage we were planning over the Tumucumaque. Once again the trip would fizzle out.

The couple's twelve-year-old daughter greeted us shyly, and seemed to be under instructions to keep us out of the house. She waylaid every attempt we made to get in the front door, and from inside we could hear her parents whispering and rushing about. It was all horribly suspicious. Also there was no sign of our canoe among the others moored at the jetty. We squatted in the yard for over ten minutes before the couple finally emerged, flushed and breathless. We need not have worried. The delay had been due to that universal phobia about receiving guests into a disordered parlour. They had obviously been using some of our equipment (and why not?), but they wanted to have it all presentable in one neat pile. The woman had even washed our blankets and sewn up an old pair of shorts. Moreover the canoe was only missing because their son had gone fishing in it up the Rio Carecaru. It was wonderful that everything worked out so well, and I was glad I had brought a few small presents to show our gratitude for their honesty and kindness.

We now had everything we needed: abundant provisions and a canoe returned to its former glory by fresh fibreglassing of the external joints. We were keen to be on our way, and under our own power. The Jari awaited us with all its usual surprises. In the stretch between the Ipitinga and Burnt Foot Camp it had presented a more serene and languorous appearance. Would it offer a bit of slack at last? We were eager to find out.

Paddling seemed hard work after the long lay-off and sickness, and even worse of course for Peter. The canoe was full to the gunwales, and we had more to pick up at Burnt Foot Camp. However, we would soon eat our way through the edible stores, and better too much than too little.

About 2 kilometres upstream we stopped to visit an Indian family Mark and I had met on the previous trip. The man was a twinkly, chubby extrovert, always bubbling into song or laughter. His wife was a serene, silent beauty and their children black-eyed charmers. We pulled alongside their jetty. I was surprised at how strangely quiet the place was, but I could see wood smoke, so someone was at home. We climbed up the steps cut into the steep bank, and walked over to a figure lying still in a hammock under a tree. It was our friend but he stared impassively at me.

'Ah, *voltou* (You came back),' he murmured, without interest or inflection. I was shocked at his appearance. He had lost more than 10 kilos and his eyes had a dull stricken look in the gauntness of his face.

'Yes, I'm back. Are you sick, Manolo? Where's Teresa, and the kids?' A large solitary tear rolled down his cheek.

'Teresa's dead.' He gestured weakly to a white wooden cross that I hadn't noticed on the edge of the clearing.

'Oh, God! I'm so sorry, Manolo! When? How?'

'Twelve days ago. She just died. Fell down and died. I don't know why.'

More tears were now coursing down his crumpled face.

'They took the children away.'

'Who did?'

'They did', and he rolled his head to one side, making it clear it was too much to try and explain.

I walked around his clearing. The pets were still there – the parrots, the snuffling baby wild pig and the tame monkey at the end of a string – but they looked neglected and pitiful, not the cheerful menagerie of a month before.

'When did you last eat?' I asked.

'I'm not hungry.'

'Well, you should be. Peter and I'll go fishing and we'll prepare you a good meal. You need it.'

'I don't want it.'

'You have to eat, Manolo.'

His voice gained the barest hint of animation.

'Look, João, you're being kind, but I don't want your kindness. I'd rather you left. I want to be left alone.'

He turned his back to us and, after hanging around feeling helpless and awkward, we fed and watered the animals, and went on our way. We paddled in silence for several minutes.

'He's just going to lie there and let himself die,' said Peter.

Yes, it looked as if he was.

We took it easy for the first few days to avoid the risk of strained muscles. That was the excuse anyway. It was still raining repeatedly in those short sharp showers that seemed to be part of the Jari dry season. They made no change in the level of the river, which was a good deal lower, but the reduced flow seemed to be to our advantage. Several times on the way to the Ipitinga we were able to wade up stretches where Mark and I had been forced to portage six weeks previously.

We reached Burnt Foot Camp four days later and found all the stuff still there. To celebrate our return we consumed a gourmet dried dinner, and spent a day organizing the gear so as to cram it into the canoe. We had to burn a few items that would not fit or that we weren't going to use, among them some of Mark's old clothing. I was just about to burn his old combat jacket when Peter told me to stop and showed me a note. *'In return for sending my combat jacket to me in Australia, I donate my Swiss Army knife, compass and any other of my personal effects left at Carecaru or Burnt Foot Camp to Peter.'* I was furious to find Mark still taunting me.

'That's a really heavy jacket. We'll have to carry it for the next five months up and over the Tumucumaque mountains. Throw it on the fire.'

Peter's face hardened.

'I promised Mark I'd send it to him.'

'Well, we're hardly a hundred metres from the post office, are we? It's bloody ridiculous.'

'I'm not going to burn it,' continued Peter, wrapping the jacket in a polythene bag.

'Well, OK, but the first time I feel we need to lighten the load, that bloody jacket will be the first thing to go.'

For the moment I had to be content with burning Mark's strange reading matter. Onto the fire went Debrett's *Etiquette and Modern Manners*, and the English grammar was designated for use as toilet paper. The opportunity to leave the jungle impeccably mannered, socially adept and smoothly erudite had been lost. And we'd better hurry up if we wanted to know what a subjunctive was.

It was a relief to leave Burnt Foot Camp, with its mosquitoes and bad memories, and journey on into the unknown. If the Jari was kind to us, we might reach the mouth of the Cuc in five weeks and be ready to portage over the hills to French Guiana in less than three months. We had a long, long way to go but we were in excellent spirits. The rapid just above the camp that had looked so formidable a few weeks before now delayed us only a few minutes. After that the river was smooth and easy for the rest of the day. Maybe the Jari felt we had passed the tough initiation test and were men enough to be allowed the chance to explore further. Suddenly there seemed to be much more wildlife. We saw a tapir, a deer, an otter and some monkeys. When we stopped for lunch on a sandbank I cast the spinner and caught a traira and five piranhas in less than five minutes. We put the piranhas back into the river, which was more than the little ghouls deserved, but everything seemed to give grounds for optimism.

Nevertheless, one should never trust the Jari to be consistently benevolent. That afternoon Peter began to feel ill, so we camped early. He vomited several times in the night, had shivers and a temperature of 103 degrees. It looked like malaria to me, though it seemed early for him to get it since we had been on the river for less than three weeks. However, Beiradão and the encampment at Tracajá would have provided the ideal conditions for the spread of the disease. I started him on a course of treatment just in case, and we stayed at that camp for four days until he felt better. It was an unpleasant camp, too, bug-ridden and surrounded by unattractive jungle. To me, the unattractive areas are those that are submerged in the rainy season – thorny, tangled and covered with debris deposited by the floods and rotting flotsam lodged in the low branches. When you look for firewood it all seems to crumble in your hands and the termites run up your wrists. I went off walking every day, but getting through such thick vegetation involved too much effort. I shot one small jungle fowl that foolishly alighted in a tree above our camp, but there was only enough meat for one, and I gutted it for Peter as he had been eating very little.

Crossing the river to see if hiking would be easier over there, I came upon a magnificently spooky place. It was an old channel of the river that had been cut off by a change of course, or perhaps by the drop in water level. The water was dark and littered with fallen debris, and trees met over the top. Cobwebs as resilient as cotton clutched my face, and a little group of bats that had been invisible against the bark of a tree detached themselves silently and flew like wind-blown leaves to another perch, immediately vanishing again.

The water had a stagnant look, but it was far from lifeless. Skirmishes and battles were taking place down there. The surface was furrowed by racing dorsal fins as big fish chased little fish, and even bigger fish chased them. Shoals of golden tucunaré cruised the shallows, causing fry to scatter in panic.

I went back to the canoe to get the fishing rod and some bait, and seated myself on a rock. It was not a place to fall in. Blasé though I am about piranha and the dangers they present, I would not trust them in a place where food was so obviously in short supply. I was also concerned about anaconda. It seemed just the type of habitat that they would love, and I glanced nervously over my shoulder at frequent intervals, imagining that heavy muscular loop of snake dropping around my neck.

I baited up a large hook with a piece of fish, and cast into the centre of the pool. I could see fish racing from all sides, but a half-kilo something got there first. Disappointed, I began to reel it in, but almost immediately a 3-kilo tucunaré swallowed the previous one whole, and I had a bit more of a struggle on my hands.

During the excitement the line got wound round a sunken branch a few metres from the bank, and as I was tweaking the line to free it I saw a massive dark shape appear from the depths, grab the tucunaré across the back and make off. I tried to hold on, but the 20-kilo line snapped with a ping and I was left shaken and fishless.

When we finally got going again we had to wade through a few small rapids but between them the river was slow and deep. The map marked seven major rapids before the mouth of the Cuc, and we thought these might help us pinpoint our position accurately. With a scale of 1:1,000,000 our map didn't show every twist and turn, nor the many islands, so we needed to take care we didn't miss the Cuc altogether. The map had been the best we could find, but was originally designed for use by pilots. Apart from the blue lines of rivers (which we hoped were accurate), it was mainly blank, with '*Relief Data Incomplete*' or '*Altitude not believed to exceed 3,000 metres*' stamped across the Tumucumaque hills. Well, that was encouraging news.

As we were eating our supper we heard a commotion in the jungle and heavy footsteps approaching. The vegetation parted and two tapirs strolled casually into our camp, grazing and oblivious to our presence. I smiled. They are one of my favourite Amazon creatures. There are a couple in Bristol Zoo near my home and the keeper says they are the most affectionate and tamest of all his charges: they follow him around begging to be scratched and petted. These two stood there blinking, deaf to the insulting comments we were making about their intelligence. Evidently we were downwind and they couldn't figure what we were. It's a privilege and a pleasure to get these sightings of wildlife and they provide the highlights of this type of trip.

Within two days we had managed to pass two of the falls; they were not especially hard compared to what Mark and I had faced. After Peter's early brush with malaria it was fortunate that the river itself was giving him a fairly easy introduction.

We got into a routine of travel. Up at first light (five o'clock), we had a large breakfast and were on the river before seven. We paddled for four hours or so, had lunch, went on for another two hours and then stopped to make camp. As we were making good progress we could afford to stop early, and Mark would have enjoyed our leisurely lifestyle, with several hours of daylight in which to relax, read, write diaries, swim, fish and get supper prepared before the sun went down around seven. After that the mosquitoes would come out and we would be driven to our hammocks and nets. Six o'clock was cocktail hour. We wished we'd brought more booze because we finished our 15 litres much more quickly than 'moderate social drinkers' should. (Aren't all of us MSDs when questioned by our doctors?) Near Carecaru we'd found an abandoned house with a tree full of limes, so for a while we concocted *caipirinhas* of rum, sugar and lime and it made a civilized end to the day. When the limes ran out the neat rum was hard to take. A very coarse, fiery spirit made from sugar cane, it is not a drink for sipping and savouring. However, toss it quickly past the taste buds and the effect is most agreeable.

The best campsites were those with an expanse of flat rock in the foreground. Here we could make our campfire as far away from the jungle as possible, so that the mosquitoes would take longer to find us. Of course if it looked like rain we had to make our fire among the trees near the hammocks, where we would rig up a shelter. It would have been nice to spread blankets on the rocks and sleep under the stars, or lie there chatting or star-gazing until late, but the bugs put paid to that. Also, judging by the number of sloughed-off skins, snakes were abundant among the rocks. There were other dangers too. One morning, when it was Peter's turn to make breakfast and mine to have a fifteen-minute lie-in, I was watching him rummage in the food bag when suddenly he leapt 60 centimetres off the ground and gave a yell.

'Ah, shit, shit, shit, shit!' he cried, hopping around and clutching his finger.

'What happened?' I giggled. The sight of him prancing naked around the fire had its touch of comedy.

'Bastard animal. It is not funny!'

'What animal?'

'I don't know the name in English.' He gave a word in German that rang no bells with me. 'You know – it is a sign of the astrology.'

'Astrology? I don't know much about that. Aries? Taurus? A bull? Twins?'

'You are very funny,' he said as he sucked his finger. 'It is an animal, that has a tail that sticks up above his back, and which stings you.'

'Scorpion?'

'Ya, that's right. Jesus, it hurts.'

A few minutes later I was searching for coffee in the food bag when another scorpion ran over the back of my hand and dropped to the ground.

Eleven days after leaving Carecaru we were negotiating a little channel that was becoming narrower and narrower when we looked up and saw a man sitting on a rock 50 metres ahead. This unexpected sight gave us quite a shock and we quickly covered our nakedness before we paddled up to him. At first we thought he must be an Indian, but from nearer we saw he was a light-skinned Brazilian. He was fishing and seemed very wary of us. We never found out who he was or what he was doing there because he evaded all our questions, then asked us plenty, which we evaded in turn. It was not a basis for a lively conversation, and there was something unsettling about his impassiveness. He squatted with his fishing line in his fingers and didn't shift his position once in the ten minutes we were there. He was not going to miss any bites through idle chit-chat. We had the impression he had been alone a very long time. His voice had a rusty, unused quality, and if he'd ever had any social graces or humour the jungle had taken them away. He gave us the creeps so, curiosity unsatisfied, we paddled on our way.

The channel we were following soon became clogged with more rocks and more shallows, so that it was easier to get out and walk, until finally we were forced to do our first portage since Carecaru. It had been a good run, eleven days without a portage; Mark would have been incredulous that the Jari permitted such relaxation. There is nothing like a portage to make you realize just how many provisions you are carrying, and we had to do three that day before we finally emerged into a wider channel. There we were faced with a large rapid which we roped our way up, a section of quiet water and then a worse rapid cascading over several drops round a jumble of islands. That took us all the next day to negotiate, with only the briefest moments of paddling and a lot of wading through fast, dangerous water.

I shouted at Peter several times. He seemed too casual when walking the canoe up rapids. All casualness had left me after that near disaster with Mark, and I preferred to proceed extremely cautiously. We would take up positions on either side of the bow, and whenever the water was very fast, or the rocks slippery, I preferred us to move forward one at a time so that the one ahead could get a firm footing before nodding to the other, who then moved up too. Without this precaution there was the risk that we would both slip together. Something went wrong with our manoeuvres that day because we both lost our footing simultaneously, floundering in the waist-deep torrent, and the bow of the canoe turned slightly across the current. That's all it takes. Just a few degrees to one side and it becomes too heavy to hold, tips and fills with water. Mercifully the channel was very narrow and the swinging bow hit the bank, which delayed its progress long enough for us to hang on. A few of our belongings started to float away but Peter managed to grab them. It was a very close shave. In Amazonia disaster is only a moment's carelessness away, and generally you are given no second chance. We had been lucky.

A short time later I noticed a piece of wood hanging from the bottom of the canoe. This turned out to be the keel, or rather half the keel – the rest had broken off and disappeared. When working on the canoe at Carecaru I had seen that there were a couple of screws missing but assumed that it was still fixed securely

enough... Well, I was wrong, so of course we had to stop, take it out of the water to dry, whittle a sapling to replace the lost keel section, then fibreglass it all down. It had been a day of hard-learned lessons. Don't be careless. And don't be lazy.

The next day started with a large rapid that forced us to portage, and continued difficult until we camped in the early evening. We had endured three days of continuous rapids, disconcertingly like the Jari that Mark and I had known and loved. We camped that night in a small gorge with huge boulders on both banks, and round the corner we could hear an ominous roaring. It was depressing to lie in our hammocks and listen to the sound of the next day's toil and misery. Impossible to reassure ourselves that we must be over the worst by now; not with the thunder of falling waters drowning the jungle chorus.

And there just around the bend were all the obstacles we had been imagining. The river had narrowed and now ran through vertical-sided rocky channels, falling over no fewer than eight drops. There was no way we could paddle or walk the canoe up there. It meant eight separate portages over the sharp rocks, dotted with dangerous blow-holes and sculptured caves. Judging by the expanse of water-hewn rock 5 metres above the present river level, this must have been an awesome place in the rainy season. Huge tree trunks had been stranded by the retreating water and were waiting for the next flood to continue their journey. Every one of these portages required six or seven trips for each of us with the equipment, before we carried the canoe and relaunched it above the fall. Then we reloaded, paddled 20 metres and did it all again. So we passed the day, and by evening had covered a kilometre or less and still not reached calm waters.

While waiting for supper to cook, I wandered upstream to check things out. I could see the need for at least three more portages in the first 200 metres, but it was a positive pleasure to stroll over the rocks in the relatively cool, low evening sun, and, for once, not humping a heavy load. From under the rocks and down inside the holes I could hear the gurgle of water, and once or twice the cheeping of young birds in their nest. The parents would try to decoy me away by feigning injury or, in one case, dive-bombing. This was a fairly small bird but the sharp whistle of wind through its feathers made me duck each time. Next I surprised a jaguar on the rocks. He paused for a second, his spotted coat glowing gold in the orange light of the setting sun, then turned and bounded for the jungle, kicking up spurts of sand across a small beach. From his tracks I paced out the size of his leaps: over 5 metres. I saw many other tracks too that evening: tapir, alligator, ocelot and deer.

Recently we had caught a new species of fish, one very similar in appearance to the tambaqui found in the Amazon, with delicious, white, firm, juicy meat reminiscent of veal. I am told that the Santo Antônio falls act as a barrier to certain fish. For example the tambaqui and the freshwater porpoise are found below them on the Jari, but not above. Also there are no stingrays above the falls, we had been told. This was a relief for men who spent an hour or two a day wading, although we never quite believed it and still took the necessary precautions.

We had 1.5 kilos of fish each for supper with rice and, although it had been a tough day, we felt terrific. Nothing like paddling and portaging to get you fit, and now that our malaria was under control we felt supremely healthy. The portages were a chore, but the scenery at rapids was always stunning: sparkling cascades, rocky islets with miniature jungles in their centres, flowers, bleached driftwood, black rocks, blue sky, herons fishing, and parrots and butterflies to provide some gaudy touches. Being fit we could carry all the gear several times and not get particularly tired, and as we hopped over the rocks with 30-kilo sacks on our shoulders sometimes we would realize that we were whistling or singing.

However, the week that followed gave us less and less to sing about. On the next day we set off straight into a portage, just a small, quick one. Then there was a big one over 100 metres, then we waded up a fast section to another portage, then crossed to the other bank and did one more. Total distance covered? About 500 metres. In front of us was another series of falls and, after getting past two of them the next morning, we reached a place where the right bank was impossible to walk over with gear on our backs. We were faced with huge boulders and large gaps between them. On the left, the jungle came right down to the water's edge so we could not portage on that side either. We decided on a reccy and found that the river looped round to the left with five or six drops in quick succession. We sat on the rocks and stared at each other gloomily.

'What are you thinking?' Peter asked.

'You remember that people told us about a rapid called Macocoara somewhere up here where you have to portage over a hillside? This could be it. It would be quicker to cut across the loop by carrying everything over this hill, wouldn't it?'

'Jeez…' muttered Peter, looking at the steep climb. 'I think we have no choice.'

We cut a trail, humped the sacks over and completed the portage by carrying the canoe across. It was a long, awkward load with which to scramble up a jungle hillside, getting wedged between trees, tangled in vines, and it was heavy enough to have us gasping.

'This is how it will be when we portage into French Guiana,' Peter panted, 'except it will be fifteen kilometres instead of five hundred metres. We are crazy, it is madness.'

We lay on the jungle floor and giggled.

'We'll also have to climb over several mountains too, not one little hillock like this one! It's utter lunacy,' I said, and we giggled some more.

We were cheerful because we felt instinctively that we had got over the worst and reached quiet water at last. However, after five minutes' paddling we rounded a bend only to discover more of the same. During the rest of the day we did four more portages, and the following day we had a 200-metre portage, a long wade, then brief peace and quiet before another portage, a little paddle, a wade and then another portage.

My feet were beginning to give me the same trouble I'd had earlier. It was a type of foot rot caused by always being in the water and always wearing wet tennis shoes with sand or small stones in them. Little patches of raw flesh developed between and under the toes and along part of the instep. It would heal quickly with a few days of dry feet. Small chance of that.

It became hard to get started in the morning, knowing the sort of monotonous activity that lay ahead. Every day was spent portaging, wading under overhanging branches, moving rocks and driftwood from channels to deepen them, dragging the canoe through the shallows, loading and unloading the sacks, cutting bushes and sunken branches, banging our scabby, infected legs and shins, getting our ankles trapped down crevices and being whipped by thorny branches while our feet rotted away. We had spent nine days like this before we finally emerged into quiet water. Nine days to cover 20 kilometres at the most. What a wonderful vacation.

8

Up the Cuc

A h, the simple pleasure of sitting quietly in the canoe all day long, with the sun on your back, feet dry, just dipping that paddle. The Jari had put us through another trial and, having proved we were worthy to see a little more, was giving us a breather. We covered over 15 kilometres in one day, passing the Mapari tributary (which enabled us to pinpoint our position on the map) and getting through two more rapids. They were kids' stuff: one tiny portage for each and on our way.

'But, Peter,' I would complain with mock puzzlement, 'the map shows a big rapid here.' I surveyed the 2-metre fall that we were negotiating. 'I see no rapid here. Maybe a few bubbles, but not what I'd call a rapid.'

Peter would agree: 'We used to do ten of these before breakfast.'

If our map was to be trusted there were only three more major rapids before the Cuc. This was greatly encouraging, but we did not dare to build up our hopes too high. Suppose there were so many rapids the cartographer had grown lazy and omitted a lot of them? And was the Jari really likely to be so sweet? We got on with our daily toil and enjoyed any respite that we were offered.

Once a week we permitted ourselves the luxury of a rest day, or as much of a rest day as the mosquitoes would allow. It hadn't rained for ten days and the jungle was very dry, but that seemed to make no difference to their numbers. Each time we arrived at a new camp it took them a few hours to find us, but once they did they stayed day and night until we left. After dusk, the only refuge was the hammock, but that meant a long, long night.

The equator runs across the river Jari a few kilometres south of the confluence with the Ipitinga, so we were dominated by the equatorial pattern of almost equal days and nights. It would be dark by seven o'clock, and dawn would break at about 5.30. Usually we had taken enough exercise during the day to be pretty tired, and that helped us to sleep quickly. At other times we lay awake for five or six hours, sweating and tossing in the airlessness of the net, with the whine of the swarms outside and the itching caused by the dozen or so that had broken through the defences. In normal life I have always been one for going to bed late, and for me the worst aspects of jungle trips are the enforced early nights and the long hours of darkness. Sleeplessness at home is a question of how you are going to feel next morning at work, but can be made more tolerable by turning on the light and reading, listening to the radio or getting up and raiding the fridge. In the jungle you can't waste torch batteries for reading, so there is nothing to do but sweat it out, think of home and make little plans or projects.

We had one more easy day, and then new difficulties arose. The Jari became shallow with almost dry channels full of rocks and only 30 centimetres of water. Frequently there was no gap between the rocks wide enough to get the canoe through, so irksome 3-metre portages were necessary. We spent most of the day either walking the canoe or dragging it. Bits of fibreglass were ripped off the bottom and floated away. Peter broke his paddle trying to fend off a rock, and the whole thing was agony on our backs and formerly on-the-mend feet. We made five long portages, and in the afternoon came to a cascade that fell over 10 metres. This forced us to do a portage of over half a kilometre, and above it the view was depressing: rocks as far as the eye could see, just like a wave-cut platform at low tide, complete with rock pools. The river was spread through so many channels that not one of them was deep.

We spent the next day and a half walking up this maze, getting progressively more demoralized and bad-tempered. Stopping for lunch on the second day we had a strange experience. I had shot a curassow, so Peter was sitting on some rocks plucking it and frying up its liver and heart with a little rice, while I repaired his broken paddle with fibreglass. Looking up, I saw a figure several hundred metres away up ahead. We waved, and he seemed to reply in kind, but made no move towards us. We were there for well over an hour, and all that time the figure stood out in the hot sun and in the same place watching us. We wished we had binoculars to examine him. From that distance he seemed naked and pale-skinned, but we could not be sure. Finally we set off wading through a difficult section towards him and he disappeared from sight. We reached where he had been, called and whistled, but there was no sign. Perplexed, we left the canoe and spent twenty minutes wandering around the islands, before we grew worried about leaving our canoe and stuff unattended, and sat on the rocks near it to have a smoke.

'Strange, isn't it?' I remarked to Peter.

'I'm thinking he is somewhere on one of those islands hiding in the trees watching us,' he said.

'Must be,' and we glanced around in apprehension.

'I'm thinking that he is pointing the arrow at you, just now. He won't shoot at me. Too skinny. But you are a nice, big, fat, easy shot,' offered Peter kindly, and we laughed nervously. We felt sure our elusive stranger was an Indian, and the situation was unsettling…

'Come out, my friend!' we shouted facetiously in English. 'Come and see the super presents we've got for you!'

Nothing stirred.

'Let's get the hell out of here.'

'Good idea,' said Peter, and we waded on our way with many a glance over our shoulders, determined to get away as far as possible before nightfall. Later we saw on the map that there was a tributary entering the Jari thereabouts and thought that the Indian could have been from a settlement up there.

We continued to see a lot of wildlife – families of capybara that gave a warning bark and galloped into the river, tapir, coatis, numerous monkeys and three giant otters. These are charming animals, and a rare sight on so many Amazon rivers where they have been widely hunted for their skins. One of them saw us coming and slipped off the rocks into the water. The other two stayed lying on their backs, paws in the air, unaware of our presence and ignoring the warning chattering from their companion. We got to within 3 metres before they saw us, and then they dived and swam around the canoe, repeatedly popping their heads up.

The river was a little deeper at last, having carved a channel through some rocky areas, and for the most part we were able to paddle although the current was swift. We learned that the difficult rapid of the previous week had not been Macocoara at all, because we came across it the next day. The river fell over 25 metres, but to get round it we found a trail cut by past travellers. Our first glimpse of the falls had taken us by surprise. We heard it first of all, and from the volume of the roar presumed it to be near. Then we rounded a bend, and the water in front of us was smooth, if fast-flowing; way up on the hillsides that bordered the river we saw a glint of white, still too far away to be easily discernible. Five hundred metres further on we were able to see that the glint was the top of the falls and that the bulk of the water was falling into the gorge from the right.

The portage was surprisingly short and painless considering the height of the falls. Yet at Carecaru this was the fearsome rapid that everyone had heard about. By the side of the trail there was a little plinth with the names of a past Brazilian expedition, dated October 1937. The Thirties seemed to have been a very busy time on the Jari. We had already seen the cross of the dead German expeditionary at Santo Antônio.

The falls themselves were magnificent, cascading in a dozen places over rocks festooned with moss and flowers. The water sparkled in the sunlight, and hummingbirds and green parrots flashed through the spray and rainbows. In the rainy season it must be spectacular indeed, although how you would get past then I don't know, as the trail would be under water and the rapids above the falls too dangerous.

The next day I felt ill again and my feet had given up on me. We had to do a portage over sharp rocks and I was hobbling along doing only one trip to Peter's three: the foot rot had spread all along my insteps, so there was no relief. It would have been all right if we had been given a day or two of calm paddling, but that day began with over a kilometre of wading, and after 300 metres I called a halt.

'We're going to have to camp for a day or two, Pete. If I don't rest them now, they'll only take longer to heal later. I'm sorry.'

'No problem,' he replied. 'If you do not rest, I would soon have to carry you as well as all the sacks,' and he grinned.

Good old Peter; he was as keen to press on as I was, but never complained. He slung my hammock for me and I crawled in. It was bliss to rest the feet, but I was also feeling decidedly rough, my temperature was rising and I recognized the symptoms all too well.

Through the mosquito net I watched Peter wading up the rapid, casting the spinner. Apart from a few minor details like his lack of clothing, the hot sun and the lush vegetation he could have been a trout fisherman on a Scottish stream. Suddenly I saw him reach into the water and come up with a .32-calibre shotgun. It was a bit rusty, but perhaps still serviceable. The result of an overturned canoe in someone else's drama, we supposed.

Later I had a classic malaria attack, shivers, temperature to 104 degrees and then sweats. I took three Fansidar. Doctors warn of the toxicity of Fansidar, saying that you shouldn't take more than three in any one week. Certainly every time I took three they did strange things to me. I felt numb and floaty, and my hearing became distorted. Sounds came in circular waves, so a wind rustling the jungle canopy would sound like the whirring of helicopter blades. In short I was stoned, and it was a welcome distraction from the miseries of malaria attacks.

In common with most people of my age, my pre-malaria experience of sickness had been no more than 'flu and the usual childhood maladies. I was unprepared for that feeling of utter misery that malaria brings, which you know could easily end in death – a new, frightening and disturbing idea to a fit young person. By the time I had this attack at Macocoara I had experienced eight malarial bouts already, yet the fear remained and I suffered the same. In some ways I had more to worry about because I was better informed about the possible complications of the disease, and aware of how different our self-medication in the jungle was from the treatment given in hospital. Falciparum malaria can cause kidney failure, permanent damage to the liver, brain haemorrhaging and death within two weeks, and in the Hospital for Tropical Diseases in London a nurse or doctor had checked on me every hour. Pete and I could monitor each other's temperature, apply cool sponges if it got too high, bring food and water, and dish out quinine, chloroquine or Fansidar, but that was it. If the medicine ran out, we'd had it.

With such cheerful topics to think about we stayed put the next day, and even with a short spell of rest my feet improved. I had a temperature of 101 degrees, but compared with the previous evening I felt positively sprightly and even went on a short shuffling walk to look for gold. Knowing that the Jari was a gold area we always kept an eye out. We didn't want to pan for it, move tons of sand or earth, or do any hard work, we just wanted to find a few nuggets of half a kilo each. Near the camp was a little creek which to our untrained eyes shrieked 'Bonanza!' and we spent the afternoon grabbing handfuls of sand and shingle to sift through. Having spent so much time walking up the river we felt it would be only fair if we stubbed our toes on the occasional golden pebble and returned home wealthy. We used to fantasize about which items in the canoe would be thrown away to make room for our cache, and of finding a goldfield up there on the Jari where in future years we could return periodically and secretly when our extravagant, debauched lifestyles needed new funding. Needless to say we never found one speck of the stuff, but it's quite possible that over the weeks we trod on it, slept on it or built fires on it.

There was a colony of hoatzin in some bushes that overhung the river near our camp. These pheasant-sized brown birds hissed and squabbled incessantly, and it was only their inedibility that spared them a few pellets up the backside. Their flesh gives off a strong, disagreeable smell and that offensiveness is their protection. Scientists regard the hoatzin as a living link between primitive and modern forms of bird, as it is the only survivor that resembles the oldest of all known birds – the archaeopteryx – reconstructed from fossil remains found in Bavaria. The baby hoatzin, I had read, has a two-clawed 'finger' at the angle of each wing. The newborn bird can creep around in the branches and, in times of danger, drop out of the nest into the water, where it swims with astonishing speed. Using its wings like hands, it then climbs to the nest once the threat has passed. I sat and watched them for a time, but unfortunately their eggs had not yet hatched, and I couldn't test these observations with some baby-baiting.

Although I had another fever that night, I felt strong enough to move on the next day. As Macocoara was the last major rapid marked on our map we had good reason to feel optimistic. The Cuc was only 75 kilometres away now, and perhaps the Jari would be moved to bestow upon us a kind farewell so

that we would remember it with a touch of affection? It was time it revealed a
sweeter nature if it had such a thing, and atoned for all the toil and hardship.

As if in answer to our prayers the river did change for the better. Suddenly
it was island-free, fairly deep and almost unrecognizable. This was the first
time since Monte Dourado that it had kept to one channel for more than
a kilometre, and the absence of islands made it much easier for us to follow
its twists and turns on the map. We now knew where we were to the nearest
kilometre and could check our progress. The chances of missing the mouth of
the Cuc because it was hidden the other side of an island had receded.

However it now became Peter's turn to be sick. There had been a strong
breeze all morning that I had found pleasant, but Peter complained of feeling
cold, put on a sweatshirt and wrapped a blanket over his shoulders. The
temperature was in the eighties. I don't know what I look like when I've got
malaria – not too good, I expect – but Peter always looked ghastly. Having a
naturally dark complexion, he got very tanned in the course of the trip, but
when he was ill his face went a sickly grey, he vomited frequently and his
temperature went over 105 degrees. That used to worry me. He might die and
leave me up there on my own! We nursed each other with concern during
these malaria attacks and fortunately they never once coincided, otherwise
we should have stopped eating for a day or two. If food was presented to us
we could eat something, however feverish we were. But preparing it would
have been beyond our strength.

I spent three days waiting for him to recover and kept boredom at bay
by doing a few chores. First I checked all our food supplies to see if anything
was damp, and which items were getting low. We still had plenty of staple
foodstuffs, but most of the luxuries like onions, drinking chocolate, alcohol
and tomato paste were finished. I washed some clothes, fished with a fair
amount of success and forced myself to read long passages from *History of
the World*. I suddenly had the urge to have short hair, so hacked away at it

with the tiny scissors of my Swiss Army knife. I cut the front and sides to 1 centimetre long all round, and Peter did the back. Finally I trimmed my beard, and finished up looking like an escaped convict. It felt cooler, and no-one was going to see me for a while anyway.

I also repaired one of our camp stools that had begun to fall apart.

'You're getting a bit old and soft,' Mark had laughed when he saw the little folding stool I had bought in London the week before we set out for Brazil. Despite excess baggage charges I had decided that a stool would be worth taking to improve the quality of life on the Jari: a little concession to luxury. I know well enough that without such a thing, at the end of a hard day, you end up leaning against trees aswarm with ants, or sitting in the debris on the jungle floor.

Mark considered it unnecessary, or so he said at first. However, the day before we left Manaus he appeared at the hotel with a big grin and a package. Inside was a folding stool – larger, lighter, cheaper and much more comfortable than my own. These stools made the period we spent together even more of a galling experience. Mine had a tendency to collapse, almost pinching my balls off, or to sink slowly into the soft soil until I was sitting on the ground anyhow. Furthermore, it was so low that ten minutes on it would cause my feet to go to sleep.

Mark's stool, on the other hand, behaved itself perfectly and, judging by his comfortable expression, had no defects on the other scores either.

After Mark and I split up, and I returned with Peter, I was tempted to tell him that for some reason Mark had bought that absurd little stool and I had bought the other. Honesty and friendship won the day, and to save a squabble every evening we designated it the cook's chair. If anything stopped us shirking our cooking duties it was the idea of sitting on the ridiculous thing I had bought. As I repaired it with a piece of wire, I thought that next time I went to Amazonia I would go one better. I wanted a folding chair with arm rests and a back. On second thoughts, I'd better take two; otherwise my companion might murder me for it.

Treks in the forest, rather grandiosely called hunting trips because of the gun slung over the shoulder, were often enjoyable nature rambles that rewarded us with some interesting sights. Apart from the usual glimpse of the rear end of fleeing deer, we saw marmosets, tortoises, the occasional sloth hanging upside-down from a branch and peering round sleepily, but not as many animals as you might expect. Usually that was because we were making so much noise, but the rainforest holds so many absorbing sights when you stop treating it as adversary and an impediment to your progress.

We came across giant trees with trunks so massive and straight that they made us giddy looking up to their crown 65 metres above. They were supported by huge triangular buttress roots often higher than our heads and only 2 or 3 centimetres thick, and it was pleasant to sit down and recline against their fibrous, russet bark and listen to the sounds of the jungle.

Woodpeckers scampered up the trees, cocked their heads to listen for the burrowing grubs and launched into an attack sometimes with an incredibly loud staccato, perhaps six strikes to a second.

A great variety of jungle sounds were familiar to me by now, but I was often not sure if they were the cries of bird or insect. These were the wolf-whistler and the knife sharpener, the football fan's rotating ratchet, and something that went ohhhhhhh-si, si, si, si, si, si, si. I recognized the squawking green parrots, the toucans and the raucous macaws which always flew in pairs conducting their screeching conversation; and I knew the whirr of tiny hummingbirds which hung suspended nearby with their wings a blur, before darting a metre or two up, down or to the side. There were beautiful iridescent morpho butterflies too, the size of a human hand, catching the occasional ray of sunlight in a dazzling flash of turquoise. They were seemingly clumsy in flight, but could fly through a tangle of lianas with ease.

The jungle could be thick and impenetrable, or as easy to walk in as an English beech wood where the tree trunks rose like cathedral pillars in the coolness of a nave of shady half-light. Insects ruled the jungle floor. Lines of leaf-cutter ants carried pieces of greenery four times their size and cleared bare paths through the debris. Termites had constructed covered tunnels up the outside of any dead tree they were working on. The foliage of the lower bushes was often totally stripped by caterpillars. If you raked the dead leaves dozens of beetles would be revealed, and always the air was filled with the hum of bees and the drone of insects. Fortunately the blood-sucking ones were fairly rare during the day.

We usually returned to camp sweaty, scratched and covered in debris and cobwebs, but each time we would have found something interesting or new to observe: a tiny bird's nest, for example, glued to the leaf of a sapling, and so small and light that it, and the three eggs it held, did not even bend the slender stem; or a tree that was obviously a favourite scratching post for jaguars. Three metres off the ground the bark would have been gouged, raked and shredded by those powerful claws. A hike also served as a pretext for each of us to get away on our own for an hour or two – important on a trip where we were together for twenty-four hours a day.

Peter was remarkably even-tempered and we rarely bickered or quarrelled. When we did it was invariably me who started it. He was very quiet and, since his English was not perfect, I felt sometimes he was just nodding his head without understanding all I was saying. But the silences were companionable, and I'm no chatterbox anyway. I would rather travel with someone who talks too little than one who talks too much.

Everyone likes to think that in times of stress and hardship they behave coolly, rationally, with good humour and in a manner supportive to their fellows. This trip really tested these assumptions, and sadly I didn't score too well. I became sulky and moody or threw little tantrums when I kicked the canoe, hurled sacks of food or hopped up and down swearing. Whenever I behaved like this a calm, rational voice would refuse to be silent in my head. 'God, you're being childish and petulant,' it would reprimand with infuriating smugness, and I would carry on with my tantrum feeling pretty ridiculous. Peter did not have many such outbursts. He would calmly take over whatever I had left undone when I stalked off to sit in the river and brood, and only deepened my shame and angered me even more.

Generally, however, we kept remarkably cheerful. We would laugh, and clown a little, and often hum and sing through the never-ending routine of daily chores. Every morning camp had to be broken, everything packed away, fire lit, breakfast cooked, items of food fetched from the stores in the canoe and transferred to the food bag, clothes washed (although less and less frequently), pots scrubbed, fish gutted and scaled. When we stopped again more fires had to be lit to cook lunch and supper, hammocks and tarpaulin put up, things repaired and machetes sharpened. All this and the trials of paddling and portaging as well. Yet not once did we argue about whose turn it was to do any of these chores. Each of us knew it had to be done, and got down to it. Pretty commendable, I think.

One night a jaguar strolled into our camp. We were sleeping on an island and had noticed numerous jaguar tracks crisscrossing a beach on the far side. Even so, we had not bothered keeping the fire going, letting it die down once supper was cooked. Jaguars were abundant on the Jari but we felt they would stay away from people. According to *The World of the Jaguar* by Richard Perry, the animal is not aggressive and is likely to attack only if wounded or protecting its cubs. Indian tribes usually revere rather than fear it. However,

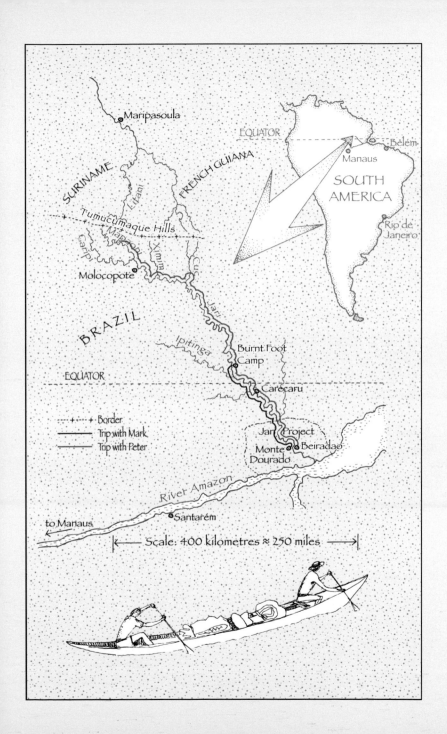

▲ Mark and our assistants launching the canoe on the Amazon

▼ River boats at Manaus

Locals skinning a Caiman

Supplies accumulating
in our hotel room

Poster warning about the
dangers of overladen boats

Our canoe

1. John with butterflies
2. Portaging a rapid
3. John with payara fish

on this page: Clearing a gap for the canoe

1. A depressing scene at low water, typical of the Mapaoni

2. Rapid on the Jari

3. A typical jungle camp

opposite page:
Peter approaching

A last look - aerial view of the Jari

owing to the terrain it inhabits and the extent of its territory, the jaguar is the least studied of the big cats. I've never heard of an instance of a man-eating jaguar, but that could be because it has never had to share its habitat with humans in the way tigers, leopards and lions have. Until recently it has had the space to move away from settlements and human encroachment.

That particular night I awoke suddenly, with the certainty that something menacing was nearby. I lay motionless, staring through the mesh of my net, but a moonless night under the forest canopy is so deep a darkness that I couldn't even see the mosquito net 2 centimetres from my face. There was a metallic clunk from over near the dead embers of the fire, and I let out the breath that I'd been holding, figuring it was Peter, having a snack or getting a drink.

'Pete?' I called, but instantly regretted opening my mouth. He would be using his torch if he was up and about. Silence returned, except for the thumping of my heart and the little creaks my ears made as they waggled around searching for clues. Five uneventful minutes went by and I started to relax. Must have been a stick falling from a tree and hitting a cooking pot. Hang on, what was that? I sniffed. Cat. I could smell the rank odour of tom cat! Then I heard the stealthy movement of a large animal taking a few paces towards my hammock before stopping again. I gulped and tried to smother the tremor of my panicked breathing that would only encourage a hungry predator. I could imagine it 3 metres away, powerfully muscled, head raised as it checked my scent, superb night vision assessing the hammock. I lay as if paralysed; any movement and it might pounce and I would be trapped in the folds. And if jaguars shared the habits of domestic cats I did not relish the idea of having my hammock swung by a playful kitty with paws as big as my hand.

I'd been lying still for ages ignoring all aches and cramps, but I would have to move soon. My throat was itching and needed clearing with a good cough. The jaguar was also motionless, but once or twice I heard it sniff the air. I had to do something or this could go on all night. I said a little prayer, drew in a lungful of air and leapt up in the hammock, emitting a banshee wail. I don't know who got the bigger fright, the jaguar or Peter. The animal leapt through a pile of our dirty plates, crashed through the jungle, splashed across the shallow river and kept on going. Peter was plucked from his peaceful slumbers by my scream and by a large, powerful form colliding with one of the ropes holding up his hammock.

Nearly the whole length of the Jari had a large frog population, and at night they began their croaking chorus, often twenty or more together. Usually I was able to ignore them, but one night, unable to get to sleep, I started to count the croaks of one frog. It had already been croaking for some time, in a monotonous rasp about once a second or a bit faster. I swear this one croaked 8,000 times before I gave up counting. Never resting, never varying the tempo, never getting the reply it must have been hoping for – 'Hey, bullfrog baby. Get your sexy arse over here.' That means I lay there for over two hours counting it, so we were both equally deranged. I rose in the dark, grabbed a torch and the shotgun and spent half an hour trying to locate it so as to blow its head off.

Peter recovered, and we moved on up the river. The Jari remained island-free, fairly deep and calm. It was about 50 metres wide at this point, serene and friendly. All day long we met no obstacles – just sat there and paddled, travelling over 15 kilometres. There was an enormous number of fish around, mainly piranha, which were probably congregating to spawn. We passed areas where over fifty dorsal fins protruded above the surface and more fish splashed in the shallows. We could never catch any when they were massed together like that. They must have had other things on their minds.

It was when we were casting the spinner among these fish in the hope of foul-hooking one across the back that our fishing reel gave up on us. The handle stripped its thread and then broke off. It was a serious blow, and there seemed to be no repair we could improvise. Fishing was our main source of food and from now on we were going to be less successful, unless we mastered the hand line like almost every other Amazon fisherman.

Our appetites were enormous, and food became an obsession. We made our diet as varied and interesting as possible with our limited pantry. We used to make rice cakes stiffened with flour and fried, porridge or oat cakes, farinha cakes, either sweet or savoury, and pancakes. A treat we looked forward to twice a week was spaghetti with an oil and garlic sauce. During the first weeks we had enjoyed onion, tomato puree and even parmesan cheese, too. We also fried up any rice left over from previous meals, ate plenty of beans, fried lumps of dough or made stick bread.

Stick bread is delicious, or seems so to the hungry expeditionary. Flour, water and a pinch of baking powder are mixed and kneaded to a smooth dough and then wound in a long length round a green stick and baked over the hot coals of a fire. It takes about an hour to cook, so you have plenty of time to yearn for civilization where you can pop into a bakery and buy something much nicer. I had been slightly put off stick bread just before our trip by reading of two travellers who died in East Africa after wrapping the dough round a poisonous stick, a danger I had never considered before. However I decided the risk did not outweigh the pleasure.

We also tried to cultivate bean sprouts several times. These are normally easy to grow by putting a handful of raw beans into a large plastic bag and covering them with warm water overnight. In the morning you prick holes in the bag to drain it, and the sprouts are ready four days later after daily watering. However we'd evidently bought a dud batch of beans. The shopkeeper in Santarém had seen us coming and flogged us his old, desiccated stock that never produced so much as one sprout before the whole lot grew mouldy and had to be thrown away. Just cooking a stew with these beans took twelve hours, even after soaking.

Fish accompanied most of the above delicacies – either filleted, fried or boiled in a soup. Amazon fish are generally very tasty but when the reel packed up we had to lift the moratorium we had imposed on hunting certain animals.

We shot a capybara one morning. There were eleven in the group: six adults and the rest youngsters, and we pursued them across the river and shot an adult female. Fortunately the river was shallow because after thrashing for a few seconds she died and sank, and it was only by wading around feeling for a furry corpse on the river bed that we were able to find her. She was as fat and heavy as a sheep, and we spent the rest of the day skinning and butchering her. Choice steaks and the liver and heart were put aside for frying. Other cuts of meat were cubed for making stew, and then the remainder was sliced into thin strips which we salted and started to dry in the sun. We had meat for many days.

We were camped in a beautiful place, a grassy hollow obviously covered by water for most of the year but now lush and dry. It seemed like a park with soft grass underfoot and a few trees to provide shade. This was a welcome break from exuberant vegetation, and there were animal tracks everywhere – tapir, capybara, jaguar, ocelot, otter, deer and alligator. To our relief, too, mosquito numbers were bearable, and we sat under a full moon with almost daylight visibility. Peter measured that we had covered 250 kilometres since the Ipitinga, which was not bad going, and he estimated we should reach the mouth of the Cuc the following afternoon.

We saw our first anaconda the next morning. It was sleeping half out of the water and we were able to paddle very close before it woke and slipped below the surface. At about 3 metres long it was just a baby. The largest anaconda ever measured was 37 feet 6 inches (11.5 metres), yet much larger ones have wriggled their way into travellers' accounts and folklore. In fact there have been so many absurd exaggerations and touched-up photos of gigantic specimens that everyone has grown wary.

For example a Brazilian told me in 1980 of an incident when he was a guide on the Juruena river.

'I know every metre of that river, Senhor,' he said, 'and every rapid and fall. But one day we rounded a bend and saw a fall that had never been there, that shouldn't have been there. Getting closer we saw that it was a giant *sucurijú* stretched half-submerged from bank to bank, with the water pouring over its back. It looked like a cascade from a distance.' The river, he said, was about 60 metres wide at that point.

Such nonsense fuels the disbelievers. They also cite the reward of $50,000 that Theodore Roosevelt offered in 1913 to anyone who could produce the skin and vertebrae of an anaconda of over 11 metres. That was an enormous sum in those days, and many people were destitute after the collapse of the rubber boom, but the reward was never claimed. While it is possible that larger anacondas do exist in Amazonia, I maintain a healthy scepticism. Colonel Fawcett, while obsessive about his quest for El Dorado, was usually restrained and matter-of-fact in describing jungle perils, until he said he measured a 62-foot (19.5-metre) specimen on the lower Amazon in 1907.

Anyway, unless extremely hungry or angry, the anaconda won't attack people. It preys on caimans, water-birds and capybaras and can swallow animals of up to 70 kilos. Contrary to popular belief, it does not crush its victim, but compresses it just enough to stop it drawing breath, and then swallows it whole. The anaconda has about seventy teeth in each jaw, the longest being about 14 millimetres and the thickness of a needle. Set at an angle towards the throat, these are used to grip the prey and to assist the labour of swallowing such a huge meal intact. An anaconda in a zoo thrives on six large meals a year, but no doubt in the wild it would hunt every few weeks.

The Jari continued free of rapids, but it was often so shallow we could walk from bank to bank with the water not above our knees. This was irritating because we could not dig our paddles in as deep as usual without hitting the bottom, so had to jab rather futilely at the surface. There were dazzling white sandbanks where we stopped to rest or swim, and where on other rivers I might have hoped to find turtle eggs. There seemed to be no turtles on the Jari. Perhaps Santo Antônio was a barrier to them too, as it was to stingrays and other fish.

There can be few creatures in this world of tooth and claw that give off such an air of benign inoffensiveness as the turtle. Perhaps it's that slow, waddling gait on land, or that rather absurd carapace. Most likely it's that wrinkled neck, bald head and myopic eye that remind us of kindly old men. There are two species of turtle in Amazonia. The tartaruga is the largest freshwater turtle in the world, living over thirty years and growing to 80 kilos. Its carapace is greenish-brown and round. The tracajá is smaller with a more elliptical, greyer carapace. Unfortunately they are both succulent and flavoursome, and the locals either harpoon them or catch them on floating lines with baited hooks under fruit trees.

Only once have I killed a turtle on my river trips. I shot a tracajá from 100 metres with a .22 rifle as it sat basking on a rock in midstream, and then paddled over to retrieve it. It was still very much alive and when I got it to the campfire I was in a dilemma as to how to finish it off. I saw a Brazilian once chop through the carapace with a machete and yank the beast out, and I recoiled at the cruelty. Yet now I was forced to consider the practical difficulties of butchering a well-defended turtle.

I placed it the right way up and stood beside it quietly waiting for the head to emerge. Sensibly the head stayed under cover for over fifteen minutes before the animal considered the danger had passed, and it headed for the river to soothe its pain. Swiftly I swung the machete and chopped the head off smoothly, congratulating myself on achieving a difficult task with the minimum of cruelty.

I then chopped the two places where the lower half of the carapace joins the upper and pulled it apart. To my consternation I discovered the heart was still pumping, the lungs still billowing, the legs waving, and even the severed head opening and shutting its mouth. My appetite was fading fast as I separated the guts and bunged the rest in a pan of boiling water, slamming the lid down shut. Even then the waving legs twice kicked the lid off before the dismembered creature consented to die. Never again.

In 1979, when I travelled by steamer down the Rio Madeira, the cargo of live turtles grew at every stop. Passengers embarked with them as extra luggage, or men paddled out and sold them to the captain. Soon even the floor space under the hammocks had its cargo of mute suffering. Laid on their backs, they were rendered helpless, undignified and pitiful. They waved their legs, extended their grandfatherly necks and spent the journey trying to right themselves. Very occasionally one would succeed if its legs could get a purchase, and many had their legs tied tightly across the underside of the carapace to prevent this.

Many had been caught weeks before and kept in pens waiting for the steamer to arrive, with no food or water. Turtles can live for much longer without sustenance, so it was deemed unnecessary. Several had the puncture hole of the harpoon in the carapace, which oozed a watery blood. Very soon nearly all had rubbed raw patches in their legs and necks from chaffing against their inverted shells. Others had bleeding wounds from the cords that tied their legs.

There was only one other gringo on board, an American, who viewed the pitiful cargo with even more outrage than I. We remonstrated with the passengers and the captain that the creatures should be watered and fed, kept untethered in the hold, should not be taken in September when some of the captives were undoubtedly egg-carrying females. All to no avail.

If we'd been richer we might have bought the lot and released them – but from talking to the passengers we realized we'd have to be rich indeed. Every kilometre nearer to Manaus their value increased. Turtles are a delicacy and everyone was going to profit from their sale, especially the captain, who had purchased several dozen.

The idea of a commando raid to release the prisoners came to us one night as we lay side by side in our hammocks passing a bottle of *cachaça* between us.

As I have mentioned before, cachaça is a fiery cane spirit that has to be tossed back and gulped with a fair amount of grimacing and exhaled breath. Once inside, however, it makes the stomach glow, the coward brave, the meek proud, the proud unbearable, the uncertain resolute and the cautious reckless. It made us embark on a foolhardy mission while the other passengers lay snoring in their hammocks with only the pilot awake at the wheel on the upper deck. We flitted about on our bare feet, shivering in the 2 a.m. chill, running our hands over the turtles' shells checking for harpoon punctures. Any without, we untied, carried to the rail and dropped overboard.

It took only half an hour and in that time we liberated sixty or seventy. That was only about a third of the total, but there seemed no point in releasing the wounded ones, and I think we hoped that no one would notice any were missing.

Some hope. By the time we awoke, hung-over and exhausted by our nocturnal mission, it was very clear that bad feeling was afoot.

Every visitor to Brazil comments on the gentleness and charm of the average Brazilian. They are a warm-hearted, easy-going, amusing race, welcoming to foreigners. Well, I can assure you that they had undergone a transformation on that particular boat. Until we got to Manaus the atmosphere was distinctly uncomfortable. Everyone stared at us with murder in their eyes, and the American and I took it in turns to go to sleep. No one voiced an accusation. Not once. But people would get up and eat elsewhere when we sat next to them at meals; stop talking when we approached; spit pointedly when we leant on the rail near them.

As for us, we felt a mixture of guilt and glee. We had deprived some poor people of a deserved addition to their meagre income – but we had thrown overboard three-quarters of the captain's personal cargo and he could afford the loss. We felt that self-righteous, persecuted glow of reformers and once we got off the boat we had no doubt we'd done the right thing.

We hugged the right bank of the river in our anxiety not to miss the confluence with the Cuc. We craned our necks round every bend expecting to see it there, and by five o'clock we were tired and keen to stop and camp. No offence, Jari, but we felt like sleeping beside another river and drinking from fresh streams, so we paddled on, and an hour later got our reward. The turbulence caused by the two currents meeting had formed a large sandbank in the middle of the Jari, and the Cuc's waters were slightly clearer. We let out a whoop of excitement and rested our weary arms. It had taken us five weeks from Carecaru. We were on schedule and pleased with ourselves.

As we drove the canoe into a small beach at the confluence Peter pointed excitedly at something in the sand. A footprint. But it was not the imprint of some splay-toed savage that had never known the imprisonment of shoes – this was a size nine boot with a heavy tread. Somehow that worried us more. A military boot perhaps?

We made our camp in the jungle behind the beach, and the coffee was brewing nicely on the fire when we suddenly heard the intrusive sound of an outboard motor approaching.

'Let me do the talking,' I said to Peter. We had been warned of a place called Molocopote where the army might stop us from going any further, though no one had been able to tell us exactly where it was. Could this be it? Would we be stopped at the scene of our small triumph? We skulked in the jungle hoping somehow that they would go right past and not spot us. Small chance with our fire belching smoke across the river. The outboard slowed its roar and turned into the Cuc. Excited voices greeted the sight of our canoe. Time to go and welcome our visitors.

Peter and I emerged from the jungle and were relieved to see that the three men were not dressed in army fatigues. They had come prepared for trouble, though. Each carried a firearm: there was one rifle that Mark would have liked, powerful enough to knock a double-decker bus on its side, one shotgun and a revolver. All were trained on us, but dropped shamefacedly when we greeted them with smiles and the offer of coffee. We sat round the campfire while I tried to find out who they were and to evade every question they asked us. We smiled a lot, shrugged our shoulders and played cat and mouse. We were two very mysterious guys.

Finally it transpired that they were from a party of fifteen geologists up there for a month doing a survey of the mineral deposits. Several years previously there had been an Indian post at the mouth of the Cuc and the airstrip still existed, but the Indians had retreated and the post had been abandoned. A military zone did start there, but when we asked if there were any troops about they laughed and assured us we would meet no one. Our fears evaporated. They were camped at the airstrip a few hundred metres away and invited us to spend the night there. However it had been a hard day, our camp was already set up and we had no further energy to face a barrage of friendly questions. We promised to call in for breakfast, and they said they would mail letters for us next time the helicopter came with supplies.

So we celebrated our arrival at the Cuc with another precious dried dinner and some capybara stew, though I felt the onset of fever again and could not really enjoy it. In the morning we called at their camp, had a coffee and handed over some letters. Then we set off up the Cuc, having learned that they were staying until late November – useful information if we met with disaster upstream. The beginning of the Cuc was all right, but after 2 or 3 kilometres we were already in difficulties. There was so little water that we were getting out every 20 or 30 metres to wade the canoe. The geologists had been measuring the water level on the Jari and told us it had dropped 10 centimetres in the past week, so we assumed the Cuc would be falling fast too. By midday we had to stop because I had a bad attack of malaria – it was disconcerting to see it back so soon. I swallowed another three Fansidar, felt better next morning and we pushed on.

The Cuc was lovely: only 10 or 15 metres wide, and twisty with abundant golden sandbanks. We saw a deer and two tapirs, and although we spent more time walking than paddling we were enjoying ourselves. Until the early afternoon, that is, when I had another bad attack of the rigours and my temperature soared even higher than the day before. The night passed slowly. When I got up now and then for a pee everything spun around, and I found my legs would barely support me. I felt sweaty, achy and very, very old. Yet the next morning I again felt stronger so we continued, but progress was slow.

'How are you feeling?' Peter asked me when we stopped for lunch.

'Not too bad,' I replied. 'I may have an attack this evening, but I'm okay for now. Just wish this bloody headache would go away.'

'Take some more of those strong aspirin.'

'I've already had six today; I'd better go easy on them.'

Ten minutes later, before the water for our pasta had time to boil, I was lying in the sun wrapped in all our blankets and spare clothing, and it was the worst attack of the trip so far. The chills came in waves that I tried to control until I was too exhausted. My teeth chattered, my body vibrated and my mind wandered off into hallucinogenic realms of nightmare and paranoia. Peter helped me to the hammock, and there I shivered, muttered, shouted and sweated until late evening. It was obvious that the Fansidar had not worked at all, so I started on a course of quinine, boosted with tetracycline – a combination that the Hospital for Tropical Diseases in London had used on me to good effect in 1980. A party of four men from the camp passed us as I lay there, and I sent Peter to ask them about helicopters. It seemed that one had arrived that day and another one would be coming in ten days' time.

We had to decide what to do. The Cuc was so dry it promised to be impassable in another week or two, especially further upstream. It was over 100 kilometres to the point where we were to begin our portage into French Guiana, and the headwaters must be almost dry. We might reach a point where we could not go any further, and by then the river would be dry, cutting off our retreat. It was now the end of October, so the rainy season wouldn't start for another month or more. Would we have to make camp until the rains raised the level of the river? If so, how long would we have to wait? Presumably it would take a lot of rain before there was enough run-off to make the river easy, so we might have to camp until January. Did we want to be inactive that long? On the river that long? Moreover we would be doing the portage and final part of the trip in the rains. And what about malaria? We only had two courses of quinine left, and if the disease returned as often as this we would soon run out of the drug and die.

Whenever malaria gave me a respite, Peter and I discussed these alarming possibilities. In our conversation, ironically, I could see similarities with that stressful time at Burnt Foot Camp when Mark wanted to quit and I didn't. Now the roles were reversed, because the geologists' helicopter was unmanning me. It afforded an unexpected chance to get off the river and out of the jungle, and I very much wanted to be whisked to the comforts and medical facilities of Belém. I put forward all the difficulties of the Cuc as good reasons for going back to the airstrip. Peter, however, would hear none of it.

'We can't give up now,' he said angrily. 'Imagine the helicopter does not exist. If it wasn't there we would have to carry on, wouldn't we?'

'But look at this little creek! Imagine how dry it'll be up in the hills.'

'You need a rest, and then you will feel better,' said Peter and set about preparing supper. I felt like crying. How could I ignore the helicopter? Why had I picked this mule-headed Swiss macho man for a companion? How could he be so stubborn? Oh, to be lifted up and away in a clatter of rotor blades, to float over the rivers and jungle, and be deposited a couple of hours later in the reassuring bustle of Belém. In a few days we could be sitting in a bar with clean, fresh shirts on our backs and ice-cold beers in our hands, making eyes at pretty girls. We could gorge ourselves in restaurants, go to the cinema, read the newspapers, listen to music. All this could be ours so soon. Surely he must succumb to temptation?

Meanwhile some strips of capybara that we had tried to dry in the sun had gone off. The weather had turned cloudy and unsettled, and the narrow Cuc was too shady a creek for producing capybara jerky. It tasted foul and had to be thrown away. Great banks of cloud rolled up from the east, though apart from one brief shower it remained dry. We began to place sticks in the river to monitor any changes of level, and we developed faith in the weather-forecasting of frogs. They had scooped out circular depressions in the sand for depositing their spawn, positioned just on the edge of the present water level, but where the sand was wet enough to fill their pools. The spawn and tadpoles were thereby safe from fish until they had matured (but why birds like the herons don't scoop up the lot I don't know). Clearly any rise in the level of the river would sweep away all this work and their offspring, so was their knowledge of the start of the rains infallible? Certainly they were still building these pools, so it seemed probable it would stay dry for a while yet.

Two days passed before I could face travelling again. Stripped of energy I lay in a delirious, paranoid torpor in the foul-smelling folds of my hammock, emerging only to take geriatric, tottering steps to relieve myself. The curious incident of the Milo happened during this period. By this stage in our journey the tastier foodstuffs were getting scarce, and little remained to enliven our jaded palates. We were also getting through our remaining sugar at a great rate, suffering terrible cravings for anything sweet. Supposedly kept for sweetening tea and coffee, or for sprinkling over porridge, pancakes and our jungle versions of rice pudding, the sugar was becoming a constant temptation. Both of us wolfed neat spoonfuls when the other wasn't looking. The last tin of Milo (a chocolate drink, fortified with vitamins) was a huge temptation. Although beautiful as a hot drink to end the day, it seemed even better eaten surreptitiously as a powder.

A little rain had recently fallen and the jungle was dripping onto our pots and pans, but as I lay in my semi-delirium I imagined I could hear Peter taking advantage of my weakness to have a few spoonfuls of chocolate powder.

'You're eating the Milo, aren't you, you bastard!' I shouted, and Peter, who was in his hammock at the time and nowhere near the food supplies, started in surprise. The truth was that he had eaten a couple of spoonfuls of sugar just before turning in, so this he confessed to guiltily.

'Oh, great! Just when we're short of sugar you start stealing it all,' I yelled hypocritically.

Feeling rather better now I drifted off into semi-consciousness, but before long I again imagined the stealthy clink of spoon on tin.

'You're still eating it, aren't you, you shit?' I yelled, quivering with rage, and Peter awoke with a start.

'John, you are going mad,' he shouted back. 'Too much malaria, your brain has cooked. Now are you going to let me sleep?'

He told me later he'd been so concerned at my behaviour that he'd got up and concealed the shotgun and machetes in the forest.

When I felt better we decided on an alternative plan. The boatmen had told Mark and me weeks before that the Mapaoni tributary would be better than the Cuc for reaching a portage point over the Tumucumaque hills. It also had the great advantage of the supposed trail cut at the top, connecting it to the Litani river in Surinam. We had rejected the Mapaoni route initially because of fears of trouble with Surinamese officialdom. Now, however, the idea that the Surinamese-Brazilian border would be a tense military area seemed extremely unlikely. We would risk it anyway. The Cuc looked impassable, and although getting to the mouth of the Mapaoni meant continuing up the Jari for a further 200 kilometres, at least the rains would have two or three weeks to do something about raising the water level on the smaller tributaries.

So back we paddled to the confluence. We had hoped to spend the night at the geologists' camp, but everyone was away on surveys except the cook and a male nurse, and they would not let us stay without authorization from the boss. The cook sat at the table nervously fiddling with a ball-point pen as he dredged up excuse after excuse for this lack of hospitality.

'We can't let you stay without authorization (click-click went the retractable pen tip) and the radio isn't working, otherwise I'd radio the boss for permission (click-click).'

On and on he went, and we simply stood there making him more and more nervous. Not deliberately – we were just tired and having a break and rolling a cigarette before returning to the canoe and finding a campsite. I made some comments about how we knew it was traditional in Amazonia for people to provide shelter to passing strangers, and mentioned how six nights previously the boss himself had invited us to the camp. The clicks of the ball-point became more and more frantic, and after enjoying his discomfort for a while we departed. Perhaps we looked a mean couple of characters by then with our wild beards, faces gaunt from malaria, and tattered clothing. I looked Peter over objectively, and he did look pretty unsavoury. We'd hoped to swap excess cooking oil for some sugar, but it didn't even seem worth asking. The cook was the type who wouldn't pick his nose without written permission.

We camped on a sandbank nearby and discussed carrying out a night raid on the cook's supplies. We had seen boxes of forgotten delights piled high over there – tomato paste, stock cubes, canned meat, tons of sugar, tins of drinking chocolate and much more. Our diet was now so bland that the highlight of our day was our candy-coated multivitamin pill. We had even gone through the medical kit and wolfed all the peppermint-flavoured indigestion tablets.

'Let's go at two in the morning,' said Peter.

'Okay, but we'd better be careful. They have a lot of guns over there, and that cook is so twitchy that he'd shoot for sure.'

We retired to our hammocks, dozed off and never woke again until dawn. We'd missed the chance. I'm sorry to say it would not have been the first time I had helped myself to someone's food…

In the summer of 1980 on the Teles Pires Andrea and I were using a home-made plank canoe – so heavy and robust that we could barely lift it. While we managed small portages we knew we would be in trouble if we hit some long rapids.

After a fairly quiet beginning the river got progressively worse. The Teles Pires had not read those geography textbooks where rivers get quieter and more sedate the nearer they get to the sea. It was calm at the source and meaner with every kilometre. It took us two weeks to get through a

15-kilometre stretch of rapids, and the weight of the canoe prevented us taking the sane option of portaging. We had to paddle through the rapids or line the canoe down on ropes while one of us floundered chest-deep in foam trying to control the bucking craft. One false move and everything would have been lost.

Finally the river dropped over a 7-metre fall and cascaded through a 2-kilometre gorge with steep sides littered with giant boulders impossible to walk across. The end had come. It would have been too difficult to retrace our steps back upstream, so we had to abandon the canoe and everything we couldn't carry and walk 100 kilometres to the nearest road.

A hundred kilometres is a long walk under any conditions; in thick jungle with 30 kilos on our backs it was nearly the end of us. Fifteen days of terrible thirst, of stumbling fight with jungle creepers, of sweat and rain and sodden nights when we slept where we fell. We were short of food and our strength went so fast that we didn't expect to get out alive.

On the seventh day we suddenly came across a faint trail in the bush. Not a game trail like so many others that crisscross the jungle, but a man-made one as shown by the machete-cut saplings and one discarded tobacco packet. It was going in approximately our direction so we willingly followed it, spared the work of cutting our way, and as dusk was approaching we came to a hollow and a deserted camp.

A trestle table held cooking utensils and one or two personal possessions. Underneath we found a pick, shovel, gold pan – and some provisions wrapped in plastic sacking. A hundred metres away were the two water-filled pits where the owner had been excavating for gold. He had obviously gone away for a day or two, taking hammock, plastic sheet and shotgun, but he intended returning soon because he had left a large monkey stew in one of the saucepans. We knew it was monkey because he had cooked it head and all, and it came as a shock to lift the lid and see the little skull grinning up at us.

I am not very proud of what followed so I shall quickly make some feeble excuses. We were in a desperate state, having eaten meat only once in the previous seven days. Rice and flour seemed inadequate fuel for such strenuous activity: we were exhausted, weak and ravenous.

It started modestly. We cooked some rice and decided to have two pieces of monkey with it. This we did, and then another piece and then another. Soon only the head was left and, deciding it would look even more insulting if we only left that, we cracked it open, ate the tongue and sucked out the brains.

'The guy will kill us if he comes back,' we said as we rooted through his provisions to see what else could be found. A tin of corned beef was opened, mashed up with rice and wolfed down.

Time for dessert, and we started on a large jar of Toddy – a chocolate drink 'fortified with vitamins', the label told us. Sounded just the ticket, and there to go with it was a large tin of powdered milk and sugar. We made a great pot of the stuff and drank it down thirstily.

'We'd better stop now,' we told each other as we discovered that if you put Toddy, powdered milk and sugar in a cup and mix it up dry it tastes as good as any Swiss chocolate bar.

Soon the spoon was clinking against the bottom of what had been an almost full jar of Toddy, and we had tried, we had tried so hard, to stop.

'We really mustn't take any more,' we'd say, and retire to our hammocks after stowing away all the temptations. 'After all, these prospectors can be very violent men. For all we know he might be on his way back at this very moment.'

Yet we knew there was no stopping us now, and soon one of us would lead a new assault on the goodies.

Eventually the stuff ran out and we began to feel apprehensive. It was unlikely the man would arrive that night as it was already dark; but perhaps he had nearly made it back and was camped a kilometre or two away and would arrive at first light? We made plans for a very early start.

In the scrubbed, empty stew pot we placed a lot of money and a good sheath knife. We thought of composing a note to go with it, but the man was probably illiterate and words were superfluous anyway. In financial terms it was a generous payment, but in jungle terms it was meaningless. It was not a question of nipping round to the corner shop and replacing the stuff. That might require a six-day round trip.

The next morning, with the sun barely lightening the eastern sky, we were on our way, and seven days later reached the road.

I still think of the poor *garimpeiro* racing against the fading light to get back to his camp, having walked 20 kilometres that day. Weary and keen to get home, he consoles himself with the glad thought that at least he had the foresight to leave some food prepared so he can eat quickly and get in his hammock.

'Perhaps a little cup of Toddy after the stew would go down well,' he muses and smiles contentedly, adjusting the load and quickening his pace through the jungle gloom.

9

The Jari Again

Our decision to return to the Jari was a gamble. It was 200 kilometres up to the mouth of the Mapaoni, and if it gave us a hard time it would add several weeks to our trip. While it had proved fairly easy for the last 75 kilometres before the Cuc, there was no guarantee it would stay that way. From our past experiences it was probable it would not.

Paddling away from the lure of the geologists' camp that morning was heartbreaking. I'd hoped that Peter would weaken and submit to the temptation of a helicopter, but he never gave so much as a backward glance. I sat crestfallen in the stern, still weak and with an appalling headache that the glare of the river did nothing to improve. I felt overwhelmed by the cumulative discomfort, the insects, the hard work, the sickness, the bland food. The whole trip had degenerated into a joyless endurance test, and I wanted to go home. We'd been presented with a marvellous opportunity to escape without having to retrace our steps, and here we were paddling away from it!

I kept these thoughts pretty much to myself. I had already suggested quitting twice to Peter, but he had rejected the idea forcefully. I didn't persist.

That was unusual: generally I make repeated attempts to get my own way. In retrospect I think I was slightly relieved that he didn't let me persuade him to abandon the trip at a moment when malaria had left me so utterly dispirited and depressed. On a more practical level I suppose I knew that a helicopter was not due for at least another week, so there was time enough to discover whether or not I would recover my enthusiasm. Meanwhile it was surely better to be on the move than hanging around the airstrip.

Next day continued easy as far as the travelling was concerned, and we gobbled up the kilometres. In the week after leaving the Cuc we saw more wildlife than at any time on the trip. The river and her creatures seemed to be trying to cheer me up and rid me of my lethargy. We drifted to within 15 metres of a puma as it reclined on the riverbank enjoying the breeze, and it watched us quizzically from golden eyes. Then it caught our scent and bounded up and away with marvellous fluid grace. It was the first time I had seen a puma in Amazonia, and the best view I'd had of one of the large cats. A superbly adaptable creature it must be to have a range that spans the high Rockies and Andes and the sweltering lowland jungles.

A few kilometres further on we saw a group of six giant otters, and could see why they are the most endangered mammal in the Amazon. They popped up a few metres from the canoe, chattering at us, and would have been extremely easy to shoot. They have a beautiful thick pelt which fetches a price comparable to that paid for a jaguar's, so they stand little chance of survival along populated rivers. They are social creatures, each group controlling a territory of up to 30 kilometres of a river. Their diurnal habits, loud calls and the way they trample the vegetation down in characteristic clearings make them relatively easy for a hunter to find. Unfortunately, once giant otters have been hunted out of an area they have no great ability to make a comeback. They reproduce very slowly – about two years between births and with an average litter of only two cubs. However, we found these enchanting animals still abundant on the Jari and other uninhabited rivers that we travelled through.

We ate well over the next few days, because we were not only viewing this abundant wildlife with aesthetic pleasure. We shot a curassow and a small alligator. The caiman, as it is more correctly known, has suffered severe persecution in Amazonia over the last century because of the value of its skin, but we shot it for its soft, fishy-tasting meat. In 1950 some 5 million caiman skins were exported from the state of Amazonas alone, which comprises about a quarter of Brazilian Amazonia. Taking into account that for every skin exported two more are probably lost owing to bad curing, or because the wounded animal sinks and cannot be retrieved, that means about 15 million caiman were killed. This figure has now dropped considerably, partly owing to tougher controls and the ban on the trade, and partly because the creature is actually hunted out. On the Jari we saw numerous small specimens that slid into the water as we approached, but the largest we saw on the whole trip was no more than 2.5 metres, which is the maximum size that the spectacled caiman grows to. The larger black caiman can reach 5 metres in length, but we never saw them on the Jari.

We were prepared to eat anything once in an attempt to vary our diet. One day we boiled up some water snails, which were revolting. Another time on a gravel bank where we had stopped for a rest we found some freshwater clams, so we collected them to make a *spaghetti alle vongole*. That was more successful, but we only found the clams once more after that. There were a lot of small crabs too, and we cooked one now and again, but we never saw enough together to make an enjoyable feast.

The new-look Jari was psychologically hard work. There were long, calm, wide stretches where we had to slog along wilting in the heat. We covered large distances but it was dull and monotonous. Silly, really, to feel that way. Not long before we'd have sold our souls for such easy travelling. I was still depressed and dispirited, aware that if we turned round we could make it back to the Cuc in time to catch the flight out. I had been taking the quinine/tetracycline mix for over a week now, and I was beginning to feel stronger. It was a complicated regime of pill-taking: four tablets at noon, two at 6 p.m., two at 8 p.m., two at midnight, two at 4 a.m. and two at 6 a.m. Considering we had no watch, there was no way I could be very accurate, especially in the hours of darkness. I just took two whenever I woke up in the night. It was only after I returned to England that I learnt of an unwelcome side-effect of tetracycline. At the time I couldn't understand why any part of my skin exposed to the sun now stung and itched excruciatingly, especially after I had been exposed to its rays for so many weeks. At night the itching and stinging continued, and I had to take anti-histamines, or get up in torment and seek relief by sitting in the cool water of the river. I thought the sun must have changed character, perhaps as a prelude to the start of the rains. Not at all: photosensitivity is a side-effect of the drug.

I must have been miserable company. I sulked in silence for much of the time, punishing Peter for being so strong-willed. Finally I suggested a rest day, and that did me good. As we did every week, we checked our supplies for any damp or deterioration, and dug out the items that we had bought to give to Indians, as we expected to encounter some soon. About 150 fish hooks, 700 metres of fishing line, spare salt, beans and some cheap mirrors and combs – it looked a sorry pile. If our lives were to depend on this trash, we'd had it. What Indians really want are knives, axes, machetes, pots and pans and colourful fabric, but we hadn't the space in the canoe for such items, or been prepared to spend the money.

By the end of the day of rest the depression had lifted away. I felt transformed: keen and eager to push on. I woke up to hear the tweets of a couple of curassow near the camp, and in my haste to put my contact lenses in I dropped one on the jungle floor.

'Peter,' I called. 'There're some *mutum* over there. See if you can shoot one.'

I had done all the hunting so far, and he had been reluctant to participate. He was still reluctant that morning.

'I never shoot an animal in my life. I don't like to kill things.'

'Look,' I said angrily, 'I can't do it because I've dropped my bloody lens and I can't see bugger all. I don't enjoy killing creatures either, but we both enjoy eating them. It's time you did your bit.'

This conversation was conducted in a fierce whisper as the birds were very near. Peter still hadn't moved.

'Peter, I'm not your bloody hired gun, you know. I won't do your killing for you. I've done it up to now, but enough's enough. Go and shoot one of those birds before they fly away.'

Off he went, and I concentrated on the area of jungle floor where my lens must have landed. Talk about a needle in a haystack – damp leaves and twigs in a layer several centimetres deep, but I knelt down and began to sift through them. I had only one spare lens, so I had to try. Peter returned, saying the birds had flown off just as he was taking aim, so he joined me in this different type of hunt. For one and a half hours we gently separated each leaf over a 2-metre square area, and miraculously in the end we found it.

Two days later we passed the mouth of the river Ximim-Ximim. At one time Mark and I had considered taking this river to the Tumucumaque instead of the Cuc or the Mapaoni. We were thankful we had dropped that idea. What a feeble trickle it was.

'I have pissed more liquid than this after a night on the beer,' said Peter as we nosed the bow of the canoe up the choked waterway, before turning back to the Jari.

Just past the confluence was a little rapid – the first on the Jari since Macocoara, which must have been over 200 kilometres behind us by now. We were developing a belated attachment to this river; it had been very kind to us lately, just when we needed peace and quiet. It was also getting lovelier by the day, narrow and twisting, with steep hillsides, sandbanks and rocks. The Jari certainly discourages the casual visitor with all the obstacles between Monte Dourado and Macocoara. The faint-hearted, the weak, the wimps – and the sensible – give up and turn back. Yet the loonies who persevere have their reward. The wildlife continued abundant. We saw several groups of giant otters and tapir, caught a glimpse of a jaguar and watched an eagle swoop and snatch a fish. Finally, draped and coiled on a fallen tree, was a 7-metre anaconda. I'd never seen one wholly out of the water before and we sat for a long time only 5 metres away while Peter did a quick sketch. It was a beautiful creature, with green, black and brown markings gleaming in the sunlight. It still hadn't moved when we left.

It came about very slowly, so slowly that we were unaware of it at first, but the mosquitoes steadily declined in density from about Macocoara onwards. They were still there, but in tolerable numbers, and we found we could sit around after dark without being eaten alive. It couldn't only be explained by the higher altitude, because on the lower Mapaoni, a few weeks later, they became more numerous again. Other factors must play a part. Martin and Tanis Jordan had found the Rio Mapuera mosquito-free, so it might be some quality of the water that destroys their larvae, perhaps.

As we approached the mouth of the Mapaoni we came across a few signs of humanity, an old shelter of the type Indians make while on hunting trips, an abandoned house and an old canoe. We checked out the ruins of the house, hacking our way across what had been the cultivated clearing, while creatures scampered ahead of us. To our joy we discovered a papaya tree with some ripe fruit. Being unable to shin up its smooth trunk, we chopped it down, which was a terrible act of vandalism, but nothing was going to keep us from that succulent fruit. The impression that the house must have belonged to Indians was reinforced by the overgrown garden being full of the little red berries they use for dyeing and decoration. We paddled on, expecting to meet Indians at any moment, so when we saw a clearing on the left bank we donned shorts and climbed up the slope to investigate. Reaching the crest, we took one look and dived for cover. There, dominating the bend in the river, was an encampment with several shelters, but it didn't appear to be an Indian village. There was a radio mast, machine parts, several aluminium canoes and other paraphernalia.

We squatted there and discussed what to do. This looked like Molocopote, the control post we had been told about, and it looked too bloody official for our liking. We debated whether to confront them openly, or sneak by later under cover of darkness. We decided on the former, and paddled round the bend. There was a young guy having a wash on a rock. Covered in soap suds and singing lustily, he did not see us until we were 2 metres away. His face was a treat. The song stopped abruptly as his mouth gaped open, the soap flew out of his fingers and Peter and I were convulsed with laughter.

We moored the canoe and went up to the camp with all sorts of stories prepared to try to bluff our way past officialdom. It proved unnecessary – they were not officials at all, just another group of gold prospectors. They responded admirably to the surprise of our arrival by piling good food on us and inviting us to spend the night.

This place was Molocopote, and there had been a FUNAI post until two years previously, with over fifty Indians living there. There was a large cleared area, the remains of some huts, a long airstrip and a herd of water buffalo that had run wild. However, another tribe had come down from the Cuc on a raid, so the survivors had moved over to the Parú river. There were also several Indian graves that one of the Brazilians had desecrated out of curiosity. He stressed that this wasn't grave-robbing, but more in the nature of a scientific exploration and an archaeological dig; nevertheless he'd chosen to hang one skull from a post of the hut. He found that the Indians were buried with a strange assortment of prized possessions: a hammock, a tube of Colgate toothpaste, shotgun cartridges, pots, pans and an empty Coca-Cola bottle. He also thought he could detect that they had been killed with shotguns rather than bow and arrow. I just hoped he was going to put it all back in the ground before a warrior party arrived to put some flowers on their parents' graves.

One of the group, Paulo, played the guitar and sang for us; he had a marvellous voice that soared in the cool, star-filled night and echoed back from the jungle of the far bank. He knew a lot of songs in English that he had committed to memory with no idea of their meaning, and he sang them beautifully. We realized that we had missed music a great deal. At the beginning of the trip, when I was with Mark, we'd had a little cassette player and a few tapes which had been an appreciated luxury. However, Mark had taken it away and Peter and I had nothing.

Four of the men had been about 30 kilometres up the Mapaoni two weeks before. They said it was really hard going with little water and many rapids. This sounded more or less what we had expected. They had a good map of the river with a scale of 1:250,000 that we made a tracing of.

We slung our hammocks near the fifteen others, and as in all Brazilian camps it was not a peaceful night. One man listened to a football commentary for two hours, and Brazilian commentators are not chosen for their reticence. Jabber, jabber, jabber they go at breakneck speed, but when a team scores the commentator yells GOoooooALLLLLLLLL! in a shouting crescendo and holds it for about twenty seconds or more in a howl of ecstasy. Well before dawn other guys were fiddling about with the wave-bands of their radios. Others coughed, spat, scratched and farted. It had been a nice interlude and a change of routine, but we were keen to depart.

Peter looked pale and continued to clutch a blanket round him long after the sun had chased away the dawn chill. He said he wanted to move on, so after some coffee we shook hands with the men and paddled away. But we had only gone a kilometre before he was violently sick and began to shake uncontrollably. He lay on a small beach wrapped in our bedding until I persuaded him that we should return to the camp. I paddled him back and found that most of the men were about to depart for a place upstream beyond the mouth of the Mapaoni where they had found gold in workable quantities. Peter crawled into his hammock and I spent the day talking to the four or five guys who had stayed behind; from them I heard some world news. It seemed that the US had invaded Grenada, which I imagined might well make the Brazilians even more paranoid about the threat of mercenaries crossing their border. However, up there in that remote spot it seemed extremely unlikely that there would be troops on either side of the border, so we were not too alarmed.

The boss and Paulo had a bitter row that evening that was embarrassing for the non-participants. I liked Elcio. He was a well-educated geologist who had done his doctorate at a university in France, and he listened to Radio French Guiana a lot, which irritated the other members of the group who were of more humble origins. He felt there should be a hierarchy in the camp, and that he should be at the apex. So he sat around giving orders, while the others felt, rightly in my opinion, that an expedition into the wilds should generate a more egalitarian society, where everyone should muck in and help. In the course of their argument Paulo brought up all these grievances, whereupon Elcio decided to quit the project and return to Belém. He told me he would only return to the jungle if Paulo were sacked. However, Paulo seemed the more capable of the two.

Everyone departed upstream next day except Elcio, who was waiting for a plane due to arrive in four days' time. Peter's malaria attacks responded well to chloroquine, and to our naïve way of thinking that suggested that he had the vivax strain of the disease. Mine would only respond to quinine, indicating falciparum. Or did it? It would have been nice to ask a doctor. It was fortunate that we appeared to have different strains because we were by now short of both drugs. I decided to stop taking my twice-weekly preventative dose of chloroquine to leave more tablets for Peter. Forty-three quinine tablets and forty-nine chloroquine remained: not even enough for two complete courses of treatment – but enough, we hoped, to keep the disease at bay and us alive. By the next day Peter felt well enough to set off again, and I had to admire his resistance to the temptation to call off the whole trip. When I'd had my last malaria attack there had been the helicopter to seduce me, and here at Molocopote he knew a plane would arrive within a couple of days. Yet he never faltered in his determination to carry on. I'd been fortunate to find a companion of his calibre.

The Jari continued quiet and peaceful and we were almost sorry to be leaving it. As we were stopping for lunch I saw a paca crouched under a tree by the water's edge and shot it. We could not understand what a nocturnal animal was doing out in the daytime until we saw that it had already been shot and wounded. I don't know how the poor thing had lived so long: it had a horrible putrid hole blown in its neck that looked two days old. It must have crouched there in agony since being shot by a hunter from the camp. This is the aspect of hunting I find most distressing: inevitably sometimes an animal or bird will be wounded and not finished off. We were glad to put this one out of its misery, and also undeniably glad of the meat it was going to provide for our dinner.

An hour or two later we reached the mouth of the Mapaoni and paused on a sandbank for a breather and to say goodbye to the Jari. We had a last swim in its green waters and gulped water from each of the two rivers to see if we detected a difference in taste. Peter was convinced the Mapaoni tasted of gold, showing optimism to the end. A few months before leaving England I had attended a medical seminar at the Royal Geographical Society which had impressed me with dire warnings against drinking untreated water. I had been scared enough to buy a filter bag and sterilizing tablets for this trip, although I had never bothered on other rivers. If a river has no towns, factories or dwellings along its banks, I can't see what dangers it can hold. Surely it is just rainwater with natural vegetable and mineral matter? Doctors shake their heads sadly at my ignorance and naivety. Anyway, our water filtration and sterilizing had been abandoned after Carecaru.

Peter discovered he had bad intestinal worms on the Mapaoni and each morning would find him prodding his deposit with a stick to see what would emerge. I was often dragged away from my breakfast to give an opinion on his findings, lucky me, and there was no doubt about the quality of some of the specimens that waved their heads at me.

'Don't take that medicine yet, Peter,' I'd tell him as he stood looking down at the horrors he had fathered. 'A bit fatter, and we'll be able to use them for fishing bait.'

When cleaning monkeys we noticed how worm-ridden they were too. Our favourite delicacy from any kill was its liver, but we had to throw away a lot of monkey livers because they were alive with thick white wrigglers. Their stomachs and intestines often contained a nauseating ball of parasites, and we made sure we cooked all game animals very thoroughly.

That first day on the Mapaoni we covered about 4 kilometres before stopping to camp. We were encouraged: not nearly so many shallows as the Cuc and a surprising amount of water for the time of year. Elcio had told us that the river had rapids, but we could not imagine them being very big affairs on a river this size. Next day we covered over 20 kilometres and, apart from a few minor rapids which we had to wade through, all was easy going. Arrogantly we mimicked Elcio and his party as we went along.

'There's no water, many rocks, many rapids. It's very hard,' and laughed. They should have seen the Cuc or the lower Jari. Obviously the poor boys had no idea what a shallow, difficult river was all about.

The Mapaoni was the most beautiful river I had ever travelled on. At the top, the Jari had become narrower and more interesting, but this was a paddler's dream. It was 10 metres wide and twisting, with constantly changing vistas, sandbanks, little rocky inlets and lovely jungle-clad hillsides. I'm captivated by jungle on hillsides, perhaps because I have travelled on so many rivers in flat terrain, where you have only one line of jungle on either bank. When it is hilly you can see the canopies of a host of trees, and really appreciate the infinitely varied shades of green. And not only green, because in mid-November there were a lot of trees in flower, showing great bursting crowns of yellow or mauve.

On the map we had measured the distances we should have to cover in order to achieve our objective. To the border was about 120 kilometres, and the last big tributary (the Caripi) entered the river about 80 kilometres ahead, leaving us some 35 which promised to be very hard, with little water.

We felt rejuvenated by the change of river. We forgot about aching muscles, the heat, the constant headaches that malaria gave us throughout the trip, and delighted in the Mapaoni. In contrast to the Cuc, we scarcely even touched the bottom or had to walk.

The second day was a little more difficult, but we still covered 15 kilometres or so. One rapid forced us to do our first portage since Macacoara a month before, but we didn't care – in between the rapids there was barely any current and the jungle wildlife continued to entertain us. Where we stopped for lunch we had a large troop of spider monkeys on one bank, as big as two-year-old children, another troop of capuchin behind us, and an otter dragged a fish on to the rocks 10 metres away and ate it, seemingly indifferent to our presence. A flock of six scarlet macaws squabbled and shrieked as they passed overhead and landed to feed in a nearby tree, filling it with their gaudiness. Later in the trip I collected some feathers from one of these birds after a Brazilian had shot one, and found that some feathers have at least five colours. Others are red on one side and blue on the other. The tail feathers are an amazing 55 centimetres long.

That afternoon I experienced a chilling moment with the shotgun. I wounded a curassow at the water's edge and, quickly reloading, cocked the gun to finish it off, but the bird flapped into the jungle before I could take aim. So throwing the gun down on the gear between us, I grabbed the paddle, thrust the canoe to shore, scrambled up a steep bank and through some thick undergrowth till I spotted the bird. When I raised the gun and made to cock the hammer with my thumb, I found to my horror that it had been cocked all the time. It was an unnerving reminder that I am very much an amateur with firearms, without the discipline and safety-consciousness that are driven into people who hunt regularly and are taught properly from the beginning. I could easily have shot Peter or myself. It was a sobering lesson, mercifully learnt without a tragedy.

That evening, after a huge meal of curassow, I tried to catch a few catfish for breakfast next day. I sat on the rocks near our camp in the moonlight, smoking, and had no shortage of bites. In fact I caught twelve piranha in fifteen minutes and put them all back. We had eaten enough piranha – we wanted something better. It was enjoyable fishing with the moonlight on the water, the cruising fireflies, the accompaniment of Peter's singing from the jungle behind me, and the nocturnal chorus swelling into full voice. There were more mosquitoes on this stretch of the Mapaoni, but they were not bothering me too much that evening. Occasional bats dipped and swept within a few centimetres of me, invisible in the dark but ruffling my hair with the beat of their wings. They were after mosquitoes and they were welcome.

I mused about the possibility of having four bats on strings, one tied to each shoulder and one to each kneecap as the ultimate mosquito-repellent. I caught another piranha, and killed it to provide a large piece of bait, then changed hook and put half the piranha on. No way would its relatives be able to swallow that whole. I cast out, gripped the line between my knees, rolled a cigarette, sipped on a mug of coffee and daydreamed.

The sudden rasp of the line being pulled out in a rush made me spill coffee down my shirt front. This was no piranha. Indeed, after a lot of mad rushes and splashes a 2.5 kilo traira was out and gasping on the rocks. When I think of all the hours I have spent fishing English rivers to catch nothing or some mere 100-gram roach, Amazon fishing really is a delight. It has also ruined fishing in England for me for ever. I dispatched the fish with a blow behind the eyes and scaled it with the back of a knife. Not a job I enjoy much, since I seem to transfer all the scales to my hair, beard and shirt. I slit out the guts, where I found a 7-centimetre fish still perfect and intact in the stomach, and tossed the mess into the stream. Then running the knife flat along the backbone I removed two juicy fillets to fry for breakfast, preserving them in a pot of brine.

Next morning I threw up my traira fillet. A bloated, dead tapir floated by just as we were eating breakfast. What a stench! The corpse caught on a submerged tree right next to us and when I attempted to nudge it along with a stick, I prodded too hard so that it deflated like a balloon, sending out a huge whiff of stinking gas and some unspeakable fluids. Retching and gagging we grabbed our gear and departed.

The geologists' party had been up here the week before and from what they told us had shot everything that moved. It seemed they did not always follow up wounded animals either. Brazilians shoot a wide range of animals for food, and tapir is the most prized for the quality and quantity of its meat – over 200 kilos on a large specimen. However, being such a large animal it can absorb a lot of shot before it dies, especially if the hunter is shooting from a distance. I've eaten peccary, deer, agouti, armadillo, turtle, macaw, toucan, snake, coati, alligator, iguana, porcupine, sloth, puma and anteater at various times when dining with *caboclos* or gold prospectors. I found them all tasty, but there is no food I won't try, and no one can accuse me of being a fussy eater. The animals on the Mapaoni had little or no fear of man and frequently just stood there sniffing at the strange, unfamiliar scent. The iguanas, on the other hand, went to the other extreme. We often disturbed them sunbathing on the topmost branches of trees. Their reaction was to let go and drop like stones into the water 20 metres below, bouncing off the lower branches and somersaulting before smashing into the water with huge splashes. How they avoided injury I don't know. Had they stayed put we would never have seen them up there anyhow. And presumably once we had passed they had to drag themselves laboriously back up again.

During these days on the Mapaoni there was still a lot of cloud, but no rain fell. The river was usually deep enough, and we certainly didn't want rain unless it was really necessary. We saw that one of our maps marked Indian villages near the headwaters; we prepared ourselves for the first contact and wondered whether a trail would still exist. We had mixed feelings about meeting Indians. We hoped they would be there because without them the trail would be overgrown from disuse, and it would obviously be an interesting experience to meet a tribe. But we were apprehensive about our first encounter because you can never be confident that Indians will be friendly. There are so many factors that can influence their behaviour – how they have been treated by outsiders in the past, whether they feel threatened, whether the tribe in question is generally war-like or pacific. Once contact was made we felt confident enough about our sensitivity and diplomacy that we wouldn't upset them by our behaviour. But we might not even get the chance to prove what smashing chaps we were and just walk into an ambush from unseen attackers. We were not too keen to go that way, but we vowed not to use guns to defend ourselves should we be attacked. We were trespassers on their land, and we were not going to compound the crime by shooting at them.

Meanwhile we were meeting bigger rapids. It's very difficult for two people to portage a canoe across rocky terrain where you have to hop from one boulder to another. Unless you try to keep in unison the canoe is yanked out of the hands of the guy at the back, or the one in front is pushed off his precarious perch. We fell frequently, but fortunately the canoe landed on something soft – us – and was undamaged. We took advantage of the opportunity to look at the state of its bottom. Not bad, considering the scraping, scrunching and abuse it had received since we fibreglassed it two months before. However, most of the fibreglass tape had been stripped off the external joints and we would not be able to leave it much longer. We had only 1.5 litres of resin left and we wanted to keep most of that for emergencies.

We had grown soft on the long rapid-free section of the Jari, but five days of rapids whipped us back into shape. Quite large rapids, too. Some of them fell 10 or 15 metres. Our progress dropped to less than 5 kilometres a day, and we waited impatiently to find the Caripi, the last major tributary. With so many islands and channels, we were worried we might miss the turn-off. Although our map was 1:250,000, it was still too small a scale to be of much use. The river was twisting and turning all over the place and most of the loops were not marked.

10
Choked Waters

Eight days after leaving the Jari we reached the confluence with the Caripi. Neither stream looked exactly imposing, but the Caripi was perhaps slightly the larger and easier. Anyhow we were happy to have reached here relatively easily. Over 80 kilometres in eight days was far faster than we had expected, but now it was apparent that the good times were over. The river was only 3 metres wide, and the main problem was fallen trees. Amazonian trees are notoriously unstable, often having roots only a few centimetres below the surface, spreading out through the thin topsoil. On a riverbank where these roots were exposed and undermined by swirling floodwaters the trees heeled over right across the stream. It was a depressing view up the diminished Mapaoni, with fallen trees obstructing the stream every 15 metres. If we were lucky a tree had fallen across from one high bank to the other, leaving sufficient space underneath for our canoe. Again, if we were lucky, the tree had broken either on impact or later after rotting, so there would be a section we could float over. Or sometimes we found a gap near the bank that we could slide under.

Sometimes the trunks stuck up only a few centimetres above the water, so we could drag the canoe across still laden. If they protruded a little higher we unloaded some of the gear before this exercise. However, if the top of the logs stuck 30 centimetres or more out of the water, we had to unload everything and balance it on the trunk while we carried the canoe across. Paddling was almost impossible, although the river was still quite deep in parts. Instead we were walking, and while walking chopping at dead branches with machetes, jumping up and down on the rotten logs to break them, and moving smaller debris out of the way.

In many places the jungle had taken advantage of these log bridges to nip over to the other bank, forming a luxuriant barricade of liana, thorns and bushes several metres thick. Standing up to our waists or chests in water full of evil flotsam that had piled up behind the barrier over the years, we slashed and sawed and cursed. The chopping and shaking of course disturbed ants, spiders, stick insects and biting flies, and cobwebby dust and bits of rotten wood rained down on us. Then we had to tug the canoe through our little tunnel, only to face more of the same.

The canoe had done very well so far, but in these conditions it rapidly showed signs of strain. The designer in England had warned us that one thing the canoe might not withstand was being hauled fully laden over logs. He advised us to put struts down from the thwarts to brace the bottom. We should have done this in Santarém when building the canoe, but we had hoped for the best and now we were taking a risk with every log. Even with the canoe empty we could see the strain we were putting on it. The bottom would bulge up as it passed over the log, the thwarts popped out of their gunwale blocks as the shape distorted, and we could only imagine what stress was imposed when we left it laden. We wired up the thwarts, but continued doggedly for another day before deciding we must take a rest day and fix the canoe up properly. The half-keel had come off too, so we had a lot of work to do.

In the afternoon we heard the warning chatter of a troop of capuchin monkeys; Peter pursued them into the jungle and shot an adult male. I heard him cursing and swearing and he yelled that the monkey had fallen dead but was lodged in a branch 10 metres up. I joined him and we tugged at nearby lianas and shook the tree to try to knock it off, but it was firmly wedged, dripping bright splotches of blood on to us and leering at our efforts with its death grimace.

Peter courageously shinned up a nearby liana like a Swiss Tarzan, while I stood anxiously at the bottom. The liana was as thick as my wrist and appeared to be well attached at the top. Or so we hoped. We were eager for the monkey meat, but a fall and broken limb would be an unacceptably high price to pay. Mark had learnt to set a broken bone while on one of his hospital visits, in theory at least, but he was now in San Francisco or playing the slots in Vegas, and Peter and I had no idea. That was the sort of disaster to which we were very vulnerable so far from medical help. One of us wouldn't be able to transport his incapacitated companion downstream unaided. More serious injuries like a fractured skull or broken pelvis would almost certainly prove fatal. Certain illnesses could choose this most inconvenient time to strike – twisted bowel, a ruptured spleen from malaria, and appendicitis, of course. We had been told that a combination of Co-Trimaxazole and Flagyl might control appendicitis for a few weeks, but the doctor hadn't looked too confident and was offering no guarantees. Anyway, liana-climbing was altogether best avoided, and it was a relief when Peter returned safely to earth clutching our supper. This wasn't the sort of expedition where help was a radio call and a short helicopter ride away.

We stopped for the night soon after, and Peter set up the camp while I skinned the monkey. Another tedious job. It is always easier when the animal is still warm, but even so a lengthy, unpleasant task. Once again we found the liver too worm-ridden to eat, but we kept the heart and kidneys. I put aside some of the guts to use for fishing bait and cut the monkey into portions. Monkeys look so disconcertingly human when you're hacking them to bits.

Hands complete with little fingernails, little penis and balls, and eyes that, although filmy in death, watched me with a sad expression. I usually closed them before I started, unsettled and guilt-ridden by the accusation in their gaze. Judging by the wear of his teeth our victim was old and would be tough and chewy. When monkeys are threatened the dominant male stays behind to cover the retreat of his family. Sorry, old boy, but I guess you had a long and full life and perhaps soon some young buck would have kicked you out to a lonely retirement.

Foolishly we decided to fry a bit of this monkey, but being elderly it was tough as an old boot and about as tasty. We nearly broke our teeth on one piece and threw the rest in a pot to be stewed up slowly.

I watched Pete carry the little skull to a nearby rock where he cracked it open by bashing it with a stick.

'You should try it,' he said as he prised out the tongue and brains. 'Mmmmm. Really good!'

Call me a fussy eater, but I turned down the offer.

My foot rot had returned and became painful as it dried out each night, so I wrapped a soft shirt round my feet to protect them from the coarse fabric of the hammock. By wandering around the jungle naked we had also collected dozens of ticks. Ideally you should let ticks suck and bloat up before trying to remove them. This way they come off more easily, but there were too many to allow such hospitality. I scratched them off with my nails, no doubt leaving a lot of heads embedded to cause further little infections.

However, the mosquitoes had suddenly vanished, this time for good. Like an animal emerging from its burrow after an early fright we waited one more night to make sure, before removing the nets from our hammocks. No more stuffy, sweaty nights worrying that heads or faces might inadvertently rest against the net. No more distractions to our view of the stars and animals that approached. Just cool breezes and better nights' sleep. Also there were certain odours that did not have to be tolerated any more. Over the course of the long tropical nights we had to urinate four or five times; getting up so often and walking a few steps in the dark, with the risk of treading on something, became a bore, and when we were sick it was just too much effort. Consequently we got quite adept at unzipping and directing the jet of urine over the edge of the hammock. Quite adept. Occasionally part of the net would get a splashing and as a result they were beginning to pong a bit.

The next day we worked long and hard on the canoe. Call this a rest day? I suppose such work is all character-building and helps you overcome your lazy, slothful personality, but we would have preferred to swing in the hammocks all day. I removed a lot of screws from the ineffective watertight hatches to secure the half-keel back on, and roughly shaped a piece of wood to replace the rest. It didn't look as though it would last for long, but would protect the bottom of the canoe from scraping. We also belatedly strutted out the centre thwart. Then we checked through our food supplies to see what was left. A lot of it was damp, so we spread it out round the fire because the sun couldn't penetrate down to the narrow stream through the overhanging jungle.

A family of capybara came swimming towards us. Two adults and three youngsters came within 2 metres before they saw us. At first I grabbed the shotgun, intending to get a juicy youngster, but I did not fire. It was such a nice family scene, and I'd had enough of killing. Instead I did some fishing with a piece of monkey gut, catching a 2-kilo traira which seemed a big fish for such a little river.

Next day we commenced battle with what remained of the Mapaoni. It might be only 30 kilometres more to the headwaters. In the morning we found we could get under or round quite a few of the fallen trees and moved fairly fast, and a lot of other trees could be scraped over without unloading. We would stand on either side of the canoe with our weight submerging the log a little more, and heave in unison, calling 'One-two-three-HEAVE!

One-two-three HEAVE!' In three or four pulls it would be over and we would be on our way again. Worse were the tangles of vegetation. We took it in turns to cut through these, the other just sitting and resting until a tunnel had been cut and before he pushed the canoe through to his companion on the other side. I was having a smoke and watching Peter swinging the machete energetically, when he let out a yell and came thrashing back through the waist-deep water.

'Electricity! Electricity!' he shouted. He looked terrified, and I guessed immediately that he'd had a shock from an electric eel. He got back to the canoe and leant against it, shivering violently.

'Shit,' he muttered. 'What the hell was that? It felt like an electricity shock!'

'It's a type of eel, Peter.'

'Eel? What is an eel?'

'A fish that looks like a snake – long and thin.'

'A fish with electricity? Are you serious?'

'Yeah. Another local wonder of nature.'

He smiled weakly. 'This fucking jungle has some surprises, eh? Well, it's your turn to use the machete.'

'Oh, I don't think so. You haven't finished your job. One tangle each, remember?'

'I'm not going back there with that electricity eel, and the land round here is too swampy for portaging. You'll have to go and finish the cutting.'

I knew that was fair, with Peter still looking so shaken, so I took the machete and cut a long pole from a tree on the bank. I then headed slowly and reluctantly for the tangle, slapping the water with the flat of the machete blade and jabbing the river bed with the pole. Electric eels can deliver a shock of up to 650 volts, more than enough to stun a man and cause him to drown, but this one must have moved on.

The electric eel is not actually a true eel, but a freshwater fish related to the catfish. It grows up to 2 metres in length, feeds on frogs, crustaceans and fish, and has to surface every fifteen minutes to take breath. The head is the positive pole, the tail the negative, and both must touch the victim to transmit the shock.

We had expected the Mapaoni to have a lot of rapids like any headwater stream, but they were not a major problem. We passed two or three little ones that day and could appreciate that fast water and fallen trees made an unpleasant combination. It was bad enough hauling the canoe and unloading sacks in calm waters, but doing so in rocky, swirling current was much trickier.

Our map marked the first Indian village about 5 kilometres ahead and we found ourselves apprehensively scanning the jungle for watching faces and checking sandbanks for footprints. Why should they attack a couple of nice guys like us (with all those super presents) who wished them no harm? But how were they to know how lovable we were? While we had long ago passed the limits of Elcio's intrusions up the river, other gold prospectors might have upset the tribes in the past. We looked out for cut branches or other signs of any lunatics trying to get a boat up here, but there were none. No doubt the Indians wouldn't use canoes on congested rivers of this sort, but really we felt they should keep their waterways in rather better condition.

We saw less wildlife now than we had before the Caripi, not because of scarcity, I feel, but simply because the ringing blows of machete on hard wood, the coarse oaths in German and English, and the splashings gave every creature plenty of warning of our slow approach. We did see monkeys and marmosets, however, and disturbed several caiman only a metre or two in front of us. Fortunately they scrambled away forward even faster than we ran away backward.

At times the river entered swampy regions with grassy banks and here progress was much easier: there were fewer tall trees along the river to topple over and block it. On the banks of one of these sections we saw signs of what seemed to be human activity – a section of broad-leaved plants had been trimmed at their base over a wide area. We got out and checked for machete cuts, but it looked on closer inspection as though the stems had been broken off rather than cut, probably meaning that the Indians in this area were as yet uncontacted and so without steel tools. We scanned the horizon for smoke, and our nervous tension increased. When two capybara suddenly 'barked' and leapt off a high bank into the water 3 metres in front of us, we jumped so violently we almost capsized.

At this time we became reluctant to use the gun at all. The sound would carry too far and alert all the Indians for kilometres around. Mindful of the lessons taught in *Etiquette and Modern Manners*, we even dug out our shorts to keep them at hand for our first meeting. This tension continued for another couple of days, but we never had the expected contact and gradually we stopped looking for human signs.

'I don't think there are any Indians in this area,' I commented to Peter.

'Oh. Why are you thinking that?' he replied.

'They are intelligent people. No one with any sense would live in this shit hole, would they?'

We averaged 3 or 4 kilometres a day up this stretch. They were tremendously hard days, made just tolerable by the anticipation of the evening's pleasures. First, the wash that had been a ritual throughout the trip now became even more of a treat. Soaping the cuts and scratches, soothing the stings and itches, removing the debris and sweat, and sluicing ants out of hair and beard never failed to restore us to a good mood. We could dress leisurely in our evening wear of long trousers and thick shirts because there were no mosquitoes to hasten the process, settle down to a large mug of coffee and our meal. Alas, the tea, Milo and powdered milk had all long since been used up, but we still had lots of coffee. We sat and discussed the day, moaned and complained, talked of the world outside that seemed so remote and far away, wrote up our diaries and I smoked a few cigarettes.

In Manaus I had bought a roll of 'Fumo'. This is compressed tobacco leaves in a long cylinder that is ideal for jungle travel, being so tightly compacted that I could shave slivers off the end with a knife as I needed it. It could get wet, and frequently did, without spoiling, and a kilo of it lasted me for over four months. It was exceptionally strong – and pretty revolting, to be honest – and induced violent coughing and the expulsion of enough tar to surface the average driveway. Unfortunately, when I returned to the jungle with Peter, I discovered that I had mislaid the huge supply of cigarette papers that I had bought to accompany it. We therefore had to rely at first on airmail paper and then on pages torn out of notebooks. Peter sensibly decided that the time was right for giving up the stupid habit and stopped after a week, but I persisted. Somehow smoking seemed one of the least important of our health problems right then, and anyway our lives were vice-free enough.

In one swampy area the river divided into several channels and we were uncertain which to follow. We separated and explored one each, in my case wading with the water up to my neck, and sometimes above my head when the river bottom shelved unexpectedly. I wished I had left the shotgun behind – it would have been easier to swim without it. As it was my feet disturbed large bubbles of foul gas from the deep slime on the bottom, and the stagnant water was too murky for me to be able to see the sunken logs, so I bashed my scabby shins and knees yet again.

I had gone half a kilometre like this when suddenly and unexpectedly I went into a funk about electric eels. This was just the sort of territory they love, and I was slap-bang up to my neck in it. I stood, paralysed with fear, convinced that if I took another step forward I would get the shock of my life. I stood still for over five minutes fighting the panic before I could will myself to proceed. I wanted to get out of the water, but the adjacent land was too swampy. The river was the only way. To distract myself I composed a silly ditty and sang loudly as I went along.

Down in the slime where my white feet tread, Oh Lordy, Lordy,
Lives a ten-foot eel, dozing on its bed, Oh Lordy, Lordy.
Will he give me a shock, will he bite off my cock?
Will he let me pass, or will he nip up my arse?

There is nothing like a coarse and banal song, sung lustily, to raise the spirits, as rugby players will attest.

I had struggled along a kilometre when I heard splashing round the bend. Tapir or Indians? Fear returned anew. The splashing was coming my way. Turning on my back I swam clumsily for the cover of some overhanging bushes, clutching the shotgun above the water, and there concealed myself among the vegetation. The splashing came nearer – whatever it was would pass very close to my shelter as it was hugging my bank. I drew even further into the cover and peeped through the fronds. Suddenly the suspense was broken by a stream of oaths in accented English. It was one area of our fine language that I'd been coaching Peter in pretty regularly recently.

'Oh, shit, you fucking bastard,' he groaned, raising a bloodied kneecap out of the water where some sunken log had removed the scab. I let him pass before I gave out a yell and sprang on his back.

Once his heart rate had dropped to a level that permitted him to speak, he told me that his channel and mine connected upstream, so that it made no difference which one we took. The last two hours had been a waste of time. We trudged back to collect the canoe.

A bit later, however, the river was so totally clogged with tedious tangles of thorns and creepers that after cutting through three we decided to portage the canoe for 300 metres rather than hack our way through five more, camping at the spot where we relaunched the canoe.

The old tick-heads I had left in my legs had turned into pus-filled pimples, and we both began to have painful sessions with the iodine night and morning. By the time we had finished anointing all our cuts, scratches, spots and abrasions we were more yellow than flesh-toned, and we reckoned the Indians might consider us tastefully decorated. Our hands were also battered from accidents with the campfire, the knife when skinning animals, or bumps and scrapes with the trees that blocked our path. Periodically, too, we had to sterilize a needle and pick out the egg sacs of the chigoes from our feet. These are deposited by sand fleas, and they announce their presence by tenderness and itching. You see a white area the size of a shirt button, with a bluish spot in its centre, and after you prise the lid of skin away a large white blob pops out, leaving a gaping hole. There was a perverse pleasure in this activity, and it was essential to pick the eggs out before they hatched, because otherwise the maggots would burrow over a large area.

We were astonished at the amount of water still in the river. Since this was the very end of the dry season and we were only 20 kilometres or so from the top of the river, we thought it must be fed by some pretty enormous springs. Or perhaps it never stopped raining up there at the source? Occasionally there were shallow sections with a sandy bottom where the canoe could not float and we would have to drag it laboriously along against the grip of the sand, but generally the water was at least knee-deep. Of course paddling was now a rare pleasure – it just wasn't worth embarking for the brief unimpeded 10 metres between obstacles.

At lunchtime next day Peter shot a monkey from among a troop that were feeding on a tree overhanging the stream. They all scattered except the victim, which stayed rocking gently and making little cries. Peter tried to put in another cartridge to finish it off, but the old one would not eject and he had to search for a knife to prise it out. In the meantime the monkey slipped, hung for a second by one hand, and dropped into the river. I waited for the current to bring it to me and saw it was still alive, jerking spasmodically, staining the water from the wounds in its chest. I grabbed it and held it under, while it kicked and struggled in my hand.

'What's happening to me?' I pondered, as I felt the little chest gulping for air, but filling only with water. Was I feeling remorse, guilt or revulsion? A little. But I'd come to regard killing as a necessary evil, part of our daily routine. Even as the creature fought for life in my hand I was assessing its body for plumpness and thinking of the meal ahead. Was this what 'back to nature' was all about? We stopped for a brew of coffee while I skinned it, and several large traira came up, attracted by the blood and offal that I was tossing into the river. I amused myself for a while by feeding them from my hand – very gingerly, because I know what large teeth they have. Tiring of that I put a hook into the next piece and after a brief struggle we had a fish starter for that evening's feast. I put everything in brine to keep it fresh until later. Then we got on with our work, and the afternoon passed in the usual wearisome way, hacking, slashing and chopping at our enemy: vegetation most vile.

In the evening when I was reaching round a tree to fix the rope of a hammock, I was stung on the little finger by a scorpion. That was the third time on the trip. The pain was excruciating and I hopped up and down cursing the Mapaoni, the Jari, the rainforest, Amazonia and all South America. After the pain diminished to a dull ache we began to laugh, and Peter hopped around the camp imitating my tantrum. As far as we were concerned at that moment the quicker they cut down all the rainforest and made one great cattle ranch the better. We vowed that when we got home we would throw out all our houseplants. We'd had enough vegetation to last a lifetime. Peter said he was going to give up his job as a landscape gardener. He wasn't going to fraternize with and care for the enemy any more. I suggested he should devote his talents to defoliant research.

I lost my cool again the next morning, this time with fire ants. They are aptly named – tiny red ants that burn like flames licking your body. I had unloaded the gear and placed it on a log in approved fashion, while we hauled the canoe over. When I picked up the bags again, dozens of ants ran on to me and began to bite ferociously, favouring the warmer, moister, tender parts of the body: my groin and armpits were on fire. I'm sorry to say I did not take this very stoically. I kicked the canoe, swore, hurled a sack of food across the sandbank and jumped in and out of the water seeking relief. I sometimes wonder why South American dictators spend so much money on sophisticated torture machines. No doubt there are foreign businessmen with briefcases and colourful brochures calling at their doors like brush salesmen, tempting them with the latest 'Shockometer Turbo Deluxe' model. What a waste of money. Two hours plonked in a fire ants' nest, or a week in the jungle without a mosquito net, and any freedom-fighter would be squealing.

We took anti-histamine tablets and after a while the torment began to ease, but not before I'd rubbed a raw patch in my groin. Peter already had a nasty one in his. I'm not sure what it was, a fungal growth perhaps from sweat and humidity, but a large area around his scrotum and upper thigh was permanently raw. He coated it with Vaseline during the day and dusted it with Mycil powder at night. But it never went away – in fact it slowly spread.

Peter already had a thing about ants that had been developing for quite a time, and I got a laugh out of his 'antics'. The large black ones would crawl over us, and then all obey some signal to sting and bite simultaneously. Peter's sense of fair play was outraged.

'For no reason! They're biting me for no reason at all!' was a frequent outburst. Earlier on in the trip he had begun to imagine that the canoe was infested with ants, which sometimes it was when they invaded the canoe at night via the rope. As we paddled along Peter began to lay down his paddle at frequent intervals to examine his body and pick off the intruders. He would stand up, shake out the towel that he had under him on the seat, and mutter, 'Little bastards, why don't you leave me alone?' I watched, half-entertained and half-irritated, as we began to drift backwards in the strong current.

Ants are no laughing matter, I will admit. Even the common black ones could make some camps unbearable. They nipped up our trouser legs, dropped from branches onto our heads to bite at the hair roots, and trickled down our necks and into any food bag left open. There were also lots of leaf-cutter ants, but at least on this trip they left our nylon goods alone. I remember one rainy night on the Rio Verde, when Glen, my Australian companion at the time, began yelling that ants were carrying away his mosquito net. I shone the torch over mine and was relieved to see that it was ant-free, because it was one of those wet, windy nights for staying under the blanket. Selfishly I lay there listening to Glen cursing and stumbling around in the dark, and saw him moving our food bags into the canoe. I dozed off.

The laugh was on me, however. The next morning I picked up my backpack and everything dropped out. The ants had carried away most of the bottom. Considering that these ants normally cut leaves to take to underground chambers where they cultivate a fungal growth that provides food, I can't understand why they are so attracted to nylon. Most probably their burrows were a little drab, and they were cheering things up with blue nylon-screened windows and wall hangings.

We estimated we were now about 10 kilometres from where we thought the trail should be. Ten kilometres is nothing in most environments – half an hour by bicycle, or two hours' walking. We reckoned we might get there in four days if everything went well.

11

Dire Straits

The canoe deteriorated with alarming speed. At our previous inspection it had seemed to be in pretty good shape. A week later it was a terrible mess. There were two places on the bottom where the plywood was completely worn through, and all the fibreglassing on the external joints had been ripped off. As we lifted it we could feel that the structure was losing rigidity – it sagged and flopped, and the whole craft was held together only by the fibreglass matting we had sensibly put over the inside. It was time for an overhaul in dry dock, so we took it out of the water that night. Next morning we found the wood was still saturated and as most of the river was in permanent shade we had to carry it a couple of hundred metres to a sandbank to catch a bit of sun. Putting aside half a kilo of resin to keep for emergencies, we used the rest to do an adequate job. It was in the nick of time. The plywood was paper-thin over much of the bottom. As we returned to our hammocks for a well-deserved rest, Peter and I discussed the situation.

'That will be the last time we can fibreglass her on this trip,' I sighed, flopping into the comfort of my smelly hammock. 'That little tin has to be kept for emergencies only.'

'I suppose when we have carried the canoe over the hills, the river over there will be similar to this one,' said Peter, gesturing at the choked waterway. 'Another hundred kilometres of fallen trees and rapids. We know what that will do to the canoe.'

'It's the sliding over logs that does it. We're as careful as we can be, but we can't carry her all the bloody way!'

'I'm thinking we do that already,' Peter muttered with a smile. 'Do you think it'll make it?'

'It's got to,' I answered, swinging out of the hammock. I'd just remembered it was my turn to cook supper. I gathered some little sticks and stuck them into the sand leaning against each other to form a pyramid. 'It'll be in a lousy state when we get to the end, that's for sure – but so will we!'

We laughed. I cut a piece of rubber from the old car inner tube that was our trusty firelighter, lit it and pushed it gently into the centre of the pyramid. The dry sticks crackled and a little flame appeared. I leaned a few slightly larger pieces of wood against the pyramid and prepared some others by attacking a dry log with a machete.

'We've got to be really careful we don't break its back, though. That tin of resin wouldn't be enough to put it back together again.'

The fire was going nicely. I began to prepare the rice and tossed over to Peter a large bird that we had shot earlier.

'Pluck that for me, will you?'

'Ah, work, work, work,' he said good-naturedly, and got up to sit on a stool. Feathers flew.

'Waiter, I'm thinking I would like my pheasant with potatoes and peas,' he said with a smile.

I raised my hands in mock regret. 'Oh, so sorry, Senhor. No potatoes or peas today.'

'Salad?'

'No.'

'French beans?'

'Very sorry, Senhor. May I recommend the rice?'

'Rice? What is rice?' asked Peter.

It was an old routine.

'Rice is a succulent vegetable from the mystic East,' I answered. I heated some oil in a pan and chopped up six cloves of garlic into it. After they had browned slightly I added the rice, stirred it up for a minute and then poured in the water and covered the pot.

Garlic had been one of our best purchases. We had bought 2 kilos and used it to spice up pancakes or rice, to make a sauce for spaghetti, and once, and only once, in porridge. At Molocopote I remembered bending over Elcio's shoulder to look at his map while he gagged and flapped his hand in front of his nose.

'Shit, John,' he gasped. 'Are you afraid of vampires, or what?'

Oh, yes, we must have stunk: a toxic combination of sweat, grimy clothing, wood smoke and garlic breath. We could have emptied a rush-hour train in seconds. As for vampires, well I think we were out of Count Dracula territory, but vampire bats were probably around. One of the risks of removing the mosquito nets was that they'd be able to bite us as we slept, but the pleasures had outweighed that risk. It was not so much a risk of blood loss, but of rabies, as vampire bats can carry that disease. Not that the blood loss is insignificant. As they bite their prey they introduce an anti-coagulant that causes blood to continue flowing for a long time after the bats have finished their snack.

Supper and coffee finished, I climbed into the hammock, but could not get to sleep for hours. I was worrying about the deterioration of the canoe. It would be so easy to wreck it in these conditions, and that one little tin of fibreglass would not be nearly enough. Without a canoe Peter and I would almost certainly perish. It was over 200 kilometres to the nearest habitation (Maripasoula in French Guiana) and to get there we would have to leave the waterways and cross the hills on foot. From my previous experience on the Teles Pires, when Andrea and I had to abandon our heavy canoe and walk 100 kilometres through the jungle to the nearest road, I knew how slim our chances of survival would be. We would be very limited in the quantity of food and equipment we could carry, and in our already weakened state we would rapidly be overcome by the exertion of crossing such terrible terrain. We would meet our end in some squalid little jungle camp and expire from hunger, exhaustion and disease.

It was not a pleasant prospect, and to shift my thoughts from such morbid contemplation I rolled a cigarette in the dark and sat up in my hammock to smoke. We'd just have to treat the canoe as gently as possible, that was all. As for meeting death on this trip, well, that had always been a possibility. One old man in Egypt had regarded it as much more than a possibility for me, and still I had come to Brazil. We might perish from the most trivial accident, from a moment of carelessness or from a stroke of bad luck. It would be a pathetic and rather pointless fate; but these had always been the odds for expeditionaries in the past, and are the essence of adventure. We had not been just quixotically romantic in neglecting the modern developments and security of a radio and back-up for emergencies. We could not afford them.

I lay back in the hammock, but still couldn't sleep. As I listened to the jungle noises my imagination began to play tricks. A strong wind was jostling the tree canopy, although no breeze touched us down below, and I seemed to hear the singing of a massed choir away in the distance. At other times I heard a radio playing, a police siren and racing tyres squealing. Were the Caipora and Mapinguary bogeymen out there too? The Caipora is a conservationist: a small, boy-like figure with his feet turned backwards. His friends are the animals of the rainforest that he protects and heals when they are wounded. Any human hunter who kills wildlife too frequently or who leaves wounded animals to suffer incurs the Caipora's wrath: they'll become lost and die.

Unfortunately not all hunters in Amazonia respect the Caipora. Many fear him a lot less than the Mapinguary. This is not your gentle, caring protector of animals. The Mapinguary just likes biting a hole in the top of your head and sucking your brains out. Instead of having his feet turned backwards, he has no feet at all on his hairy, ape-like body. He has one eye in the middle of his forehead, and his scream is so loud that it can knock you over at close range. He is especially active on Sundays.

I've met quite a few homesteaders in Amazonia who believe in these two characters. I suppose there might be some Yeti-like figures in that huge area. Certainly I have heard some distant roars and screams that might have been the Mapinguary on the prowl for my brains. And what about those eerie moments when the jungle goes deathly quiet, and those background chirpings, warblings, croakings, rustlings and whoopings cease? They are usually so omnipresent that the sudden silence is alarming. You can imagine all these little birds and beasties pricking up their ears to some sound you can't hear. Could it be the bogeyman?

'Nonsense,' you mutter, but the little hairs on the back of your neck are not convinced.

I got up and stuck the coffee pot on the embers of the fire. It probably was not even midnight yet, so there were five more hours to dawn. The frogs croaked repetitively and in the distance I heard the rasping grunt of a hunting jaguar, but as I sipped my coffee I became aware of a breathy whistling that I had never heard before. Immediately I thought it must be Indians, which seemed to be confirmed when from the other bank I heard an answering whistle. Nearer and nearer the sounds came, and although I tried to reassure myself that no Indian would attack in pitch darkness (in the westerns it's always at dawn, isn't it?), I began to get frightened. Soon I could hear actual footsteps approaching, and a stealthy swishing in the undergrowth.

There then came a colossal fart from a few metres away, followed by the rumble of dung hitting the deck. Only one Amazon creature produces that amount of wind and excrement: our old friend the tapir, and my galloping heartbeat eased as I remembered being told how they whistle to each other. I relaxed and listened, amused by their seeming inability to get together. This one walked through our camp whistling forlornly, and was answered from the other only 100 metres away on the other bank. Yet I knew they were rather intellectually challenged animals and their attempt at a rendezvous seemed doomed to failure. The situation became pitiful as they both crossed the river, whistling all the time, but ended up again on opposite banks. Poor lonesome tapirs. When I last heard them they were still calling plaintively to each other, further apart than ever.

I returned to my hammock, but was still awake when the howler monkeys started their chorus just before dawn. Weighing up to 15 kilos and standing a metre tall, they are the largest of the South American monkeys (although the gangly spider monkeys look bigger). Their chorus is an extraordinary sound – especially when heard close to. Audible for 4 or 5 kilometres, it sounds like a roaring wind when the monkeys are distant, but from nearby you can hear far more subtleties. The male starts the proceedings by gradually cranking himself into action. He utters long, rasping, vibrating exhalations, followed by almost equally powerful inhalations. After ten or so of these he attains a crescendo that becomes a sustained roar. When this falters slightly, presumably as he is drawing breath, you become aware of a falsetto trilling in the chorus. This must be the females. The chorus ends after three or four minutes with a last few coughs from the male. Peter and I found their almost nightly performances both wonderful and comforting. Many travellers disagree. 'It touched some secret chord of long lost fear, when speech was yet unformed. While it lasted, the sense of peace which had been inspired by the calmness and silence of the jungle gave place to a hidden portent of evil,' wrote C W Beebe dramatically. Mind you, if you did not know it was monkeys making that racket, then you would be alarmed.

We set off pretty late the next morning. I felt drowsy, and we spent some time improving the strutting of the canoe. However, we made reasonable progress, managing to squeeze under or round more trees than usual, and during the morning we only unloaded the canoe eight times and portaged twice. Easy stuff. After lunch I heard the alarm call of curassow and clambered up the bank. Sure enough, there were four of them and they flapped up into the low branches as I approached. I fired and one toppled dead to the ground. The others seemed unaware of what was going on, so I reloaded and bagged another. By now it wasn't just a case of relieving the boredom of our diet. Our stocks of food were so low that we couldn't afford to let slip any opportunity to live off the land. Tired of bloodshed though we were, we couldn't stop now.

You might imagine that after three or four months of celibacy our thoughts would be repeatedly turning to women and sexual activity. Not at all. We lusted and craved for only one pleasure: food. Our conversation and yearnings were wholly concentrated on the titillation of taste buds and orgies of gluttony. We lingered and slobbered in masochistic detail over the great feasts of the past and those we planned for the future. This had been a feature of every jungle trip I had done in the past. On the Teles Pires, Andrea had taken me each night on a gourmet tour of Italy's provinces, discussing intimately the regional dishes and the wines, and telling me how they are prepared. 'You take the oil, onions and garlic, and fry them gently ('sssssssssst' he'd hiss softly) until golden brown…,' and I would listen, drooling as I spooned down my boiled white rice.

That afternoon we glanced up and saw a large, hazy outline towering over 300 metres above us. For a while we were not sure if it was cloud or mountain, but since it didn't move, it had to be a mountain. After seeing nothing higher than a few little hills for so long this mountain mass seemed pretty awesome and we realized with excitement that it was part of the Massif de Mitaraca. Our portage! There are two major peaks in this massif – Paloulouniméenepeu (try saying that after a drink or two), 707 metres, and another of 690 metres. We would be portaging over the lesser Mapaoni-Epoyane (300 m) and Temomairen (453 m), which still gave us more than 100 metres of climbing, but might even seem easy after the last couple of weeks. Imagine being on dry land and damp only from sweat. Elated at being so near our goal, we camped early and gorged ourselves on curassow. They have a lot of meat on them and roasted in the oven with stuffing, spices, and regular basting I'm sure they would be absolutely delicious. Boiled too quickly in river water they emerge tough and tasteless, but we did not care. We ate half a bird each with a good helping of rice. Next morning we had fried rice with curassow pieces, and still had plenty left over for lunch and supper. The Mapaoni had become a tiresome little creek, but it was bountiful.

We were expecting to find one last tributary coming in from the left. According to our map the trail over the mountains started 4 kilometres up that. The trail might have become overgrown by now, but we thought there could be some sign of its old starting point, like abandoned tin cans, bits of plastic or a collapsed shelter perhaps. By lunchtime, after a morning of unloading and carrying, the river veered west, which would mean (if we had identified our position on the map correctly) that our tributary was further ahead than we thought. A little later we saw another place on the bank that seemed to have been cleared by man, and that encouraged us, because we needed Indians now. Our earlier fears of meeting them had been replaced by positive eagerness for contact. If there were no tribes on the upper Mapaoni using the trail regularly it would be completely overgrown, and Indians would be able to save us time by showing us the way. Also, we had a couple of heavy bags of junk (sorry, I mean presents) to hand over, which we were getting tired of humping around. To warn them of our approach, and to attract attention, we fired six shots into the air, and made camp cheerfully hoping that we would receive visitors.

We were in good spirits. The end seemed to be in sight – well, far from the end, but at least the end of the second stage. Now everything depended on the trail. Did it exist? The idea of the Surinamese and Brazilian governments deciding to connect two rivers in this remote region seemed unlikely, yet the boatman said it had been done when the frontier was surveyed and demarcated. More likely the Indian tribes of the region had found a route to cross the watershed and reach another river system so they could visit or raid other tribes and extend their hunting grounds. After all, they were here long before the white man came and drew his boundaries. As for our initial fears that we would stumble on garrisons of crack troops resisting the Cuban-inspired invasion of Brazil from Surinam – well, that seemed laughable. Perhaps we might meet a few soldiers on the Surinamese side because access to the border was a little easier over there, but it wasn't an idea we could take seriously.

In this mood we set off enthusiastically the next morning, but after a couple of kilometres our hopes were dashed. There was a tributary entering from the right, which according to our map should not have been there at all. It was also much too large to ignore. This was the sort of development we had feared. It made us doubt our position and shook our faith in the map. Once a map has proved unreliable, you never trust it again.

This was not the sort of terrain over which to drag a canoe if you were not dead sure you were going the right way, so we tied it up and set off on foot up the larger of the two streams. (Force of habit that – to tie up the canoe. But just how far could it drift away?) We covered over 4 kilometres wading the shallows, swimming across the deep pools and sometimes walking through the jungle, all the time checking likely places for some sign of the trail. Once we thought we had found it because on high ground near some rocks we discovered an old saucepan. Completely rusted through, it had obviously lain there for many years, but it was the sort of rubbish we expected to come across. We climbed up the hill behind, looking desperately for any further signs, but had to give up when the compass told us we were heading south rather than north. Bitterly disappointed, we carried on upstream, the only consolation being that someone had been up here before. Half a kilometre further on, the river again divided in two, making our confusion complete. We had three maps and none of them coincided with what we were finding. We had expected the 1:250,000 scale one to be more help, but it too was letting us down.

We returned to the canoe and made camp. It had been a tough and miserable day, only marginally improved by Peter shooting a curassow so we could have a meat supper. While we ate we decided to push on up the way we had walked that day and take whichever fork of the river looked to have the most water, as long as it went approximately north. After all, if the trail did not exist we would have to cut a new one, so the further we travelled in the right direction the better. Still, it was worrying that no big peaks were visible. If we were only a few kilometres from the planned portage point shouldn't we be seeing high ground by now? To the northwest there should have been a peak rising 300 metres above us, like the one we had seen three days before. It should be only 10 kilometres away at the most, and clearly visible over the tall forest. Yet through the breaks in the cloud we saw only flat scenery in that direction.

The following morning we took the canoe with us and camped a little way along the right-hand fork that we had discovered the day before. With each subdivision the river became still smaller and shallower. There were a few deep pools, but in many places there was not enough water to float in. The obstructions remained as numerous as ever, and that day we were treated to a new and particularly unpleasant experience. As Peter was slashing through a tangle of vegetation, I saw a large dark mass, which I'd assumed to be a bird's nest, suddenly separate and drift outwards in a cloud.

'Look out, Pete!' I yelled, but he had already heard the buzzing and seen the size of the insects heading his way. He began to run like hell for the deeper water, but was a bit too slow. Just before I dived under the surface he let out a scream and clutched his head. We stayed in the water for over five minutes, only popping our heads up briefly for air. The hornets continued to fly about agitatedly, and they were massive and terrifying. Peter told me later that sting had been far more painful than that of the scorpion a few weeks before.

'Ten of those stings, man, and you'd be dead,' he said with conviction, fingering the swelling on his head. 'Shit, that hurts!'

The hornets had now formed a new swarm, and I had to volunteer to go and retrieve Peter's machete from where he had dropped it. I crept towards my quarry, eyeing that seething mass and debating whether we could do without the machete after all. The hornets were still angry and unsettled, and many cruised around looking for trouble. With their legs trailing below them, they reminded me of Harrier jump jets and I crawled through the shallows keeping as submerged as possible. I grabbed the machete almost directly below the swarm and retreated with considerable relief.

At this juncture we decided we'd better portage the canoe through the jungle rather than risk any more stings, and that turned into a bit of an epic. Hauling the canoe up a steep bank, finding a fallen tree in the jungle that necessitated a lengthy detour, struggling through creepers that hooked up on our loads and pulled us back meant that the little detour took us more than two hours. To get our revenge on the hornets that had caused us all this trouble we foolishly decided that they needed to be punished.

Sneaking up to within 5 metres of the swarm, we fired the shotgun at it, then turned and sprinted for our lives. But in our haste we collided with each other and fell in a heap in the shallows as the first of the hornets reached us. One landed on my arm. I remember seeing it alight a split second before I submerged, and washed it off just in time. The water was only 50 centimetres deep, and we crawled along the bottom, heading for a pool upstream. Lungs bursting we clawed our way over the shingle, concerned above all that our bare arses should not stick above the surface. We reached deeper water and surfaced at last. All clear. We looked at each other, gasping and pop-eyed from the fright, and burst out laughing. That would teach us to mess with hornets.

As we had come across two half-mouldy onions mislaid at the bottom of the food bag, we decided to treat ourselves to one of our dried dinners, and use the onions in style. The next dried dinner had in fact been earmarked for celebration when we found the trail, but we were in need of encouragement here and now. Tired though we were, we went to great lengths to prepare a memorable meal. We made a dough from flour and rolled it out on a paddle blade using an empty bottle, then wrapped it round some fried rice with onion and garlic, and fried the patties until crisp before serving them with a curry sauce.

Next morning we began to haul the canoe up the tributary, but after battling with our worst kilometre to date we stopped to reconsider. This stream was surely impossible. It held almost no water, was more rocky than usual and there were fallen trees everywhere. We could not move more than 5 metres at a time without having to lift the canoe over an obstruction, usually after unloading all the gear. Our cheerfulness was wearing thin. You can keep in moderately good spirits for the first ten times you unload and load the canoe (four sacks, two backpacks, two bags, one large sack of bedding, one sack of cooking utensils and Peter's two smelly monkey skins that he was intending to cure, not to mention Mark's army jacket). You can force a smile for the first ten times you carry the canoe over obstructions and get stung again. You can manage to twitch the mouth corners when dragging smaller logs out of the way, or pulling 200 kilos of canoe and gear against the grip of sandy shallows. But, try as you may, no smiles can be mustered when you cut through 10 metres of tangled creepers and thorns that seem to leap back into place however frenziedly you slash at them. Try cutting a tunnel through a tangle like that and then meeting rocks and logs in the middle so that you have to unload all the stuff, haul the canoe over and reload while you're bent double and throttled by creepers. Ants drop all over you, sticks gouge those old, festering wounds and you collect a new crop of scrapes, bruises, bites, scratches and cuts. Just see if you smile.

Nothing was more guaranteed to produce flaring tempers than such tangles of vegetation. The person at the bow of the canoe had to do the cutting, while the other shoved the canoe up the tunnel behind. The bow was 6 metres away in front, so it was not easy to see how near it was to your companion floundering amid the vegetation. The danger was that you shoved enthusiastically and rammed him in the back or pushed him on to that column of ants he'd been trying so carefully to avoid.

'Wait! Wait! Wait, you stupid bastard!' came the muffled scream of rage. 'Pull it back, you've got my leg trapped. Ouch! Shit! Ouch! Why the fuck don't you wait? I've got enough trouble in here without you pushing me on to these thorns!'

We decided to leave the canoe once more and reconnoitre on foot. We walked about 5 kilometres, I suppose, and managed to establish nothing definite, apart from the fact that getting a canoe any further up there would be sheer torture. There were sections difficult enough for us to walk through unladen. I thought we would be lucky to advance a kilometre a day in those conditions. Fortunately, anyway, the stream seemed to be bearing mainly east, and that seemed to indicate it was the wrong tributary. Hunger forced us to return to camp, but we decided to have a better look at the terrain next day. We set off at dawn armed with a plastic bag of rice cakes and the shotgun. We walked all day, explored every likely place for a trail, checked the compass frequently and climbed any hillsides to gain a better view. No luck. Not a sign of major mountains either to the northeast or to anywhere else. What was certain was that the stream carried on running east, which ruled it out. Thank God. It was a bitch of a stream. We turned back for camp.

Peter's malaria returned that evening and he had a night of shakes and vomiting. What a wonderful holiday we were having! Who the hell wants to stay in some beachside hotel with a temperate, dry heat, a game of tennis before a breakfast of orange juice, crunchy croissants and coffee with creamy milk? What pleasure could be found in a morning of beach, reading and swimming, followed by a light salad and siesta in an air-conditioned bedroom? Then more beach, a shower and an evening of good food, wine, dancing and moonlight strolls? How boring. How mundane. How fantastic.

As I sat staring into the embers of the fire, smoking and reflecting on life and leisure, I heard a jet pass overhead. At one stage of the trip, near the mouth of the Cuc, we must have been on the main Rio-Miami-New York route, because we would hear three or four jets a day (without actually seeing them). Now it was over six weeks since we'd heard one, and perhaps this was Air France's flight Manaus-Cayenne-Paris. My flight home. It was a Thursday, about 7 p.m., and I could imagine the passengers up there nursing their pre-dinner drinks, served by pretty attendants, with a film showing later. God, how I wished I could be with them and on my way home. I wanted to see my family and friends, sample some home comforts, eat varied food and get some intellectual stimulation.

I sighed, prodded the fire with a stick and thought of Raymond Maufrais who had disappeared not so very far from here in 1951. I had come across his journal, *Journey without Return*, in a second-hand bookshop years before, and found it a very moving story. When he was seventeen, Maufrais had been awarded the Croix de Guerre for his bravery with the Resistance in World War II, and he later became a parachutist in Indo-China. Then he embarked on a career as a journalist and joined an expedition to the Mato Grosso in 1946. In 1950, at the age of twenty-four, he set off on an ambitious expedition through the jungles of French Guiana to attempt a lone crossing of the Tumucumaque hills. An Indian found his diary, rifle, camera and other possessions on the banks of the Tamouri river in early 1951, but Raymond Maufrais was never seen again.

His father published the unedited diary to raise money for his own attempts to find his son, who he was convinced was still alive. This humble workman-turned-explorer undertook several expeditions of his own in the search, and became the first westerner to cross the Tumucumaque from French Guiana to Brazil, travelling with Indian guides.

To impartial readers of the diary, it seems that his son must have perished. By the end Maufrais was suffering from dysentery and starvation, and decided to swim the 75 kilometres downstream to the nearest village.

> I feel it's going to be an amazing experience. This, after all, is the real primitive life that I love. A civilized man turned into an amphibian on a river in Guiana with nothing to rely on but his skill, his strength, his willpower, with no firearm, half-naked, no roof to return to… it's fascinating.

These lines are rich in morale-boosting bluster and courage. They come on the last pages of the journal that recount his sufferings over six months. Reading the account, you cannot help but feel that he was ill-equipped and his plan too ambitious. People advised him to head straight for the Tumucumaque via the Oyapok or the Litani (the river Peter and I were planning to cross to), rather than taking the difficult, exhausting route that he chose. He was plagued by lack of funds and forced into delays that made him miss much of the dry season. He could not afford a light canoe which would have saved him so much hard work, and right at the start he had to sell several items of useful equipment.

More important, he planned a trip across the jungle mostly on foot, and that is far harder than any journey by river. There are limits to the supplies you can comfortably carry on your back; Maufrais was soon wholly dependent on living off the land and found the jungle an erratic provider, over-generous one day, miserly the next.

> In the forest, providence is my maitre d'hotel... You can walk for hours and days together, exploring every inch of the forest without finding a thing, and then when you pause for breath at the foot of a big tree you see a hocco [curassow], a tortoise or a partridge.

He journeyed up the Maroni river from the coast, then up the Ouaqui in the company of the bush negroes of the interior. He was then on his own, and crossed from the Ouaqui to the Tamouri rivers by land. His only companion a little terrier called Bobby.

The intense solitude of the forest quickly began to affect his spirits, and he poured out his homesickness, fears and uncertainties in the diary. Perhaps if he had survived he might have edited out these passages before publication and concentrated more on the moments of cheerfulness and confidence. If so, we would have lost a moving and unique account.

> I hunted once again – drew blank. Yet I want to live, I want to be strong. I want to come through all this. I want to eat. I want to see my parents again and make them rich and happy. I have such great stores of love for them; it doesn't matter if we're rich or poor, so long as we're together. Oh, God, let me live. Suffer me to return to France!

His search for food became more and more desperate, and it took up all his time. He ate snails, tortoises, palm hearts and grubs, but on many days he found nothing, or not nearly enough to prevent his physical decline. On 3 January 1951 he killed his dog.

> I killed Bobby this evening. I was just strong enough to cut him up in front of the fire. I ate him. I was ill afterwards; my constricted stomach caused me agonies of indigestion. I suddenly felt so alone that I realized what I had just done and began to cry. I was angry and disgusted with myself.

Two days later he wrote:

> I thought of Bobby and realized how necessary to me was his silent
> companionship. There's nobody in camp now to welcome me in the
> evening. No more barking, no more eager licking. Poor Bobby!

Poor Raymond. The borderline between recklessness and audacity is a narrow
one, and the determining factor is success or failure. If he had succeeded he
would have been considered extraordinary, brave and daring. But he failed,
and it is easy to be unkind and unsympathetic to failure. 'That unhappy,
deluded young Frenchman, who in order apparently to prove to himself that
he was not a coward, persisted in adventuring on various expeditions, virtually
without equipment, into the most inaccessible South American jungles . .'
said one writer. Reckless he was, but he had courage, tenacity and the ability
to bounce back from the black moments.

He reached the banks of the Tamouri, but by then he was in severe
trouble. He camped there and began to build a raft, a task that took him a
couple of weeks, as he had to spend most of the day scavenging for food and
was often too weak to work afterwards. Most of what he ate aggravated his
dysentery or would not stay down. Even when he did finish the raft and set
off, he travelled only a kilometre before it was wrecked.

> I ought to have realized that a raft would never get far on such a creek.
> You need a light, narrow boat that can slip along anywhere.

He started work on a dug-out, but soon realized that it was beyond his
strength. He could not walk any further on land because his shoes had
disintegrated, one ankle was swollen and painful, and his backpack had fallen
to pieces. He decided to swim, leaving the gun and hammock behind.

> I can only count on providence to give me the chance of knifing a
> sleeping crocodile, or a serpent on its liana, or a ray in a shallow pool,

or a fish sleeping between two rocks. All these are entirely speculative of course. I promised to come back; and come back I will, God willing.

It was a desperate move, but his situation was equally so. Swimming or wading down a creek would be less arduous than walking through the jungle, or getting a canoe through, and he would cover more distance each day. However, the decision to leave his rifle was a bad mistake. Perhaps he should have made a small raft to carry the gun and pushed in front of him?

After the Indian discovered Maufrais' diary and belongings in February 1951, the Prefect of Guiana organized an expedition to look for him. In October it was found that he had reached a point 50 kilometres from his last camp, and had built a native shelter. This was only 22 kilometres from the nearest village, but he was never seen again.

It was a small consolation that he left the journal, and in his moments of loneliness and discomfort he wrote many touching entries:

> I'm rather ashamed of my weakness. I feel that I'm behaving like a washed-out, fretful creature. But I'm a man after all, and I've a loving heart inside me. I'm not like an animal that thinks only of getting something to eat in the fields. And I've nothing to love in this forest.

> There's always a struggle inside me between my continual need for affection and my love of solitude and adventure. I've nobody to stretch out a hand to me, nobody to smile and wave me on, and so I talk to myself and curse myself. I've got to get out of this apathy, this dreamland; I've got to break through. When I don't think, I'm happy; and I take delight in the way of life – free, pure and primitive – that we all long to experience, even if only for a while.

I sat by the fire trying to imagine what it would be like to be alone in that place. Days of struggle with no one to moan or joke to, and no one to share the work. A crushing solitude that would stifle the song on my lips, that would make the shadows menacing and the imagination lurid. Any accident would mean death, and the idea of Indians around would be much more disturbing for someone alone.

I did one short canoe journey in Amazonia by myself and I found it a very lonely experience. Yet the Rio Guaporé had a few houses, so I could spend some evenings in company. Up here it was different. You were beyond help, prey to any accident or illness. A tree might topple and crush your canoe (one of my recurring nightmares, that one), or you might fall on a knife, or cut an artery when the machete slipped in your wet palm. Admittedly the same mishaps could occur to a pair of you with equally disastrous results, but how comforting to have someone to share the worst – even to die with.

I looked over at poor Peter, who was retching over the side of his hammock. We were both exhausted, plagued by headaches and sickness, never-ending toil, painfully slow progress and now confusion as to exactly where we were. We had been on the river for fourteen weeks, and while we wanted to achieve our objective it seemed to be degenerating into a joyless endurance test. The fate of most expeditions, I suppose, as they go on for too long or too far.

12
Dilemmas

Peter had a bad night and in the morning did not feel up to doing another long reconnoitre, so I decided to explore the left-hand tributary by myself. I crammed some tobacco, cooked rice and cartridges in a plastic bag, strapped the compass on my wrist, picked up the shotgun and machete, and departed. This stream was substantially easier than the other one: deeper, with fewer fallen trees and no rapids. It also seemed to be heading in the right direction, northwest, so after about a kilometre I decided to cut through as many of the tangles as I could to save time later when we returned with the canoe. Indeed it was often the only way I could walk through.

After an hour I came to a bend with the deepest water we had seen for a long time. Holding the gun above my head I was swimming awkwardly across and got the fright of my life when what I had taken for a piece of driftwood suddenly thrashed the surface and duck-dived 2 metres away. A caiman. I kicked my way to shallow water, aware what a tempting target my waving legs must make, and pulled myself on to some rocks, heavy with relief. As I stood up, a squawking flock of large birds legged it into the jungle. I threw the gun to my shoulder and snapped off a blind shot as they began to get airborne. Miraculously I hit one. It was an attractive bird that I had not seen before – mainly black with a long elegant neck and head, pale blue legs and a half-dozen rainbow feathers on its breast. A common trumpeter, I learned later. There seemed no point in continuing with the shotgun, as we had our supper and it was heavy and awkward to keep dry, so I left it and the bird in the fork of a small tree and continued relatively unencumbered.

It occurred to me that I was running a grave risk of bumping into Indians while by myself that day. That first contact would be preferable if I were accompanied by Peter. I wished I had waited until the next day when he would have been feeling stronger, and I peered into the undergrowth apprehensively for the rest of the way. I walked for five or six hours and must have covered over 7 kilometres. The direction of the stream seemed right, but there was still the perplexing absence of mountains. They should have been towering overhead by now. I scanned the horizon but saw nothing larger than a few low hills.

At one point I was crawling under a tangle of creepers when a swarm of bees set upon me and stung me ten or fifteen times before I could scramble out. Cursing and smarting I edged back to see where the nest was. I soon spotted it hanging from the tangled vegetation and effectively blocking any attempt to pass. I was looking gloomily at the prospect when the little shits set on me again and gave me half a dozen new stings. I had to cut a lengthy detour through the jungle to get round and continue on my way. To my consternation the stream gradually narrowed down, getting more and more choked with vegetation, although it still had a few chest-deep sections. At about 3 p.m. I had to turn back to be sure of reaching camp before dark. Even so, I only just made it, arriving at dusk, weary, rubber-legged and carrying the bird for our supper.

When I retrieved the bird four hours previously I had found it aswarm with the little black bees that seem to be the first agents of decomposition in Amazonia. They soon find any fish or meat and collect in hordes. Fortunately they are stingless, because there must have been several hundred to shoo off the bird and they had already nibbled away quite a bit around the eyelids, anus and shotgun pellet wounds. Their honey must be delicious.

It made me ponder just how long one's own body would last on the jungle floor. A meal for the bees, wasps, maggots, ants, beetles, not to mention the carrion-eating rodents and birds. I would not be surprised if everything were devoured within two weeks: skeleton, the lot. Maybe even sooner. There were some mean, ugly little rodents around at night. We often heard them crunching up the discarded bones from our supper, and for small creatures their jaws must be disproportionately powerful. By shining the torch we obtained only a glimpse of glowing eyes and a small, furry outline. We had to wait until a visit to the zoo in Manaus before we saw them clearly. Now I am in general quite sentimental about animals. I find most of them attractive in some way or another. Not all are cuddly, but they usually have something appealing – a lustrous coat, an inquisitiveness, an alert intelligence. Well, these creatures were the exception. They were shifty-eyed, mangy-furred, bare-tailed, vermin-ridden and foul-smelling, with pointed snouts full of yellowed teeth. They were quarrelsome and aggressive to each other, and made the brown rat look sweet and cuddly in comparison.

Back at camp, I found Peter had recovered enough to move himself from his hammock to a stool by the fire. He slumped there looking ghastly. The malarial fevers of shakes and sweats are bad enough, but I think the immediate aftermath is the worst part of the whole cycle. Your temperature has returned to normal, but you feel an overwhelming weakness. Every joint and muscle aches and the hallucinations and delirium have left you with a sense of unreality and depression.

I prepared the bird, and Peter forced a bit down before he returned to his hammock. We decided that if he felt up to it the following day we would take the canoe up this second tributary. It seemed the best option, and at least it was heading in approximately the right direction. However, if we still hadn't seen any mountains within two or three days we would have to rethink and assume that somehow we had gone wrong.

Next morning after progressing only a couple of hundred metres we had holed the side of the canoe. We were pushing it through a narrow gap at the time, and Peter saw that it would not fit.

'Don't push any more, John. It will not go through here.'

I continued obstinately shoving. The alternative was a portage, and it was too early in the day.

'Stop pushing, for Christ's sake!' shouted Peter.

Too late. A sharp piece of wood pierced the thin plywood just above the waterline.

'There, see what you did!' said Peter angrily. 'That was bloody stupid.'

'Oh, shut up!' I was in no mood to take criticism. 'If we're talking about stupid mistakes what about you the other day chopping the canoe with your machete? That was a fucking smart move!'

The incident had happened while Peter was chopping at some vegetation and the canoe had drifted a little too close, so that his swinging machete cut a chunk out of the bow – but well above the water line. We had laughed at the time.

I notice that when under strain I get increasingly sensitive to criticism. The most extreme example occurred on the Teles Pires. We were paddling down a rapid, and I made a cock-up which caused us to crash into a rock. Andrea turned around in his seat at the bow.

'Come on, John, get it right!' he said angrily. 'We had plenty of time to avoid that one!'

'It's all right for you to sit there in the bow – you don't have to do any steering at all!' I snapped. 'In fact if you'd done a draw stroke you could have pulled us away from that rock.'

There was still a lot of rapid left and the canoe was picking up speed. 'If you think you can do better, come back here and try it.'

I stood up in the canoe and waved him to take my seat.

'For Christ's sake, John, this isn't the moment to change seats!' cried Andrea, as the first waves sent spray over his lap.

'No, come on. If you're so bloody clever, you come and try it, smart arse!'

'Not now, John. Steer the canoe or we'll turn over!'

I sat down reluctantly and picked up my paddle.

'After eight fucking weeks I make one little mistake and you start shouting at me. You're welcome to sit back here any time you like!'

'Okay, John, I'm sorry. I'm sorry. You're a marvellous steerer. I couldn't hope to match you. You're the tops. Now look out! That rock!'

It's sad to see yourself reacting so poorly in times of stress. Where were the noble spirit and the stoical, long-suffering good humour you always liked to think were just below the surface? These trips put me to the test, and I was found wanting. I wasn't a figure of heroic stature after all. It was a tough truth to swallow.

We covered about half the distance I had walked the day before. On one high section of bank we found a very rusty piece of metal. It crumbled in our hands, but we thought it had once been a kerosene can. There were no other signs of a camp or trail, but at least it meant that some other poor devils had been up here years before. Perhaps we were on the right tributary after all.

That night it rained very hard, which did little to lift our spirits. It hadn't rained seriously for so long that we had grown lazy about erecting the plastic awning. This time the rain came suddenly and torrentially, dowsing the fire before supper was cooked, soaking our hammocks and the clothes we slept in. We turned in hungry and cold, and the next morning we awoke to a disaster. The canoe was three-quarters full of water; in fact it would have sunk completely if the stream had been deep enough. The combination of the leaks and the rain water had weighed it down until that hole was below the water line, and then the canoe had rapidly filled.

All our gear was submerged or floating, and the food sacks had been under water for several hours. Even the triple-wrapping in plastic bags had not been enough to protect our stocks: the rice was swollen and damp, the spaghetti had congealed into solid lumps, and the beans were soaked. It did not matter about the salt and the sugar, they would not spoil, but we had to dry out the rest immediately, and that wouldn't be easy on an overcast day on the upper Mapaoni. We made a large fire and spread out all the rice and beans. The spaghetti had definitely had it. We ate it up over the next three days – boiling it for five minutes and then cutting it into thin strips which we fried until crisp. These were moderately palatable eaten with salt or sugar.

We reckoned we had food for only another two weeks, and it seemed likely that a lot of the rice and beans would spoil and be wasted. Game seemed quite plentiful and we felt we need not starve, despite the lesson of Raymond Maufrais, but we hoped to avoid a total dependence on living off the land.

It was the worry that we might be up the wrong creek that was beginning to undermine our resolve. If we could just find the trail, or discover where to cut a new one, we'd get stuck in and do it. This uncertainty was causing delay and virtually ensured that we would run out of both food and malaria pills. We decided to give it just four more days and if we had found nothing in that time we should consider returning back downstream. We pulled the canoe out of the water to start drying her off prior to some more repairs, and set off walking. We examined every possible place for signs of a trail. We climbed a large hill: excited by the glimpse to the north of a higher hill, we wondered if we could be standing on Mapaoni-Epoyane, and hoped the bigger one might be Temomairem. But there were no hills visible to the northeast, not even from 100 metres above the river and with a reasonably unobstructed view.

We had been wandering around up there, following a ridge and looking for a place to get a good view, and I had been taking only casual glances at the compass bearing. When the time came to return to the river the direction seemed totally wrong and to be heading right away from where we thought the river should be. How easy it is to get lost in the jungle – a moment's distraction or the pursuit of an animal, and you suddenly have no notion where camp lies. The compass is an absolutely essential guide, but at that moment it needed all our self-discipline to believe in it. Contrary to expectation, it did lead us safely back to the river and we were so relieved to get there that I totally forgot about that bees' nest: we were severely reprimanded.

On another trip I once spent a very uncomfortable and frightening night in the jungle after getting lost. I'd had the compass with me but had not bothered to check it. I felt confident that I knew my way back and I had not intended going far. It was a troop of howler monkeys that led me astray. In my attempt to photograph them I pursued them avidly as they swung through the treetops always tantalizingly too far away. I gave up as the sun was going down. It was time I headed back. I strolled confidently towards a section of sparser forest with more sky showing that I assumed was the riverbank, but instead I hit a huge area of swamp, something I had not seen on the way out and which was impassable. I felt the first stab of panic. The sun was on the horizon already and the light was fading. I hurried along the fringe of the swamp, tripping and stumbling, scrabbling at the vegetation. Then I headed off in a new direction. But by the time night fell I was hopelessly lost. It was a terrifying experience. I could have been 200 metres from camp, but it might as well have been 2 kilometres. I fired the rifle into the air to try to attract my companion, but the crack of the little .22 was absorbed by the jungle.

Fortunately, being a smoker, I had matches on me so was able to build a fire for comfort; but the mosquitoes ate me alive that night. By morning I had so many bites on my eyelids that they were closed to two little slits. During the night I had controlled my panic, and at dawn I headed north, marking my way as I went. After covering over 2 kilometres on that bearing and finding nothing familiar, I returned to the starting point and headed south for a similar distance. Again nothing. Back to the beginning and off east. To my joy that led me to the river. It's all so simple when you keep calm.

I staggered into camp expecting to find my companion pacing up and down in panic and concern, but he was fast asleep in his hammock.

'Hey,' I shouted, giving his cradle a rock. 'Sorry I'm back so late. One hell of a party. Went on all night!'

'I stayed up for three hours, calling and whistling and banging saucepans but when you didn't show up I thought, what's the point? And I went to bed.'

Peter and I walked for another two hours without finding anything conclusive, then returned to camp. We were absolutely wiped out, stumbling like zombies, and we had spells of dizziness when we had to sit down for a while. We were in need of a good long rest. A total sort of rest that we were unlikely to find in the jungle. We reached camp and flopped out in the hammocks for an hour or two, contemplating the effort of making a fire and cooking supper. We had no meat, so when we heard the commotion of a troop of monkeys (chattering, swishing of branches and the plop of discarded fruit), Peter grabbed the gun and set off in pursuit. After fifteen minutes I heard two shots and assumed he'd got one. A bit later he returned, but instead of a monkey he carried a dead fawn – a spotted, limp-eyed bambi. I looked at him in surprise, and with a smidgin of reproach. Until a month before he had not been willing to hunt at all, and here he was shooting a creature that would have made the hardest man's finger hesitate on the trigger.

'It was hard,' he admitted sheepishly. 'I saw it lying there in the little hiding place that the mother make. I stop there for five minutes or more, thinking shall I, or not?' He shrugged. 'Hunger won.'

It was such a pretty creature with its silky coat and soft eye; but at the same time the saliva was bursting out at the prospect of supper. Most of us have eaten lamb and veal from animals not much older than this, we thought, trying to justify the death to ourselves as we began skinning, and I've never eaten any meat more delicious. It was so tender that even the bones could be chewed up and eaten.

Because the canoe was not drying out with any speed we built a large fire next morning and propped the canoe up beside it. We then fibreglassed over the holes, and I fixed another keel. By the time we had finished it was too late to do another reconnoitre so we had a day off. Peter did some sketching and I started to re-read parts of *History of the World*, but I could not concentrate for long. My mind kept drifting off to thoughts of the world outside the jungle. We were becoming bush-crazy and the idea of life outside seemed more and more attractive. Entertainment, food and drink, social life, girls and a rest from all the repetitive toil. Sunshine was something we missed, too. We had been living in gloom for weeks, and our skins were pale and soggy.

I lay in the hammock thinking of food. Nothing very fancy (after all, you can't get anything much fancier than milk-fed venison, I suppose), just good solid fare: potatoes, either fried, sautéed, baked or mashed, bread, eggs, cheese, fruit juice, cakes, chocolate, a nice variety of puddings and some jam. Sweet things dominated our cravings. Normally I'm a savoury man myself, and rarely eat sweets and desserts, but now I was dreaming of crumbles, chocolate, cakes, apple pies and biscuits. We joked that if we were unexpectedly presented with the choice of a night in the best restaurant in Manaus or a night with the most beautiful girl in Manaus the restaurant would win. No contest. Things were that bad.

I have to admit that despite my general familiarity with the jungle, on a mental level I find it hard to shake off a nostalgia for the people and activities of home. The harder the going, the more escapist my thoughts. Conversely, when life at home is dull and routine, my thoughts find their way up Amazon creeks.

My yearnings right then were for domesticity. Having reached the age of thirty-three without accumulating more worldly goods than could be fitted into a small saloon car, on sleepless Amazon nights my thoughts were now dwelling upon how nice it would be to own more than one duvet cover; how my wardrobe really was scruffy and inadequate; and how I should invest in a clock radio and a machine to make me a cup of tea when I woke up.

Anyhow, next morning we had to get up without the aid of either, and before dawn, because we'd decided to push fast upstream on foot. To avoid returning to camp we took the minimum of gear with us for staying the night up there: our hammocks, two small plastic sheets, the coffee pot and an Amazon picnic of cooked monkey legs and rice. It all fitted into one backpack, and off we set. This was going to be the final push and exploration. If we found nothing that looked right by the end of it we would obviously have to conclude that we had gone wrong somewhere.

We donned our shorts just in case we bumped into somebody. Twice the previous day we had fired a volley of shots to try to attract the Indians we still hoped might be in the vicinity. We needed their help now, and did not want to offend their sensibilities by arriving naked. On the other hand the canvas uppers of our shoes were flapping and separated from the soles, we were grizzled and hairy in appearance, pale from lack of sunlight and sickness, gaunt of face and covered in a welter of scratches, scabs, infected cuts and pimples. We would certainly give anybody a nasty turn if we took him by surprise.

Our attempt to look decent did not last long. We had gone a couple of kilometres when I paused to rest on a log and smoke a cigarette, and Peter began to laugh. Looking down I joined in. My shorts had been damp for so long that they had rotted and split during my exertions of clambering over logs. The split completely exposed my genitals in a manner that looked far worse than if I'd just been naked.

By midday we had passed the spot we had reached on previous walks and were now on new ground. The river was becoming more and more choked with vegetation, and we needed to cut our way through. We found one very small tributary coming in from the left, but it seemed too small to be likely and anyway it would have been impossible to get the canoe up, so we ignored it. There was then a long marshy section where the course of the stream had almost disappeared among grass and reeds. We squelched along with the mud sucking and dragging at our tired legs.

It's strange, but I have never seen a leech in South America, and Martin and Tanis say the same. People associate them with rainforests and in Southeast Asia they are always present. A crossing of a marsh like that would have collected twenty or more. We should be thankful for small mercies.

By nightfall we had covered another 6 or 7 kilometres and still could not see any mountains, but we realized we must be near the source of the tributary. By now it was less than 2 metres across and shallow. We slung our hammocks and had our supper, discussing the situation and knowing that tomorrow would be make-or-break day. It rained for over an hour. There had been cloud around all day and for the last week we had heard thunderstorms rumbling in the distance. The rainy season was overdue, and seemed to be on its way at last.

We started at first light and moved as quickly as we could. There were a few small hills to the north, which we climbed to get a view from the top.

Nothing. On we went. There were a couple of cascades, but they were small affairs. The stream would be too shallow for most of the way to float the canoe. Still no hills. We walked until after midday, then stopped for some coffee and a gloomy discussion. We were a tired and dispirited pair. There seemed no point in continuing. It would take several hours to walk back to camp, and if no hills were visible from where we were, it was probable they were not up this tributary at all. Where had we gone wrong? We must have taken the wrong fork somewhere. But where? This one seemed to flow in the right direction, and we had followed our route approximately on our maps. When making the tracing of Elcio's 1:250,000 scale map, had we missed copying a crucial fork at the headwaters, or was that map no more accurate than the others?

It would make no sense to start cutting a trail before finding the hill and being reassured we were in the right place. We could, I suppose, have wandered off towards the north on foot to try to find the streams on the other side of the divide. But that would take a week at least, the cutting of a trail a fortnight and the carrying of the gear another week. If we were on the wrong tributary it might be a 30-kilometre portage instead of 15. Even if we crossed to the Litani, it was sure to be as difficult as the upper Mapaoni had been, and we would certainly not arrive at Maripasoula, the first town on the French Guianan side, for at least two months.

We barely had enough quinine and chloroquine for controlling one more malaria attack each and we would be guaranteed more than one in those two months. We would be totally out of food in less than a fortnight. Did we wish to prove that we were more proficient in hunting than Raymond Maufrais had been? The jungle was an erratic provider. While we saw a lot of game when we were not particularly needing it for survival, no doubt it would immediately become scarce the moment we finished our last rice. The combination of weeks of very hard physical effort, sickness and shortage of food would put us into that fatal survival trap that had killed Maufrais.

Using all our dwindling reserves of strength to hunt, and rarely killing enough to replace the energy expended in the effort, we would soon be reduced to a standstill. Our growing weakness would make a portage of the canoe impossible, the malaria would rapidly debilitate us further and the time spent just searching for food would leave no time for anything else. We would find ourselves camped for weeks in one place, unable to push on, or even to retreat, each day growing weaker.

The continuous toil of the past few weeks had already weakened our resolve. If we'd been sure enough of our position I am certain we would have cut the trail and completed our mission, yet all the uncertainty and fatigue had toppled the magic of crossing the Tumucumaque hills. What had seemed a noble objective at home, as I pondered the map on a winter's evening, now seemed daft. Mark had been right, I thought, as I looked at the jungle around me. So what? What for? The work involved in cutting a trail over the hilly jungle was enormous. Carrying a 40-kilo canoe and all our equipment for 15 kilometres was sheer folly. If we had been fresher it would have seemed different, but we had been on the river too long already. Too much strength, enthusiasm and motivation had been eroded by exhaustion and ill health. We wanted to get out. We were disappointed, and felt we had failed, but above all we wanted out.

We stumbled back to camp, only just making it before dark, and had a gloomy supper.

'If this was a big expedition,' Peter sighed wistfully, 'we'd radio for a helicopter to find the correct small river from on high and tell us where we've gone wrong.'

'The pilot could drop us some malaria pills, some beers and food, and then go away,' I added. 'Hell, I don't want to turn back now. We're only 10 kilometres or less from the border with French Guiana, 250 kilometres from Maripasoula. It seems silly to give up after so long.'

Peter had calculated we'd been on the river for precisely 100 days and had paddled over 650 kilometres against the current. That seemed an awfully long time and distance only to end up thwarted and disappointed.

'The problem is we don't know where we've gone wrong,' said Peter. 'We can walk up every little river, and two more weeks would pass. I hate the idea of giving in, the same as you, but we know we'll have big trouble if we continue for two more months.'

He was sitting naked on the stool by the fire, preparing some coffee. He'd lost most of his tan, and his skin had taken on an unhealthy yellow hue. The geologists had commented on that a month before, and said it was probable due to his liver being full of malaria parasites. Might he have hepatitis too? He was also having a lot of trouble from heart palpitations. He was always conscious of a fast and erratic heartbeat and complained of breathlessness. I'd become aware of this a few nights previously when, with our hammocks almost touching, I'd been listening to his breathing. It was noisy and fast, as if he had a fever. I asked him if he felt sick, and he replied, a bit surprised, that he felt okay. When I mentioned his breathing, he replied that he was having a spot of trouble with palpitations, but no worse than usual.

There was also one suspicion that I had not voiced yet. Among the cuts, scratches and sores on his forearms I had noticed two little ulcers with raised edges that looked alarmingly like leishmaniasis to me. This is a horrible disease, spread by the sand fly, that starts off with skin ulceration and then spreads to attack the mucous membranes. The palate, nasal and throat cavities become obstructed and are eventually destroyed; and death from secondary infection may occur after years of suffering. It is difficult to cure. I felt a certain responsibility for Peter's wellbeing. After all, it was my crazy schemes which had lured him away from his original intention of hitchhiking through South America. I knew that he had valued the experience, but he seemed to be in danger of permanently ruining his health. The crossing of the Tumucumaque certainly was not worth such a price.

Disappointment was therefore mixed with relief when we agreed to return to the geologists' camp at Molocopote and beg a flight out. The trip had not been a total failure. We had kept going over some pretty tough weeks. We had travelled two of the most beautiful rivers in the world, and seen most of the wildlife of the region. There was plenty to be grateful for, and not a little to feel proud of. The prospect of retracing our steps to Molocopote, through all those tangles of vegetation and fallen trees yet again, was not much fun. However, it had been sheer chance we had met the geologists there at all, and of course without their existence we would have been forced to continue, or to return all the way to Carecaru, six weeks downstream.

We stayed put the next day sorting out our gear and chucking out the presents for Indians that we had carried so unnecessarily for so long. As the fire consumed the cheap combs, and we dug a hole and buried the mirrors, we were grateful that we had been spared the embarrassment of handing over such gifts. We also dug the second shotgun out of the pack, where it had been stored all the trip, and found it seriously rusted. As we were hoping to pay for our flight out of Molocopote with the guns, we scrubbed it with sand and coated it with cooking oil, which made little difference to its appearance. We hoped the geologists would have some emery paper and gun oil.

There were a couple of heavy showers that day, and in the evening we had our first serious rain of the trip. The clouds boiled up all afternoon, advancing, retreating and encircling, and by nightfall the distant thunder and lightning got us rushing our supper and hastily repacking the rice and beans we'd spread out in an attempt to get rid of the musty, mildewed smell. The wind increased and the jungle began to sway and groan. This is when you begin to inspect the trees around your camp for the ones that are tired of life and might feel like lying down on you. Twigs and small branches often did fall near our camps, but nothing larger, although many times we heard large trees coming down with a sustained smashing noise as they toppled several others on the way, or barrelled down a hillside cutting a swathe of destruction. A couple of weeks earlier I had gone for a hunt and returned the same way to find a large tree had fallen since I had first passed. We hoped the storm would not blow a lot of new trees across the river to add to the enjoyment of our return trip.

We could hear the rain coming – the roar of millions of drops hitting leaves, advancing steadily towards us, louder and louder. Peter and I shouted our last messages and snuggled into our hammocks, pulling the blankets up to our chins. The tarpaulin lifted and strained in the gusts of wind and the rain came, drumming and deafening. In a lot of books about rainforest ecology, I have read that the jungle canopy is all-important in protecting the thin soil from erosion. The rain merely hits the forest floor in the form of a fine spray, say some scientists who have obviously never sat out a storm in the jungle.

The noise of the rain makes conversation impossible. You retreat into a world of your own, and it's quite pleasant for as long as the hammock remains dry and snug. But there seems to be a limit of about an hour on the tarpaulin's impermeability, and then the water starts to creep up the ropes and gradually to soak the hammock, making it cold, clammy and uncomfortable. That night it rained for over seven hours without a pause.

13

The Retreat

I awoke shell-shocked from the roar and din of the storm, feeling depressed by our decision of the previous day. The jungle dripped but the sky had cleared. I strolled sleepily to the river to collect water and let out a cry of surprise.

'Hey, Peter! Get out of your Swiss roll and have a look!'

'What?' he grunted, swinging his feet to the ground.

'Look at the river. The majestic Mapaoni!'

The river had risen at least 20 centimetres overnight, and was lapping around the items we had left on the sandbank. It had always seemed to me that after months of dry season when the jungle is tinder dry it would take several weeks of rain before the river level rose. I had been wrong.

'We'll go now easier downstream,' smiled Peter. 'We'll float over many logs.'

'Yeah, but there may be others we won't get under any more,' I countered negatively. We loaded the canoe and turned her round. No traveller likes to retrace old paths, especially with the taste of defeat rank in the mouth, and we hesitated for a few minutes.

'Shit, this is a very bad day,' said Peter, and we both had tears in our eyes. 'I think our journey deserves a better ending than this.'

'It sure does. One hundred and twenty kilometres back to Molocopote, over those same logs, through those same tangles. At least we had the excitement of entering the unknown on the way up.'

We sighed and began the gloomy wade southwards. We soon realized that those extra centimetres of water would make an enormous difference to our progress. Of course one or two logs we had squeezed under before were now impossible, but generally on the way up we had gone over far more logs than we had gone under. Also there were now no shallow areas where the canoe couldn't float. We still couldn't paddle – we walked all day – but we covered over 7 kilometres, three times the speed of our progress upstream.

In the afternoon I shot a monkey that fell mortally wounded but refused to die. I tried to insert a new cartridge to shoot it again, but the cardboard was damp and swollen and the spent cartridge would not eject. (This invariably happens when you need a quick second shot.) I tried to pick the monkey up by the tail to swing and brain it against a tree, but nearly got bitten. I searched around for a stick, but all the wood seemed rotten, so I used the gun butt on its head. Even that did not seem to work. It was a horrible experience with the monkey trying to drag itself away, emitting heart-rending little cries, with me in pursuit clubbing it with the gun butt. In the end I could take no more. I lifted the gun up by the barrel and brought the stock crashing down on its skull. The skull fractured and so did the stock. I sat down and leant against a tree to roll a cigarette with shaking hands, tears running down my cheeks. I had dealt with a Rasputin capuchin, participated in a murder where the victim keeps getting up. I had also ruined one of the guns. But at least the monkey had stopped making those cries. I was looking forward to leaving the jungle and being able to buy my meat dead, cleaned and cellophane-wrapped.

It rained again most of the next night and the river kept rising. The Mapaoni was transformed: we had to carry the canoe only twice the next day, and once again covered more than 6 kilometres. If only we'd had this easier going during the previous two weeks. It's difficult to choose the optimum period for ascending an Amazonian river by canoe. Go too soon after the rains and the river is still too full and the rapids too dangerous. Go too late and it becomes too rocky and shallow. Only the months of August and September seem to be perfect.

We hoped to reach Molocopote on the evening of 14 December, allowing us nine more days to get there. We knew that all the geologists' team were leaving for Belém and Santarém before Christmas, and the 15th had stuck in our minds as the date the plane would come. We did not fancy having to wait there until they returned in January. Also, there was the risk that they might decide to leave for the duration of the rainy season, which would leave us over 500 kilometres of paddling back to Carecaru. This was a life-threatening prospect with our shortage of food and malaria drugs.

The next morning lingers in my memory as one of the worst of the entire trip. The creek had deepened enough for us to have our first spells of paddling for over two weeks, but it also meant we had to leap out frequently into deep water. It was a cloudy, drizzly day, and we were soon blue and shivering with cold. Our spirits reached a new low. We made a fire at lunchtime to get warm and stood around it like workmen round a brazier on an English winter's day. It seemed a waste to spray piping hot urine into the bushes. Better to let it dribble in lovely warm streams down the thighs.

That evening we reached the place where we'd carried the canoe through the jungle to avoid the tangles, repeated the portage in reverse and camped. My temperature had risen to 102 degrees, so I swallowed some Fansidar and sat wearily by the fire, reasonably warm at last. We had no meat to cheer us up at the end of an awful day, only a bowl of boiled rice. Boy, had we eaten a lot of rice. Peter and I had worked our way through more than 35 kilos of the stuff over those weeks, and surprisingly we still liked it. However, our remaining 5 kilos had got damp and tasted sour and nauseating, and we spooned it unenthusiastically into our mouths.

'How long do you reckon that portage was we did this evening?' I asked Peter.

'Oh, three hundred metres I think,' he replied, laying down his plate.

'Can you imagine carrying the canoe for fifteen bloody kilometres! What a crazy scheme that was!'

'We are too tired and old for those games. I'm just waiting to get to Belém and go into a supermarket and push a cart down those shelves full of beautiful things. I'll take some bread, cheese, tomatoes, mayonnaise, chocolate, biscuits, cake, orange juice, jam... shit, I will take everything!'

'Imagine sitting in a restaurant, dressed in clean clothes, sitting on a real chair with a back to lean against, and have someone cook a meal for us!' I dreamed aloud. 'Look at those two girls there with us, sweet-smelling, soft skin, velvety as peaches, laughing eyes, our knees touching under the table...'

'Yeah, okay, very nice,' interrupted Peter laughing. 'But what food do we order?'

'The big city,' I mused, drawing deep on my rank cigarette. 'Supermarkets, shops, restaurants, cinemas, bars, clubs, museums, beers, real cigarettes, noise, bustle, pollution, litter, squalor, degradation, filth, human misery and suffering. Mix it all together and you've got paradise. You've got Belém!'

That night it rained again, which gave us moderate pleasure because we needed the river to stay high for a while longer, but we were sick of the gloomy dripping jungle. We wanted unlimited horizons of fields and moorland. Once we joined with the Caripi the river widened out and the sun could reach us at last. I had to start from scratch with protective cream, because all vestiges of my tan had vanished over the past weeks. We had the rapids to negotiate again, and they'd got much bigger and more menacing since the rains. But they did not delay us for long: we walked the canoe down some, lowered it empty on the rope down others, and the portages, if any, were brief. The extra water made the river unrecognizable. On the way up it had flowed round numerous sandbanks. Now it must have been 70 centimetres higher and they had vanished. The water reached right up to the banks, and the Mapaoni looked a substantial river. It was still pretty, but it had been much prettier before. Or maybe we now looked at it with jaded eyes?

The beginning of the rains brings high mortality. Many of the sandbanks are riddled with wasps' nests in the dry weather, all of which are flooded out by the swollen waters. Millions of ants, termites and other insects must be swept away and eaten by fish, but we weren't going to cry for them. Plants that have misguidedly taken root on the sandbanks now stand forlornly doomed in swirling water. Though it is a bonanza time for fish, most animals must dislike the rains as much as we do.

In one pool we disturbed two adult giant otters with their two youngsters. We did not pause to watch these lovely creatures. We barely broke the rhythm of our paddling as we passed by. We had seen it all before, and nothing about Amazonia could give us much pleasure or excitement right now. Our indifference must have offended the adult otters, because they surfaced near the canoe, chattering and hissing. I had heard that they can be very dangerous when they have young, and certainly they are big and powerful enough to inflict serious injury. We kept on paddling, pulling a bit harder now while they swam around us, diving under the canoe and popping their heads up to hiss some more. They were getting uncomfortably close. We yelled at them, waved the paddles in their faces, and looked with alarm at those large, yellowed teeth. The otters would have been quite agile enough to climb into the canoe, and the idea of 2 metres of muscle hopping onto my lap made me stop to pull the shotgun within reach.

We had left the pool by now, but still they followed, and we were paddling at full speed. Gradually they dropped back and we could begin to relax. Or so we thought. We leant on our paddles for a breather and to look behind us at where we had last seen the otters, but they had disappeared.

'They've gone,' said Peter.

The words were no sooner out of his mouth than two snarling heads appeared out of the water a metre away and gave us a hell of a shock.

We paddled on. We were in mosquito country again, and had to put the nets back on the hammocks, making them stink of mildew, dirt and urine, and seem airless and suffocating. All our clothes were also in a filthy state and we'd got very lazy about washing them over the past few weeks. We wore clothes only in the evenings and at night, but they were covered in soot from the open fires, and of course we wiped our greasy fingers on our trousers. We'd also spent many hot, sweaty, malarial nights in them. In short, they stank – but there seemed no point, or we had no time, to wash them now.

We started to shoot a lot of the rapids, to save time, and through laziness, and for the excitement too. If they were short rapids we did not bother stopping the canoe to check them out, just stood up in the boat, made a snappy decision as to whether they were possible, and if so, which line we should take. Quite frequently the quick look had missed some surprises and we shipped a lot of water, but at least it gave us a little thrill. In between the rapids we had long spells when we had no interruptions to our paddling. How many times over the past weeks had we said, 'Oh, for just one day paddling in the sun!' Now we'd got it, we found it hard in a different way. Our paddling muscles had grown soft, and although we paddled along at a brisk pace we found it both boring and strenuous. It also gave me hours in which to contemplate Peter's efforts with a critical eye. One of the inevitable consequences of sitting in the stern of a canoe is that I develop an obsession with my companion's lack of effort. I've sat behind five men on different trips, and not one of them seemed to do his share of the work. Each dip of their paddle produced a whirl of water that passed me on my left: feeble little whirlpools that betrayed the desultory stroke that had propelled them that way. I pulled hard on my paddle, and compared the magnificent swirl of water with their puny creations. I would scowl at their backs, growing bitter and savage as the ferocious sun caused my head to hum and as the hours passed. On a bad day I could work myself up into quite a state.

We stopped on a rocky islet to prepare a batch of pancakes with the last of our flour. It was my turn to cook and of course everything went wrong. The islet was just too small and uneven. I needed space for the bowl of batter, for the fire, for me to sit, for the plate with the finished pancakes. At first the fire wasn't hot enough, so the pancakes didn't cook right. Then the stones that I had placed around the fire needed shifting, and without thinking I moved one by hand and burnt my thumb. Soon the fire was too hot, scorching my hands and burning the pancakes. I'd had enough. I kicked the fire into the river and sulked.

Peter, with infuriating Alpine calm, took over from me, started again and turned out a dozen perfect pancakes.

'Of course he's not as tired as I am,' I thought to myself, 'he hasn't been paddling as hard as I have, has he?'

I had to cajole him along during this period to do slightly longer days. I often felt like a school teacher chivvying along a reluctant pupil – and there was much sighing and casting of wistful glances at possible camping places after 2 p.m. I felt much more urgency. I preferred to paddle an hour or two longer every day rather than run the risk of missing the flight out by a day just because we felt tired and lazy. But they were long, long days.

However, at least we ate well, because we were in prolific fishing waters once more. As long as we had some bait, fishing was laughably easy.

We'd stick the bait on a large hook with some fencing wire for a trace, attach that to a nylon cord, heave the whole lot into the current and tie the cord to a tree. Within five minutes, before we had even got the hammocks up, the branches would be shaking and we would have landed a traira of 2 kilos or more. It was hardly great sport, but it gave us large pots of fish stew and soup.

Fruit was not very abundant at that time of year, but we experimented with any we found. In case they were poisonous we took it in turns to have one good bite, while our companion watched curiously for any unpleasant reactions. Occasionally we got stomach ache, more often the taste would make us discard the rest, and very occasionally we found something delicious. We found some orange-coloured soft fruits reminiscent of apricots, and it was my turn to be guinea pig. I took a bite.

'Mmmm, great!' I said, resisting the temptation to eat more. 'Let's gather a lot to take with us.'

We filled our largest saucepan and carried on paddling. When an hour had passed, and I wasn't rolling around clutching my stomach, we began to tuck into the fruit, putting aside twenty for supper but eating the rest. We agreed they were the nicest thing we had eaten for weeks.

About one and a half hours later, I felt a pressing need for a toilet break, and told Peter I'd have to pop into the jungle for a moment. I emerged five minutes later.

'That was a profoundly moving experience,' I commented as I picked up my paddle.

Ten minutes later it was Peter's turn, and then mine again, and then his. Each time was becoming more painful, and by the fourth, we were clutching our abdomens as the cramps shook us. There seemed no point in continuing our travels. We squatted in the forest waiting for the effects to pass.

'Bloody fruit,' groaned Peter.

'We've made a discovery for science,' I said. 'The world's strongest natural laxative. Move over, senna, your days of supremacy are over.' It was over three hours before we could move from that spot.

One day we collided with a tapir. The dumb beast lumbered into the water followed by her youngster, fixed us with an unseeing eye, submerged and swam straight underneath us. We stopped paddling, but she suddenly realized we were there and tried to get out. Her broad, muscular back rose below the canoe and tipped it sideways, half filling it with water. The tapir then panicked, dived again, made a bee-line for shore and finally belted off into the jungle. Her youngster meanwhile ended up on the opposite bank, and knowing tapir they probably never found each other again.

If the truth be known we weren't particularly competent at paddling downstream. We had adjusted our skills to the slow pace of upstream travel when there is ample time for manoeuvre. Swept along by a swift downstream current, we often found that our efforts at making a quick sharp turn to avoid a tangle of thorns and creepers ended us smack in the middle, scratched and cursing. Frequently we shot alarmingly under fallen trees with only a centimetre or two to spare. Peter is smaller than I am, so he could crouch down lower. Several times I failed to get low enough and scraped my back on the log as we skimmed under. At other times I would lean backward over the stern of the canoe and go under the log in limbo style, praying I had gauged it right and wouldn't be decapitated.

At midday next day, when we thought we were still about 20 kilometres from the Jari, we rounded a bend and emerged abruptly into the wide river. We now knew we could easily reach Molocopote that night, dead on schedule, because it was 14 December. We stopped for lunch and caught some piranha to grill, before starting a very boring paddle down to the airstrip. The Jari was so deep and wide and incredibly dull after the small streams we had grown used to. It rained heavily but we paddled on.

Rain on a river is very pretty. Each drop causes a droplet to jump above the surface, and the effect is of a sheet of bouncing pearls. However, we were not at our most appreciative that afternoon. We were cold, and the rain stung our bare skins. Moreover, we had paddled or walked over 120 kilometres in the past ten days, and we just wanted to arrive at Molocopote, tie up the canoe and never paddle again.

We recognized a small rapid which we knew to be a kilometre from camp (Peter had thrown up his breakfast hereabouts) and quickened our pace. Round a couple of bends more, and there it was. No canoes were moored there, so it looked as if everyone was still at the gold-workings. That was a relief. The worst scenario would be to find all the canoes moored, and no hammocks hanging in the shelters. That would have meant they had already flown out. With a last shove of our paddles we ran the bow up onto the sandy shallows and grinned wearily at each other. We'd made it and in damn good time. Christmas in Belém, here we come!

14

The Long Wait

Confident that the place was empty we had not bothered to put on our shorts, but as we stepped out of the canoe we were surprised by a welcoming greeting. It was Fernando, standing with a blanket over his shoulders, hugging himself in the sunlight and looking far too ill to be shocked at our nakedness. We had met Fernando there over five weeks before, but he was a shadow of the jaunty twenty-year-old joker we had known. He loosened his warming self-embrace for a moment, letting a chink of cold air through the blanket long enough to stretch out a hand to us, and then retired to his hammock.

We grabbed a few things from the canoe and followed him up the slope to the shelter where we found three more men cocooned in their hammocks. Malaria was now rife in Molocopote. When we had passed before there was none, but it's very hard to stop the spread of the disease in a jungle camp. Elcio, the manager, had pursued the policy of making everyone sleep under a net and isolating anyone with the sickness. Perhaps since he had left everyone had grown more careless. Or perhaps Peter and I had been responsible for bringing it here? Anyway, we learnt that ten men

had already been flown out for treatment, and these four were waiting for the next flight.

We sat and chatted with them; they commiserated with us for not having achieved our goal, but agreed we'd had a good stab at it. We also learnt that there would possibly be a flight to Santarém on the 18th, and certainly two to Belém on the 23rd. It seemed we need not have hurried quite so much. One by one they ceased talking as they embarked on their evening ordeal of the rigours that, as one man commented, came regularly at six o'clock 'like cocktail hour'. Knowing they would prefer to endure the attacks alone and hearing four sets of teeth chattering and the hammock strings vibrating, Peter and I took ourselves off to raid the cashew trees along the airstrip. The cashew is an apple-shaped fruit, some red, some yellow, bursting with juice and with an appealing bitter-sweet taste. It also has the bonus of a cashew nut at one end – but these we discarded as they needed to be roasted.

The presence of the sick men was something of a disappointment. We had hoped that we would be alone at Molocopote if we were to wait a few days for a flight, so that we could be spared the friendly curiosity and efforts at conversation. After weeks and weeks of solitude it takes a while to be at ease among groups of people. As no one else was interested in food, we cooked up some rice for ourselves and flopped into our hammocks. We were exhausted, and it was a good feeling to know we would never have to make or unmake another camp. We didn't even have to get up the next day and paddle. If we so wished we need never paddle again.

We were awoken at midnight by the arrival of another canoe-load of men waiting to take a plane which was apparently due the next day. This had been requested over the radio from the gold camp. It looked as though there'd be no room for us, and the number of men with malaria had risen to seven. By way of consolation they had shot a paca on the way down and we sat around the fire preparing and eating a late-night stew. We were up at first light to get our gear more organized, in case we were able to squeeze on the plane. Everything was filthy and in a chaotic state. We gave our clothes a good bashing on the rocks, stitched up the rips in the seat of our pants and felt we were perhaps now ready for the bright lights of the city. We cleaned the two shotguns with emery paper and diesel, and they turned out quite presentable, apart from the broken stock. We then sorted through all our belongings and distributed what we didn't need any more – torches, batteries, fishing line and hooks, rope, plastic sheets and some of the more useful (and less dangerous) items from our medical kit. The men enthusiastically grabbed the ampoules of local anaesthetic and used some on the spot to extract someone's tooth with a pair of pliers.

The men all had lousy teeth – what few were left – and most smiles would reveal large gaps in the front. It's strange how the absence of teeth can transform a handsome man. After a smile you feel a sense of relief when the lips close over the wreckage. Others had a form of decay that ate all round the edges of each tooth, making them look as if they were widely spaced. Glen, the Australian dentist with whom I had travelled on the Rio Verde, called it the 'rip-saw smile'. When you see the amount of sugar they eat, you understand where the teeth go. Coffee without at least four spoonfuls of sugar provoked indrawn breaths and puckering of the lips, as if you had offered them a lemon to suck. '*Muito amargo* (very bitter),' they complained, and added two more spoonfuls.

Well, things were very *amargo* at Molocopote. They had run out of sugar and we only had one cupful left. There was no tobacco, either, so they pounced on my remaining stash and that was gone by the end of the day. It seemed the time had come at last to kick the weed; at least until we got out of there.

There were seven people wanting to go on the plane to Santarém, and the others were waiting for the Belém flight. The plane could take 700 kilos if the pilot agreed, and as the Brazilians were small lightweights there was some hope.

'What happens if the pilot only agrees to take one of you?' a man asked. 'Who stays and who goes?'

Peter and I looked at each other. We'd grown close over the past few months, but...

'John, would you stand aside and let Peter take the place?' he continued with a smile. I fidgeted uncomfortably on my stool.

'Well... I'm sorry, Peter, but I don't think I would, no,' I answered.

'Dear me, John, what selfishness!' He turned to Peter. 'How about you? Would you do the decent thing and insist John go first?'

'Not a chance,' smiled Peter. 'We decide with a coin I think.'

In any case the plane did not arrive that day: a disappointment, but we were still confident it would not be long. There were some nice people

in the camp, above all Mineiro and Cabeça Branca. Mineiro's real name was
Ernesto; he was called Mineiro because he came from the state of Minas
Gerais. He had been a student of physics until the previous year, but when
his bank went broke he lost his savings and had to give up his studies. He
had a lot of easy-going Brazilian charm and the ability to converse easily
with everyone whatever their background. He had been at school with one
of the investors in this project who invited him to take the job as supervisor.
Ernesto regarded the whole thing as a holiday and an adventure, writing
notes on his impressions and making a collection of jungle curios.

Cabeça Branca (white head) was a prematurely grey man of forty-five
who was in charge of one gang of workers. In contrast to Ernesto, he was
illiterate, but with a native shrewdness and intelligence. He had an impish
smile and amused us every morning by singing songs in the *repentista*
manner. A simple melody is used and the lyrics are inspired by the events
of the moment and the people around. In the northeast of Brazil you see
incredible performances of this art that needs continuous rapid thinking
for half an hour without hesitation, all the time choosing the words for the
rhyme. Cabeça Branca was an amateur, but his witty and acidic comments
on our situation got us up with a laugh. He was also the best hunter in
the group and was passionate about it. He wanted a lot of information
on the Mapaoni, saying he was thinking of taking a canoe up there and
becoming a *gateiro*. I could well imagine him returning with plenty of
furs, so I deterred him a little with the addition of at least twenty major
rapids. That did not seem quite enough to kill the sparkle in his eye, so I
invented a contact Peter and I had had with a fierce band of Indians. I think
the jaguars, ocelots and giant otters of the Mapaoni owe me a thank-you
present, because all the men were scared stiff of Indians.

Round the fire that night we talked about Indians for several hours
and met a sad, blind ignorance and prejudice on the subject. Indians were

'dirty', 'thieving' and above all 'treacherous'. The original American frontier clash was being re-enacted 150 years later in the southern hemisphere. The Indians and the rough, tough adventurers would not find a way to live without conflict and, their undeniable qualities apart, these characters were ill-suited to the delicate mission of first contact, trust and compromise. They all had some second- or third-hand account of treachery and murder to back up their intolerance, and our appeals fell on deaf ears. The fact that we had supposedly had a contact with Indians and emerged unscathed and without having killed any aroused a mixture of admiration and consternation. Of course it had all been a lie, but from what we knew of the two tribes in that area – the Wayana and the Akuriyo – it seemed we would have been in little danger.

The Akuriyo were totally nomadic until the early 1970s, hunting and food-gathering in the forests of southern Surinam, French Guiana and across the border in Brazil. They avoid the big rivers, being unable to swim or build canoes, and move around in the forest staying at the most a couple of weeks in any one place. Hunting and fishing provide them with protein and fats, and additional food takes the form of honey, palm fruit, palm nuts and various tubers. The Akuriyo are able to distinguish some thirty-five kinds of honey and are constantly in search of nests. As these nests are often located high in trees, falls are a major cause of death.

The Akuriyo were unable to make fire, so the women of the tribe were responsible for carrying the precious embers from camp to camp. If the fire of a band was extinguished, there remained only two possibilities: to get fire from another band quickly, or to die. According to Peter Kloos, who has lived and worked among them, the expression 'His fire has gone out' is a euphemism for 'He is dead'. Since the early 1970s most of the Akuriyo have moved into the Trio and Wayana settlements and forsaken their nomadic, stone-age existence. However, there are thought to be one or two small groups who have chosen to remain in the forest, and there would have been a slight chance of our bumping into them on the Mapaoni headwaters, although they would probably have merely spied on us from a distance.

Hunting and fishing were extremely poor around Molocopote, due, we were told, to the past proficiency of the Indians in these pursuits and to the use of dynamite by the prospectors. Lots of us tried fishing, day or night, and we caught nothing, not even a piranha. This was extraordinary on the Jari. To stand a chance you had to go to the two small rapids a kilometre upstream. I got my first taste of the equally poor hunting that day when I went for a short walk. I saw a small troop of capuchin monkeys, which scattered in every direction, bounding from branch to branch, while I was still well out of shotgun range. These monkeys really knew that man was bad news. Otherwise the jungle seemed strangely empty.

Having plenty of time on my hands I walked fast to put distance between me and the airstrip, hoping to enter less trodden pastures. I found a tree that had been dropping its large fruit – and there were four toucans and a mob of green parrots tucking into the crop in the canopy. A lot of discarded pieces had been chewed by monkeys, pacas and agoutis, and there were tracks of deer and wild pig. I seemed to have hit a well-visited tree.

I remembered an Indian technique for attracting animals, and cut a sapling. The idea was to imitate the fruit being blown off the tree by a breeze. The falling fruit would hit a few leaves – so you swished the vegetation twice – it might hit a branch – so you knocked one – and it would make a good thump as it struck the ground – like that. The idea was that the agoutis and pacas in their burrows would rush out, but I felt pretty self-conscious and foolish as I slapped the leaves and branches and stamped my foot for 15 minutes to no avail.

The next morning being Saturday, we were informed that the pilot would not be coming, as he was a Seventh-Day Adventist and did not work on

Saturdays. The morning passed fairly quickly as we got up late and made breakfast for everyone. There was plenty of farinha, so we made fried farinha cakes which everyone was curious about, but which no one really liked. Brazilians are pretty conservative about food. If it's not meat, fish, rice, beans or orthodox farinha they are suspicious. Apart from the farinha there was not much food left at Molocopote for so many of us. We had 2 kilos of rice, a little spaghetti and beans. However, with so many men either out hunting or making fishing trips along the river in the motorized canoes, we ate a lot over those first few days. Each time someone caught a fish, or shot a monkey or bird, it would be cooked immediately and everyone would partake, filling the meat out with farinha, which swells up in the belly giving a warm, bloated feeling for a while. That way we ate nine or ten times a day.

Molocopote was situated on a bend in the river, and round the corner from the main camp was an attractive sandy beach where few people went. At first I thought it would be the ideal place to be alone. However, when I went there with a book to do a bit of sunbathing I found that thousands of little ants drove me away within half an hour. It was Amazonia in a nutshell: relaxation marred by insects. So to get a bit of privacy Peter and I would go hunting or for walks along the airstrip and around the old Indian clearings. It had been a very large site – there were acres of old plantations that had now run to secondary growth. Scattered around were the ruins of the old huts and some old graves, several of which showed clear signs of the disturbance caused by Ernesto in his 'archaeological digs'. In fact one had been left almost open with a thigh bone protruding from the soil, and we tidied it up.

As predicted, the plane did not come on Saturday, nor on the Sunday, and time was really beginning to drag. We sat around and chatted, had a few swims, re-read a little of our well-thumbed books, tried to write and ached for tobacco. One guy went round collecting all the old dog-ends and emptying them into a cigarette paper. I confess that I had sunk so low

I too queued up for a few puffs of that tarry, germ-filled cigarette. A period of such prolonged inactivity is not ideal for breaking the smoking habit. Once 3 p.m. had come and gone each day, we knew the pilot would not be coming because he would not have time to get back to Santarém or Belém in daylight, so then we could wander away from the camp to stretch our legs. The bulk of the time we just lounged in the hammocks, trying to resist the temptation to sleep during the day as it would cause insomnia in the night.

Next day, the 19th, was a Monday and we all got up optimistic that a plane would arrive. The more confident among us untied our hammocks, rolled them up and sat with ears cocked for the distant drone. Peter and I discussed which of the restaurants we knew in Santarém would receive our custom that night, although clearly we had no cause for much hope unless two planes came. We were way down on the waiting list.

Fernando was the only man still suffering from malaria rigours. I had handed out a lot of Fansidar, and it seemed to do the rest of the men good. Mind you, with the dosage they took it was kill or cure. The doctors advise three at one time and no more for a week. These prospectors preferred to take four the first day, three the second, two the third and one the fourth. All survived. Yet poor Fernando showed little sign of improvement. He carried on getting a fever and the shakes every night, and his companions told me he had been ill for over a month and taken over forty Fansidar in that time. I thought of giving him some of my remaining quinine tablets, but decided to leave it for a while. I was due an attack of malaria and did not want to leave myself with no effective treatment.

Midday came and went, and our optimism began to fade. We replaced our hammocks so we could lounge in them. Later I went down to the river and chatted for a couple of hours with Ernesto while we swam, shampooed and sunbathed. He was one of the men who had been suffering from malaria, and was delighted with the resultant weight loss.

'This is fantastic,' he chuckled, running his hands over his flat stomach. 'I must have twenty pairs of trousers that were too tight for me before. Now I look like a teenager again. I think I'll ask a chemist to prepare me some malaria pills so every time I want a quick diet I just pop one down, retire to bed for three days, and shake and sweat it off. Malaria is the best slimming aid ever.'

He was thinking of spending Christmas there by himself as he had no real desire to spend it in civilization and looked forward to a period alone. He was also pondering whether to quit the job in January.

'This *garimpeiro* stuff is only worth it if you earn big money. I mean a lot of money – six or seven times what you could get out there in the wide world. It's not worth doing for less. Think of all the things we miss out on – girls, entertainment, good food, music, comfort – for six months at a time. If you earn a fortune it's worth the sacrifice.' He submerged to rinse the shampoo out of his hair. 'There's gold up there, but not in big quantities. None of us has earned much yet, and I don't think we'll ever get rich. So once you've experienced the *garimpeiro* life and had your adventure, it s best to go back home. That's what I say.'

They had all the necessary machinery upstream, and Ernesto explained the method they used. They have two pumps, one more powerful than the other. One sucks water from the river and blasts it under pressure to break the gold-bearing shale, and the second sucks the rock and water and squirts it into an inclined trough with metal grids to separate the large pebbles. The trough is lined with sackcloth to catch the gold. (This is a method used since ancient times, though in Europe a sheepskin was used instead of sacking. It is believed by some to be the origin of the legend of the Golden Fleece.)

There was also one diver in the team who would take the hose down to the river bed so that gravel could be sucked up to a trough mounted on a raft. Cabeça Branca had been a diver on the river Tapajós and, although the water was not usually more than 10 metres deep, it was a dangerous job owing to the strong currents. Once he had lost the mouthpiece that supplied him with oxygen and had passed out before the team on the raft realized anything was wrong and hauled him up. Generally the men worked in teams of six or eight, were provided with the machinery and their food, and rewarded with 50 per cent of any gold found. Other prospectors preferred to work for a daily wage of about $15 a day, which is four or five times the usual wage for unskilled work in Brazil.

A few men wander off to explore new areas and retain vestiges of the old romance of gold prospecting, at least to the uninitiated observer. Certainly their ability to survive in the jungle with the absolute minimum of provisions is a lesson to most of us. All they seem to take with them are sacks of farinha, a machete, fishing lines, a gun and cans of kerosene. (I have never met a caboclo who bothered to light a fire without a splash of kerosene to help him.) Their proficiency at hunting and fishing guarantees them enough food. Although Peter and I had journeyed in a very unsophisticated and uncluttered way, we had a comprehensive medical kit and many, many more luxuries than they. Men like these had no doubt covered every river and creek in Amazonia with no fanfare, and some had probably disappeared unnoticed.

Certainly some gold prospectors in Brazil make considerable fortunes, judging by their subsequent spending sprees in the nearby towns. On the other hand, there are plenty of people ready to relieve them of their fortune – from the pilot who flies them the 70 kilometres for $600 one way, to the whores, and the stores where a bottle of beer costs $40 and a chicken $100. In a way, it does not seem to matter, because to many the idea of making a fortune and getting out with it is considered bad form. One should treat one's friends to a party with glorious girls and luxuries flown in from Rio or, as one man did a few years ago, have a Cadillac flown in from the States to drive up and down 100 metres of mud at the camp. In short, the pattern is two or three years of backbreaking labour in the jungle, with a handful of malaria attacks, in order to make enough money to spend on celebrations, only to return penniless after a week and start all over again.

All previous gold finds shrank into insignificance with the discovery of a bonanza at Serra Pelada (east of Marabá on the Brasilia-Belém road) in 1979. It is estimated that over 50 tonnes of gold a year were extracted from this area 2 kilometres long and 300 metres wide. Twenty-five thousand prospectors flocked there before the government began to impose controls. The authorities wanted to make sure that the gold was sold to the Central Bank, rather than through illegal channels, but it was also feared that so many men, with so much money at stake, could erupt in serious violence. Now, no more prospectors are permitted and a police force is on the spot. One man found 19 kilos of gold in one day and sold it for a quarter of a million dollars, and several others have found over 100 kilos each in their time there; the largest nugget found weighed 6.8 kilos, but of course many others don't even manage to cover their expenses.

In 1983 the prospectors of Serra Pelada won an amazing victory. A group of powerful mining concerns were pressuring to be allowed in to work the area more efficiently (it is estimated that at least 40 per cent of the gold at present ends up on the slag heaps, owing to the inefficient methods used). They argued that, given Brazil's enormous foreign debt, sentiment about the livelihood of a few thousand prospectors should not stand in their way. However, President Figueiredo promised the *garimpeiros* that they could stay – at least until conditions got too dangerous to continue with their present methods. This was an extraordinary triumph for the little man, especially in the South American context.

Well, the plane did not arrive that day, or the next, or the next. The men were infuriated by the delay. They had requested a plane for a handful of sick people and it seemed that the pilots could not be trusted to appear promptly when summoned.

'What would happen if we had a serious accident?' they asked. 'A broken limb, or appendicitis? Just because the pilot can earn more money doing a run elsewhere they leave us until last.'

On 21 December, a week after our arrival, we at last saw the first plane circle the camp before landing on the strip. Could we get on it and escape from this boring place? Everyone said we should go and speak to the pilot and beg a flight. He was a glum fellow and his eyes were invisible behind the mirrored sunglasses so favoured by the South American machos. He answered that he was already taking six people and could not arrive at Belém with any more passengers because it was against regulations. We had heard of this, so I countered that he could easily take us as far as Macapá, where he would have to refuel and where controls were lax. He refused, and when I attempted to persuade him by pleading ill health and urgency, he was unmoved.

'You came up here through choice. So you can get yourselves out again the way you came up.'

In the mirror of his glasses I could see myself fighting the urge to punch him on the nose, rip the stupid, affected, tough-guy things off his face and stamp them into the dust. Reason won. He might be returning in a day or two, and we could not afford to antagonize him. I turned on my heel, walked back to camp and kicked hell out of a tin can.

Ernesto saw our impatience and disappointment and apologized for not helping us out with a word to the pilot. He told me that we'd been dealing with the owner of the Aero-Taxi firm, and not one of the usual pilots who were more prepared to bend the rules. I asked him if he really thought we'd manage to get out before Christmas, and he assured us that there was no doubt of that.

That night we watched, to our dismay, the arrival of another canoe-load of men, swelling the numbers yet again. Many were sick and must have had a miserable two days' journey, especially as the canoe had overturned in a rapid. One of the least attractive prospects I could imagine was to be dumped in cold water in the middle of malarial shivers and forced to swim for your life. They had also lost a lot of provisions, so now we were almost out of food. We had been eating so insanely since we arrived that the prospect of reduced rations seemed quite attractive. As I wrote in my diary on 20 December: *Now midday of yet another exciting instalment in this waiting game. So far have eaten three times – beans and farinha, fish and farinha, and just now another catfish and farinha – and I turned down an offer of monkey and farinha. Everyone has round little bellies, Pete and I included, and we no longer feel the healthy, fit, lean creatures that arrived here six days ago. And we haven't even got to a place with beer, cakes, chocolate, biscuits and everything else yet!*

We passed the morning of 22 December in increasingly futile hope, and when nothing had come by 3 p.m. I set off in our old canoe to go fishing. We'd sold it to one of the guys for $10, and he came with me. I was regretting giving this character so much stuff – he had been greedy and grasping when we had been sorting out our things while the others had been more retiring. I learnt that he had sold off a lot of the gear that I had intended as a gift for everybody. He was unpopular and over the past week we had seen why: he was lazy, never stirring to hunt, fish or prepare food, but leaping out of his hammock with agility when it was time to eat. He then piled his plate to overflowing with all the best pieces.

He had been cajoled into going fishing for once, and feeling in need of some exercise and wanting a last paddle in our canoe I went with him. We set off the 3 kilometres to a rapid downstream, and after half an hour I was regretting it. All my muscles were already lazy and out of condition,

MOLOCOPOTE

and the Brazilian was not pulling his weight. It was a morose, ill-tempered fishing excursion, especially when he had the nerve to tell me he had just sold the canoe to Ernesto for twice the price he had paid me. I was livid. He had whined that he really needed a canoe, and all the time it was only for him to trade. The frustrations and irritation of this week of emptiness came pouring out of me and I shouted and swore at him, and he answered in kind. We almost came to blows.

'No one speaks to me like that,' he shouted, 'not even my father.'

'If your father had done it more often you might not be such an unpleasant, lazy, selfish son of a bitch,' I replied.

We arrived at the rapid, and he was obviously expecting us to stop above it to fish from the rocks. However, out of a perverse need to scare him and get a bit of excitement after so many days of tedium, I headed for the worst section and yelled at him to paddle. We had nothing in the canoe except the shotgun, and that was tied on, so even if we overturned not much would have happened to us, but I got a kick out of the frightened, wide-eyed glance he gave me over his shoulder before we swept, bucking and bouncing, over the waves that slapped over his lap and put 15 centimetres of water in the canoe.

He was nicely quiet and subdued after that. 'Crazy gringo bastard,' I heard him mutter as we pulled to the shore and tied up.

We then fished for two hours, caught nothing and paddled wearily home against the current. On the way he asked me if I had any drugs to control epilepsy, as he had run out of the tablets that he had been taking for the last fifteen years. He said he had been trying all the drugs in our medical kit, and had found some bitter-tasting ones. That was enough for him. His epilepsy tablets tasted bitter and these tasted bitter, so they must work the same, he thought. When I got back to camp I found several quinine and chloroquine tablets were missing. Also Peter had lost his Swiss Army knife, and my sheath knife had disappeared. Peter went up to him and accused him outright of thieving, which was a good sign that the strain was telling on him too, and soon the knives were miraculously 'found' in some place where we had never used them.

December 23 dawned, and we were all up bright and early. Two flights were due that day, and we were going to be in Santarém wining and dining that night. Cabeça Branca composed a witty little song about us all and we were as excited as school kids. The grizzled prospectors dug out little slivers of mirror and rusty razors and retired to the river to perform their grooming. Unruly hair was wetted and combed flat, moustaches trimmed, fingernails cut, and out came the hats. Generally around the camp people wore old straw hats or went hatless, but for the return to the city suitable headgear was required. These must normally have been preserved in plastic bags and mothballs, but that morning was the big day. Stetsons, homburgs and fedoras were lovingly brushed and placed at jaunty angles. The *garimpeiros* were going to town. Sadly, though, only a couple of men had the sort of face to carry it off with panache. The rest looked a bit silly. What is more, they bore the flashing sign on the head to all who lay in wait: 'I'm a *garimpeiro*. Fleece me.'

At 9 a.m. the other men heard the drone of an engine several minutes before Peter and I could hear anything. We grabbed our gear and raced up to the airstrip to fight for a seat. It was not that important to get on the first plane, although a restaurant lunch and some cold beers would be nice. The plane taxied to a stop and a different pilot stepped out. This was the Seventh-Day Adventist, apparently, a young man in his late twenties, and we jostled good-naturedly around him. He said he was taking nine people with him this flight, which seemed a very full load. Fourteen of us wanted to fly out, so we had expected him to take seven each trip. Then he dropped the bombshell.

'I'm not going to do a second flight today,' he announced. 'I'm afraid the rest of you will have to wait until 5 January when I'll be back.'

Those of us not included in the nine stared at him in horror. Twelve more days here? Christmas Day here? New Year's Eve here? Peter and I had Fernando dangling between us with his arms around our shoulders. He was too weak to walk unaided by this time.

'Aren't you going to take this guy?' I asked. 'He's had malaria a long time.'

'He hasn't got enough money,' was the reply, 'and anyway, I'm full already.'

I turned to the men who had been chosen to go.

'Fernando's really sick,' I said. 'We need to get him to hospital right now.' They wouldn't look me in the eye, so I took it out on the pilot.

'All these men are desperate to spend Christmas with their wives and families and girlfriends,' I said. 'They've been in the jungle for six months. Most of them are sick, this man particularly, and maybe he'll die before you return.'

No one else said a word. Brazilians perhaps are accustomed to being let down, to the cruel whims of fate or the callousness of the powerful. I was the lone voice. And I went over the top.

'They tell me you're a Seventh-Day Adventist,' I went on, gathering momentum and bile as he shrugged his shoulders indifferently. 'You should know that there's more to a Christian life than endless praying and church-going and Bible-beating. Christmas is a time to lend a hand, to help the sick, to re-unite families, to put aside the thought of profit and to be altruistic and caring.'

He got into the plane, but not before I had seen a twinge of guilt flicker in his eyes. The departing men shook our hands and looked embarrassed; the reprieved leaving the condemned. Peter and I carried the boy back to camp, laid him in his hammock and tried not to look up as the plane roared overhead, heading south. We just wanted to cry.

15
Christmas

Twelve days! Another twelve days with nothing to do, nothing new to read and not much to eat. It was the excruciating boredom that had really eaten into us during that past week. The waiting, those blank hours swinging in the hammock curbing our impatience, the sudden inactivity after months of adventure. We were so bush-crazy and suffocated by the jungle that we were beginning to crack up. How could we survive these extra days? We deserved a Christmas in civilization, and Molocopote was no place for festivities.

Ernesto and some others decided to head back up to the goldfields for the next eleven days and urged us to accompany them.

'There's food up there,' Ernesto argued, 'and hunting and fishing are much easier. We won't be able to leave you much stuff here and you'll go hungry.' We were too depressed to be persuaded. Partly because if we had to spend another twelve days hanging around, we would prefer that everyone left so that we could be by ourselves. Partly because we were expecting more malaria, and it seemed likely that one of us would have a canoe trip while suffering from it if we went with Ernesto. Partly because there was an outside chance that another plane might arrive before 5 January.

'You won't even have a functional canoe,' Ernesto went on. 'We're taking all of them with us – including yours – except for that one over there that has a big hole in it.'

We didn't care. We had two shotguns, lots of cartridges, fishing tackle and there were always the cashew trees to stop us starving altogether. Ernesto left us 2 kilos of pasta, two of farinha, a kilo of beans, one of wheat flour and a small tin of powdered milk. That lot, rationed carefully, would go quite a long way.

However, we would have the sick youngster, and to our dismay the character that everyone now cruelly called Epileptic announced he would be staying too. (I later learnt that he stayed because Ernesto had refused to take him.)

'Are you sure you want to stay?' Ernesto asked us one more time as we said goodbye.

'Yes,' I replied. 'We'll be okay.'

'We'll be back on 4 January,' he said, started the motor and departed.

I went down to the rocks to do a bit of sunbathing and to try to shake off my depression. I didn't succeed. If we had known we were going to have more than three weeks waiting at Molocopote, we might perhaps have continued over to French Guiana, or even have carried on paddling downstream to Carecaru. Both those courses of action would have been foolish, and we had made the right decision, but in our black mood either alternative seemed preferable to continuing this enforced inactivity.

After a couple of hours I returned to camp and found Peter making a big stack of pancakes, and with a pot of milk on the boil. I controlled my temper with difficulty, but in my diary I wrote, '*Barely three hours after a good lunch, and Ernesto leaving, Peter used up half the wheat flour and a third of the milk. It pissed me off quite frankly, especially as he is becoming really fat and lazy. He hasn't been hunting or fishing once since we arrived – just swinging in his hammock like a big cuckoo waiting to be fed. At this rate all the food will be gone in two or three days, and then what?'*

Not having been for a hunt or fished, Peter couldn't understand just how difficult it was at Molocopote. He had grown accustomed to a bountiful river and forest and simply assumed there would be no problem, even if our food stocks were exhausted.

The next morning we were awoken by a shaking of the hut that made all our hammocks shudder. It turned out to be Epileptic having a fit while lying in his hammock. We checked that he did not swallow his tongue or hurt himself, but it was a mild affair and he was in no danger.

Peter went over to the fire and finished off the rest of the flour with another batch of pancakes. Oh well, I thought, he'll learn soon enough. But we put aside the rest of the powdered milk for Fernando, who by this stage could not eat much in the way of solids. In fact he couldn't get out of his hammock unaided, and seemed to be deteriorating fast. I felt guilty withholding the quinine from him, but I knew I would need it myself. It was a horrible decision to make, and one I still live with. Would ten quinine tablets have made any difference? Did he have hepatitis as well as malaria? Certainly he was very yellow, but that may just have been due to prolonged malaria.

I went for a long hunt, saw some monkeys and spent three-quarters of an hour stalking them. I was having a good day at this game and sneaked along in true Indian fashion. I wriggled under bushes and from the cover of one tree to another until I was below them. They still had not seen me and were stuffing their mouths with some berries. Feeling overconfident, I got a second cartridge ready, hoping to bag two, cocked the gun, took a bead on a plump one and pulled the trigger.

'Phuttt' went the dud cartridge, a billow of smoke erupted and the lead shot went up 2 metres, then showered about me. I snapped open the breech to eject, but no luck. Which genius had thought of making cardboard cartridges for a damp forest environment? The monkeys chattered in alarm and disappeared, leaving me hopping up and down in a fury.

I returned dejected to camp and found there was a big pot of spaghetti cooking on the fire. This time I rounded on Peter.

'We had a bloody big breakfast, so why do we need another meal so soon? Why not save it for tonight?'

'I didn't cook it,' he answered. 'It was Epileptic.'

'Didn't you say anything and try to stop him, though? You've got a tongue, haven't you?'

I went up to Epileptic and with icy rage asked him why he needed to finish all our food so soon. He grew sullen.

'Ernesto left us this food. For me too. I'll eat it when I damn well please.'

'Oh, no, you won't,' I countered, and the control slipped away. 'You'll eat it when we decide, and unless you pull your weight you won't eat at all. We're prepared to share what we hunt and fish with you, so long as you share some of the work and control your greed. But we owe you nothing, we don't like you and you're dependent on our charity. It's us who make the rules.'

'Who the hell are you to give me orders?'

I put my face up close to his.

'I'm a big, mad gringo,' I answered comically, although perhaps I didn't look too comic at that moment, 'I weigh 20 kilos more than you, and I'm 12 centimetres taller than you. I could knock your head into the river. You're also an epileptic,' I added viciously, 'and if you want to make sure I pull you out of the fire or the river when you have a fit, you'd better obey me.'

His stricken face made me feel thoroughly ashamed of myself, and Peter rebuked me too, but I wasn't ready to shut up yet. The concept of rationing was alien to the Brazilian mind and seemed to be alien to the Swiss mind too. You ate what you had and only worried when it ran out. I turned on Peter. I was furious at him for saying nothing when the Brazilian had begun to cook the spaghetti. It was time to establish some rules and common sense, and I didn't care how unpopular it made me.

'I know it's a Swiss custom to sit on the fence and not take part in any conflict around you. But you're not in Switzerland now, and there's no room for neutrality here. If you got off your arse for a change and went for a hunt, you'd see why we have to go easy on our food.'

A few minutes later he picked up the shotgun and went off, and while he was gone I felt bad about shouting at him. I seemed to be alienating everybody. I need not have worried about Peter, however, because he returned empty-handed and from then on his attitude changed.

A bit later, Epileptic asked if he could use the shotgun. I agreed reluctantly because there was a risk that he might have a fit while in the jungle. I wasn't worried that he might shoot himself, but that he might lose the shotgun.

He'd been gone about half an hour when we heard two shots in quick succession. We waited eagerly to see what he would bring on his return. It was Christmas Eve, after all, and a bit of meat would be welcome – otherwise it would just be boiled pasta. Epileptic emerged into the clearing and the sun struck the plumage of the two scarlet macaws he carried. If we'd had a camera it would have made a prize-winning shot for an environmental campaign – 'The Earth in Our Hands' or a theme like that. He held them by the legs and their wings hung limply open, dragging the ground; the brilliant colours contrasted with his dark skin and the greenery behind him. I had not realized that these macaws were quite so beautiful until we examined these two. How sad to kill such gorgeous creatures. By the time we had finished plucking them the ground was brilliant with blue, yellow, green and red feathers, and we were left with two skinny little carcasses that made their murder even more poignant. Brazilians and Indians often shoot these birds, the Indians more for the feathers than the meat.

Of course old Epileptic was quite insufferable in his triumph at being the breadwinner for a change, especially so soon after my tirade. I got a pleasure, however, out of informing him that he had shot two birds that retail illegally in the States for $1000 apiece. Alive, of course. The meat in fact was so tough that it was hard to gnaw it off the bones without loosening our teeth, but at least we had something for our Christmas Eve dinner.

We fed the broth to Fernando and I sat and chatted with him for a while. He told me he was engaged to be married and had come to the jungle to earn money for the wedding. He was twenty years old and lived in Santarém. He reached weakly into his pocket and pulled out a well-thumbed photo of a plump girl with a mischievous grin, who he informed me was his fiancée. Tears ran down his cheeks as he talked about her and the five years they'd known each other, the house where they were going to live and the six or seven children they planned to have.

'I don't think I'm ever going to see her again,' he sobbed. 'I'm going to die before the plane comes back.'

'Oh no you won't,' I answered with forced cheerfulness. Secretly I agreed with him. I was more and more convinced that there were some complications beyond the malaria. His urine was very brown, the whites of his eyes were yellow and he was very anaemic. But my lack of medical knowledge left me helpless. I gave him two chloroquine, two quinine and two Fansidar to see whether there would be any improvement the next day. If there was we would give him more. If not, all we could do was to get some nourishment down him and hope he survived the next ten days.

'Can you promise me something?' he whispered next time I went to sponge his face.

'Sure, Fernando.'

He showed me a brass shotgun cartridge with its end stuffed with paper.

'Take this to my girlfriend in Santarém, if I don't make it.' I had to look away to hide the tears in my eyes.

'You'll be able to do that yourself in a few days' time. Don't think like that.' The cartridge was quite heavy and I peeked at the gold inside. Not heavy enough to compensate for a death, though. No way.

'Promise me.'

'OK. I promise.'

'Thank you. The address is on the back of the photo.'

He closed his eyes and seemed to sleep.

I turned in at about 8 p.m. because the mosquitoes were fierce. Now that they were concentrated on just four of us instead of the fifteen who had been in the camp before, Molocopote was becoming a very unhealthy place. Even if Peter and I had had only one strain of malaria each when we arrived, we were certain we would have a second before we left. That proved to be true.

Christmas Day. I went for a walk to savour the early morning coolness and to enjoy the view of the mist over the river. This blanketed the Jari every dawn and lasted until 7 a.m., by which time it would be burned off by the sun. We wished each other a happy Christmas and then tried hard to forget what day it was. This we almost succeeded in doing apart from one unwise discussion of Christmas fare in England and Switzerland, which drove us hunting and fishing in an urgent attempt to find something good to eat. Using damp farinha as bait on a little cane rod with a tiny hook, we managed to catch eighteen little fish of whitebait size. These we gutted and grilled over the fire and shared out four and a half each. They were bony and tiny but that was Christmas dinner. As we ate we discussed the pilot.

'I bet he's in church now,' we snarled, 'thumping the Bible, holier than thou, feeling self-righteous and one of God's chosen. He's probably put us out of his mind and his conscience feels sweet and pure.'

Fernando was showing no signs of improvement from the pills, and while I was feeding him there was the sound of liquid falling to the ground; I saw that he'd urinated in his hammock. He didn't seem to notice, and it was an indication of how weak he'd become. From then on, we cleaned, washed and changed him several times a day.

I went for a hunt that afternoon and had more bad luck. I wounded a monkey, and again the cartridge failed to eject and it got away. A few weeks before I would have felt wretched about a wounded animal suffering a lingering death, but now I was just unhappy that lunch had escaped. In fact the way I had shot at it marked a departure from usual practice. It had been a bit outside the safe killing range, and on the run, but I had snapped off a shot in the express hope of wounding it and slowing its flight. Hunting had reached such a degree of necessity that there was now no room for either sentiment or sportsmanship. We needed to kill, and if animals were wounded sometimes and escaped, that was just too bad.

As soon as it was dark we climbed into our hammocks and tried to sleep. The more we could sleep the better, and the days would be shorter. Epileptic had two annoying traits to add to all his other faults. He farted explosively dozens of times a day and each fanfare would reduce him to helpless mirth. Peter and I were hardly prudish, but we found everything about Epileptic tasteless and irritating. The other thing he liked to do was swing in his hammock, singing in the most tuneless voice imaginable the most trite, maudlin collection of ballads penned in Brazil over the last ten years. We told him to shut up. We ourselves had stopped singing long since, and we could see nothing to sing about, especially with his voice.

The next day we busied ourselves repairing our backpacks, clothing and mosquito nets. After that we went hunting for the cashew nuts that had been discarded under the trees. When we had fifty or sixty Epileptic showed us how to roast them. Using our old, solid frying pan, he heated them over the fire, and there were little puffs of smoke as they released their oil. He stirred them around as they began to blacken and until the bottom of the pan became lined with oil. He then deliberately let it all catch fire, which it did explosively with the nuts letting out jets of burning gas and oil until all the shells were blackened and charcoaled. They were then ready to eat. The shells could be crumbled away to reveal the delicious nuts inside.

That first time we made the mistake of sitting around the pile of nuts eating communally. Definitely not the thing to do when dining with Epileptic. His tempo rapidly increased until he ended up eating most of them. From then on we counted the nuts and shared them out equally so that we all had the same number and could eat them with leisurely enjoyment.

Later Peter went out for a hunt and shot a monkey. It cheered us up and we kept Epileptic on tenterhooks all afternoon while we forced ourselves to wait until the evening before we ate it. When it came time to serve up, there were more scenes of brotherly goodwill when our friend helped himself to both legs and an arm and was forced to return them to the pot for a more equitable share-out. We had to watch the bloke like a hawk. He took his plate to the other side of the shelter in what we assumed to be a sulk, but which we discovered the next morning had been a planned move to enable him to finish off nearly all the farinha without us noticing. The farinha that had been put aside for fishing bait.

I think we would have hit him, but he'd just had a serious fit, kicking up the dust and writhing and foaming on the floor. Much as we hated the guy it was no time to thump him, and anyway he was really rather appealing in the hour after the attack. He would wander around afterwards as if in a drunken daze, and however many times we guided him back to his hammock and suggested he rest, he got up again and came stumbling over to us.

'Who are you?' he would ask.

'I'm João and this is Pedro.'

'You are my friends, and I am your friend,' he would murmur charmingly, and put his arm around our shoulders like an affectionate child. We felt quite warm towards him at these moments, but unfortunately the fits just weren't frequent enough.

On 28 December we finished the last of the food that Ernesto had left us. From now on we would be totally reliant on hunting, an occasional cashew fruit and the slim chance of catching a fish on a spinner. (In all the time we had spent at Molocopote the spinners had produced nothing.) It promised to be a hungry eight days. Peter and I made plans to go fishing in the old canoe that we had caulked up with rags, and to try our luck at the rapid upstream where perhaps spinners would be a novelty to the fish. However, that night I got malaria again and couldn't face the exertions necessary for such an expedition. I told Peter and, wrapping myself up in my blanket, I surrendered to my sufferings. I heard Peter depart, punting the canoe as we had no paddles, and assumed that Epileptic had gone with him, but when I peeked my head over the edge of my hammock a couple of hours later I saw he was still there.

'Why didn't you go with Peter?' I asked.

'I didn't feel like it,' he answered.

Ah, give me strength, I thought, as I lay back. Peter hadn't said anything, so why should I? Bugger the lot of them.

Contrary to most of my malaria attacks of the trip I did not feel any better the morning after. The fever lasted all day and intensified that evening. At least I was not feeling hungry, though, and did not mind when Peter returned in the afternoon having caught nothing. We ate three cashew fruit each, and Peter pulped some for Fernando.

'He is looking worse,' he told me. 'Only just conscious and his temperature is 104 degrees.' He tucked the blanket around him to keep out the cold and damp, and got up in the middle of the night to change him and feed him some warm milk.

Epileptic also had a malaria attack and made quite sure we all knew it. He groaned theatrically and noisily all night, keeping us both awake, but getting no sympathy from us.

'Oh my God in heaven, I'm going to die,' he moaned at one point, and in one voice Peter and I answered, 'Well, for Christ's sake hurry up then!'

'I've got malaria,' he cried, 'I feel so sick.'

Hell, as if we needed to be told how sick malaria makes you feel! Peter and I were very reserved and stoical in our suffering. Northern European stiff upper lip and all that. The occasional whimper might slip out, but no more. Epileptic was just less inhibited. He let it all hang out and, being the unpleasant character he was, groaned to an indifferent world.

16

Last Days

D ecember 30, and the year was coming to a close. I made a chart at the back of my notebook of the remaining days, and each morning savoured the small pleasure of crossing out one more. One week to go. We were pinning our every hope on 5 January, but there were doubts that the plane would arrive even then. After all, most of the men had departed with malaria and two weeks might not be enough for them all to have recovered completely. Perhaps they would decide to prolong their holiday a bit, in which case the pilot was unlikely to fly up to Molocopote empty just for us. Money was the prime concern, it seemed, and such a trip simply would not be economic. Still, we had to pin our hopes on something.

I decided to set off for another hunt, only to realize very quickly how much the malaria had sapped my strength. Of course a diet of three or four cashew fruits a day was no fuel for strenuous activity either. I saw a commotion in a distant tree-top where a troop of spider monkeys were feeding. Big, gangly, 10-kilo beasts they were, and despite the malaria, hunger and weakness I broke into a trot. They had seen me coming and were already in retreat. The only hope seemed to be to run as fast as I could in an attempt to get within range. I floundered through the jungle, tripping and scrabbling in the undergrowth, and with only a pair of underpants on I was soon scratched and bleeding. My heart was thumping in my chest, there was a bitter dry taste in my mouth, my empty stomach was flapping against my spine, but I was gaining on the monkeys. The chase went on for several hundred metres, until I staggered within range. One monkey was running along a branch and about to leap to another tree when I fired. It was a hurried snap shot, but the monkey faltered as it was about to leap and missed its handhold, toppling head first 20 metres down to the jungle floor.

Between me and the place it had landed was a fallen tree, and I needed to sit down and rest before I could go on. When I did, there was no sign of the monkey. I walked around searching for half an hour. Either the monkey had been not too badly wounded and had dragged itself away, or else it had missed its handhold from shock at the sound of whistling pellets, recovered and nipped up another tree. At all events, it was our last hunt at Molocopote. After that we conserved our strength by spending most of the time in our hammocks, with the occasional foray to the cashew trees. In the evening when I took some of the last of our milk to Fernando I found him lying with his eyes closed and his breath rasping from his open mouth. His thin face with the adolescent beard was gaunt and shiny with sweat, and the lips and the corners of his mouth were caked with dry white spittle.

Down the ropes of his hammock ran a column of ants. They crossed his cheek and disappeared into his open mouth. I called Peter over. Brushing the ants away, we bathed the boy's face and squeezed some water into his mouth, but apart from the occasional groan he didn't react. We sat helplessly by his hammock for the next few hours as his breathing became noisier and noisier until it rattled deep in his chest. Finally, at about ten o'clock, the breathing faltered, his chest quivered and then relaxed. He had gone.

We pulled the blanket over his face and went to our hammocks. Poor boy. We hoped St Peter had written a little entry alongside the pilot's name for the Day of Reckoning, to greet him when he turned up pompous and pious and oh so damn sure of his appointed place in heaven.

Next morning we awoke to find Epileptic had been busy. Somehow he had manoeuvred the body out of the hammock and laid it on a board between two trestles. Candles burned at head and feet, the hands were crossed on the chest and he had wound a bandage around the boy's jaw to keep it closed. The face was horribly yellow and the ants were back. I wiped them off the cold skin with a shudder.

There was no way we could leave him unburied for long in that climate, so after an hour or two we grabbed shovels and set about digging the grave. We looked for a place with some nice views around, and where the soil might be less compacted and easier to dig. The best places were near the Indian graves, so we began to dig there. A Brazilian *garimpeiro* and some Indians were going to lie companionably together, in death if not in life. It was back-breaking work under a scorching sun, and we suffered badly from having no pick to loosen the soil with. Rocks and the roots of long-dead trees made us fight for every shovel scoop and when we got down a metre Peter and I thought that it was deep enough.

'Oh, no,' said Epileptic. 'A good grave should be at least 2 metres deep. Otherwise animals can dig up the bones, and it is disrespectful to the dead.' Typical, I thought. When Fernando was alive Epileptic had done nothing to look after him. Now he was dead, everything had to be by the book.

By late afternoon we finally finished, and it was a fine job. Two metres deep, sheer, smooth sides, and 2 metres long. We leant on the shovels and admired it.

'Seems a shame to fill it again,' I muttered, and went down to the river to wash off the sweat and dust. An hour later, as the sun was setting, we lifted the boy up in his hammock and carried him up the hill. It was a rather scruffy funeral cortege – the three of us wearing just shorts or underpants – but Peter got down in the grave and we passed the body down to him to lay in the bottom. He uncovered the face for a moment while we all said our farewells, re-covered it and then we filled in the earth. Peter picked some flowers to lay on the top and the job was done.

'One down, three to go,' I commented sickly on the walk back. 'Who's next?' and giggled. A reaction to the exhaustion and the death, I suppose. Peter looked shocked and angry at my lack of taste, but I could not stop.

'At least there'll be one less waiting to get on the plane now, so our chances are improved. Imagine if the plane had come this morning! They'd have laid him out flat, occupying at least four places. We couldn't have really sat on him, could we, or rolled him up in a ball?' Then, after a pause, 'Pete, I want to tell you that if I'm next, don't bother going down more than a metre, eh? I wouldn't regard it as a lack of respect, and I know you'll be weak and tired. But, could you put a piece of wood over my head and face before you fill it in? I don't like the idea of all that weight pressing down on my nose.'

Ah, it was a festive New Year's Eve. We ate six cashew nuts each and then turned in. We were not waiting up for midnight to sing *Auld Lang Syne* or some Swiss equivalent. I had time for one last shaft of brilliant wit before I fell asleep:

'Don't worry, Pete. I think a plane will come next year.'

Over the next four days we got up only to drink water, urinate or do a shuffling tour of the cashew trees with little success. By now we no longer felt the same ravenous hunger; just an emptiness and lack of strength. In fact I've felt hungrier in England by the mid-morning tea break on a construction site. Nature's safety valve, I suppose. Peter and I both suffered more malaria attacks and that reduced our weight and strength even further.

We may not have been ravenous, but we did think and talk of food a lot. I particularly remembered the ten-week cycling trip I had done with a friend the summer before down to Sicily and beyond. We had eaten unrestrainedly to fuel our muscles, and what magnificent spreads they were with cheese, paté, fruit, raisins, dates, figs, crusty bread, croissants, butter, jam, salami, milk, fruit juice. That was a real holiday. All the same, our hunger was easier to bear than the crushing boredom. We should have liked a fat novel or two to read, as much as a meal to eat.

Epileptic began to have a fit per day, and we had to keep an eye on him when he went near the fire or the river. He became quieter and quieter, as we all did, and we lay for hours on end in our hammocks without exchanging a word. The rain continued to fall frequently, approaching the rainy season pattern of a fierce storm every evening, and the river was over a metre higher than when we arrived.

On the evening of 4 January Ernesto returned with three others.

'My God, you look like shit,' he said when we got up to greet them. 'So skinny.' He glanced around and noticed Fernando was missing. 'Didn't make it, eh?'

He took me by the arm and told me in a whisper that the boy's father was among those who had just arrived with him. He then went over to one of the men and led him away from the camp to stop by the water's edge and talk. I saw the father's face crumple into tears; he sat down abruptly and stayed there sobbing for a long time after Ernesto returned to us.

'Let's go for a walk, John,' he said. 'I want to talk to you and I fancy a cashew.'

'You'll be lucky to find one,' I answered, but we set off slowly. The slope up to the airstrip seemed steeper every day, and my heart hammered in my chest. Ernesto slowed his pace to match mine, and I told him our news.

He found one ripe cashew that we had missed, and we sat under the tree and chatted, about Epileptic mainly. I learnt that he had been sacked from the goldfields five weeks before for laziness and had been hanging around

at Molocopote since then waiting for a flight. However, the pilots refused to take him without payment.

'I've brought some food with me from the goldfield, but we've only a little and I've decided that Epileptic is not going to have any.'

'What'll he live on, then?' I asked.

'That's his problem. He should have thought about that before he turned everyone against him by thieving, and by doing damn all to help. At least six men have come to blows with him. We're just not prepared to carry him any longer. It could be another ten days before a plane comes and…'

'What?' I cried, snapping out of my contemplation of Epileptic's fate and thinking of my own. 'Ten days! But there's one due tomorrow isn't there?'

'Well, it might come, but I can't imagine those sick men being ready to return just yet. Anyway,' he smiled, 'if that same pilot comes back he might not take you after the things you said to him. They were well said, I never liked those evangelical bastards but you upset him, and he's a powerful man.'

I was on the edge of tears and my voice shook.

'Oh, shit, Ernesto. I don't think Peter and I could take another ten days of waiting here. We'd go crazy. We're not too good now, but we've managed to hang on in the hope of getting out tomorrow. Hell, we'll buy the canoe back off you and paddle downstream! Anything's better than staying on here.'

Ernesto looked at me, his expression a mixture of concern and amusement.

'That would be stupid. At least we've got some food here now, so it won't be so bad for you. It's only ten days, after all.'

'It's not hunger, Ernesto. You don't understand. We've been here twenty-three days already, and another ten days would be just too bloody much.'

I was pacing up and down shouting, and he got up and put his arm around my shoulders.

'Well, let's wait and see if the pilot comes tomorrow or not, before you go paddling off heroically downstream or blow your brains out, okay?'

We returned to camp and told Peter the news. He reacted much as I had done.

'Ten more days! No way, John! Impossible! We would go crazy!'

We had a supper of paca meat that the men had hunted on their way downstream, and turned in with our bellies full for the first time in ten days.

When we got up the next morning Peter and I were nervous, but still forced ourselves to act with confidence. We untied our hammocks and rolled them up, gave away our mosquito nets and blankets, gave the shotguns one last polish and packed everything up. We were leaving that day, we reminded ourselves optimistically.

'Tonight a good steak with fried eggs, potatoes and salad. Six cold beers and a chocolate dessert.'

We sat around for the next four hours, and finally one of the men cocked his head and announced, 'Plane coming.' We hadn't heard it, but we let out a whoop of excitement, grabbed our gear and began to scramble up to the airstrip. We'd only gone a few paces when a figure raced past us carrying a shotgun. It was Fernando's father.

'Stop him,' I yelled, shrugging the pack off my shoulders and beginning the chase. 'He'll shoot the pilot!'

That was evidently the man's intention. As far as I was concerned, he could do the deed whenever he pleased in Santarém, but not here, leaving us with an unmanned plane. Ernesto gained on him and tripped him with a rugby tackle. The gun flew out of his grasp.

'Leave me alone,' he shouted, twisting and fighting furiously. 'I'm going to kill him. He left my boy to die.'

Peter and I joined Ernesto and helped to hold him down.

'You can't do that,' Ernesto told him. 'It wouldn't bring your son back or change anything. It would just put you in prison for ten to fifteen years. Think of your other children – the ones who are still alive and need you.'

The man weakened and his struggles subsided. Soon he was sobbing and safe to let go. We continued up to the airstrip and the plane taxied up to us. To our relief the pilot was a new face to us and we were able to calm Fernando's father with the news.

'You're the gringos old Cabeça Branca has been telling me about,' the pilot said with a smile before we'd even introduced ourselves. 'He's been pestering me every day, persuading me to take you out. You've got a persistent friend there.'

'Are you going to take us then?' I asked nervously.

'Yeah, I'll take you.'

Peter and I did a little dance of joy.

'He told me you would pay with two shotguns,' he went on. 'Have you still got them?'

We showed him the guns and he seemed content enough, though he muttered 'Out of all the rich gringos in Brazil right now, it's just my luck to end up with the only two poor ones.'

We loaded our packs and heard Epileptic pleading with the pilot to be taken.

'Have you any money?' the pilot asked him.

'No.'

'I'm not a charity,' the pilot retorted. 'If you get on a bus you'd expect to pay, wouldn't you? Why should a plane be different?'

'He's not very well,' I said. 'He's got malaria and has finished his pills to control his… (I paused)… his illness.'

It suddenly occurred to me what it would be like to have to deal with an epileptic fit in a small, crowded plane. If Epileptic was taken I vowed to sit very close to him.

'No money, no travel are my rules,' said the pilot.

'I'll pay for him,' said Peter, and I stared at my saintly companion in awe. 'I can get some money sent from Switzerland in a day or two.'

I couldn't switch from loathing to such charity in the space of a few minutes, but thought I'd better offer something nonetheless.

'We've got some medical equipment that you'd be able to sell to prospectors, some other stuff too….'

'What about that gold dust?' Epileptic remembered suddenly, eagerly turning to me. 'That gold that Fernando gave you!'

'He asked me to give it to his fiancée,' I protested. 'It was one of his last requests.'

'I need it more than she does,' he argued. 'Fernando was my friend, he'd want me to have it.'

I doubted that somehow.

'What do you think?' I asked Peter, keen not to make the decision alone.

'I think you've really got to follow Fernando's wishes,' he said. 'He entrusted you with that task, didn't he?'

'His fiancée need never know! Don't tell me you were actually going to seek her out!' protested Epileptic, unerringly choosing the one argument that hardened everyone's hearts against him.

The pilot was growing impatient.

'Come on, or we won't make it to Santarém before dark.'

'You can't leave this guy here all alone with nothing to eat!' Peter protested.

'Oh yes, I can,' he replied. 'Some of his mates are coming back in a week or so to continue prospecting and they'll bring supplies. When he's earned his fare like everyone else he can leave. This guy's always broke and always begging favours. I don't like him.'

Before we had time to think of a solution he signalled us to get in, slammed the door and started the engines. Peter and I averted our eyes from Epileptic who stood forlornly on the grass. Our intense dislike had turned to pity.

The plane taxied to the far end of the strip, revved its engines in a rivet-popping crescendo, released the brakes and bounced down the runway into the air. As it dipped its wing to turn southwards we caught a final glimpse of the hut where we had spent so many days and the little figure of Epileptic trudging dejectedly down the red smear of the trail.

Postscript 2011

After we left the forest it was confirmed that Peter did, in fact, have leishmaniasis, as well as falciparum and vivax malaria, and he spent a long period in hospital. I got off lightly with just the two strains of malaria.

He seems to bear me no grudge for almost wrecking his health. In fact, like me, he looks back at the trip as one of the most wonderful experiences of his life. In 1990 we returned to the region to make a TV film for *National Geographic*. Peter now has three young children, runs a farm near Bonn with his partner, and has a landscape gardening business. As he likes warm weather he hasn't been tempted to join me on a new passion – canoe trips to the tundra of northern Canada – but he did go on a six-week float down the Duero/Douro river in Spain and Portugal a few years ago

A lot has happened in the twenty-five years since I wrote this book. The world has changed, attitudes have changed and I've changed a bit as well. Like any author faced with a work he wrote years before, there are passages that I was tempted to edit or remove. I've resisted the temptation. In particular, the hunting scenes make me ashamed of myself. Mind you, I'm reading them with a belly full of tasty food and unlimited choice available down the road at the local supermarket. It's a long time since I was faced with dwindling supplies, hunger and having to butcher my own meat.

And of course the Amazon has changed too. An enormous tropical wilderness that once seemed boundless now seems finite and shrunken. The rivers I canoed in the Mato Grosso in the 1980s are fringed with ranches and farms instead of virgin forest, and Brazil is booming. With a growing international market for its food and raw materials, its future looks assured. It can still expand its acreage of agricultural and pastoral land by clearing forest. Exports of beef, soya and timber have increased massively year on year.

There are two new threats to the remaining forest. The recent completion of the Interoceanic Highway from the Brazilian state of Acre to the Peruvian coast has finally given Brazil access to ports on the Pacific Ocean. This will inevitably lead to more destruction as produce is sucked from western Amazonia (and the largely intact rainforests of Peru) to the insatiable markets of China.

Secondly there are plans to build up to twenty-four hydroelectric dams along many Amazon tributaries in the next decade, costing $100 billion. The largest of these – Belo Monte on the Xingu river – will be the third largest in the world. All of them will displace people, drown virgin forest and interrupt fish migration.

There has also been bad news from the region travelled in this book. The government has given the go-ahead for a 373-megawatt hydroelectric dam on the lower Jari at the falls of Santo Antônio. This will power the pulp mills that Daniel Ludwig constructed at Monte Dourado.

But there has also been excellent news. On 23 August 2002 the Brazilian government announced the creation of the Tumucumaque Mountains National Park along the border with Surinam and French Guiana. Totalling 38,874 square kilometres it will be the world's largest tropical forest park – larger than Belgium. When put together with the adjoining Guiana Amazonian Park in French Guiana, the protected area totals 59,174 square kilometres.

It seemed probable that the creation of the new park would give Molocopote airstrip (where this book ended) a new role. It could become a base for scientists while they study the region and catalogue the species that live there. Later, when the park is opened to limited tourism it could make a perfect site for an eco-lodge.

However, until the national park gets the staff to enforce its protected status, the government thought that the airstrip was just attracting the wrong sort. Drug smugglers, gold prospectors, foreign canoeists and the like.

I've flown back to Molocopote three times. To film on the Ximim Ximim tributary; to use it as a starting point for my wife's initiation to the Amazon, when we canoed down the Jari to civilization; and finally when we made another attempt on crossing the Tumucumaque – a trip that's told in the book *Into the Amazon: an incredible story of survival in the jungle.*

In February 2010, a group of federal policemen used 1,700 kilos of dynamite to blow craters in the runway of Molocopote, and the nearby Anotae and Cruzado airstrips, rendering them unusable. This will help keep the area undisturbed for a while longer, but sadly rules out any more trips up there.

SEPTEMBER 2011

THE LAST TIME JOHN HARRISON VENTURED INTO THE JUNGLE A MEMBER OF HIS GROUP DIED. THIS TIME HE BROUGHT HIS WIFE.

'superb... an example of what the human body and mind can achieve'
Dervla Murphy

'An absorbing account of an obsessional journey into South America's unknown dark heart'
Matt Dickinson

www.summersdale.com